PRIYANKA CHOPRA

The Dark Horse

PRIYANKA
CHOPRA
The Dark Horse

Bharathi S Pradhan

Om Books International

First published in 2018 by

Om Books International

Corporate & Editorial Office
A-12, Sector 64, Noida 201 301
Uttar Pradesh, India
Phone: +91 120 477 4100
Email: editorial@ombooks.com
Website: www.ombooksinternational.com

Sales Office
107, Ansari Road, Darya Ganj,
New Delhi 110 002, India
Phone: +91 11 4000 9000
Fax: +91 11 2327 8091
Email: sales@ombooks.com
Website: www.ombooks.com

ISBN: 978-93-5276-625-3

Printed in India

10 9 8 7 6 5 4 3 2 1

For Sanjaya, Siddhesh & Paddy,
the three boys in my life who better me every day

To see what few have seen
You must go where few have gone

Anonymous

It was the year 2000. On November 30, at the spanking
new Millennium Dome in London, more than ninety lovely
leggy girls had put their best foot forward.

Five stunning finalists stood still with bated breath.

The pressure on Contestant No 23, Miss India, was like
that of a volcano waiting to spew lava.

The previous year, India's Yukta Mookhey had won the
Miss World title.

Pradeep Guha, the big daddy of *The Times of India*
group back in India, was looking at a repeat act in more
ways than one. This was the millennial year and he wanted
something special.

In 1994, his entries, Miss India Sushmita Sen and 1st
Runner-up Aishwarya Rai had victoriously brought home
the Miss Universe and the Miss World titles, respectively.

In 2000, Miss India Lara Dutta, sangfroid and confident,
had already won the Miss Universe crown in Cyprus.
Another Indian beauty, 2nd Runner-up Dia Mirza was the

front-runner at the Miss Asia Pacific pageant in Manila; the crown was tipped in favour of India in December.

One crown home, two more to go. Guha had his fingers crossed. He wanted all three.

Contestant No 23 didn't have to be told how high the expectations were; how much Guha, *Femina* and India wanted an epochal year like 1994, a double whammy. Three hundred million Indians were estimated to be watching the event.

In the judges' row sat a familiar face: Hemant Trivedi whose gown she was wearing.

But Miss India at the Miss World pageant wasn't looking at him.

What mattered was what presenter Jerry Springer was asking her: "Do you feel the pressure?"

"There's always pressure," replied the self-assured Miss India. "I operate best under pressure," she added with a lopsided grin.

Then came the clincher. The eighteen-year-old Miss India was asked, "Who do you consider the most successful woman living in the world today?"

Miss India answered, "Mother Teresa."

Mother Teresa had died three years earlier, in 1997.

But the gods, perhaps Mother Teresa herself, were on her side as Priyanka Chopra beat the odds, the pressure and the wrong answer to give Guha his dream moment – the coveted second world title from his lineup of beauty queens – as she stepped up to become Miss World 2000.

That was the beginning. Would her luck hold out in the next round which would be held back in Mumbai?

She had to jump a few hurdles to get there. Despite the title of a beauty queen, Priyanka Chopra was never a natural stunner like Aishwarya Rai in whose footsteps she unwittingly trod as she found herself in the film studios of Mumbai. Snagging a film offer wasn't the tough part for a beauty queen; getting it off the ground was the strenuous stretch.

Miss World 2000 was launched to the blinding pop of flashbulbs in a Mumbai film studio. It was a dream debut for any aspiring actress that year. Mahesh Manjrekar was basking in the glory of his blockbuster gangster film *Vaastav* (1999) and was the most toasted director of tinsel town. Bobby Deol, the second son of Dharmendra, was a hot-selling celebrity kid. The producer was Vijay Galani who was introducing fashion model Bipasha Basu along with Hindi cinema's genetically-famous Kareena Kapoor in *Ajnabee*, a film that also co-starred Akshay Kumar and Bobby Deol and was being directed by Abbas-Mustan, famous as makers of stylish thrillers.

Miss World's debut couldn't have been in a more impressive set-up: produced by Vijay Galani, directed by Mahesh Manjrekar, co-starring Bobby Deol. Another popular producer of that time, Pahlaj Nihalani, gave the mahurat clap.

Priyanka shot for six days.

The film was shelved. Worse, the word that went out was, the new heroine's nose job was a botch-up.

Another film, this time with Bobby's older brother Sunny Deol, reportedly repositioned her from lead heroine to second lead.

Two major worries at that stage of her life would've made anybody else reach for a strip of Restyl. Would she make the grade as lead actress and would the nose correct itself?

The gods were benevolent once more. Nothing could halt her march to more fame.

She went South to do *Thamizhan* (2002), a Tamil film opposite Vijay; she came to Mumbai and signed yet another Hindi film titled *Andaaz* (2003) and voilà, the heavens ensured an award-winning debut this time. Priyanka Chopra's perseverance had paid off and this was only her first baby step.

But in 2004, she hit an unexpected roadblock. Priyanka had just about begun to clamber towards stardom when Akshay Kumar, the only hero with whom she was making a commercially successful pair, put an embargo on working with her – a disastrous turn of events for any growing actress. But again, the forces above didn't think so. Even the self-willed ejection of the most important hero of her life at that time, didn't make a whit's difference to her stardom. Like a speed breaker that merely required a shift in gear, she negotiated the bump, increased speed and turned into one of the most interesting actresses of her time.

Thirteen years later, Priyanka was poised among the creamy layer when there was a heartbreaking repeat of the 2004 act. Shah Rukh Khan, the biggest box-office name of his time, the only top-draw Khan with whom she had a special chemistry, dropped out of her career and life.

Had the ones above finally abandoned their favourite child? The answer came swiftly – not one to be easily squelched, Priyanka became an international star.

It has been the gold standard of Priyanka Chopra's life – with every blow, the stumble was momentary, the return to stance stronger. For the next bout.

In December 2017, having acquired the status of a global icon who embodied an empowered woman, Priyanka Chopra delivered an annual lecture (available on YouTube) backed by NDTV, the television channel. She filibustered from the podium and the women in the audience were lavish with their hurrahs as the actor enumerated the twelve rules that could make you Priyanka Chopra.

She fiercely upheld the 3Fs of her life – failure was not one of them.

"Be Fearless, be Feisty, and a little Flawed," she said.

She was all three.

Evident right from the time she wore a school uniform.

The $100,000 prize money Priyanka brought home with the Miss World crown was welcome but not a drastically lifestyle-changing amount.

Whatever the restraints or reversals, hers was not a rags-to-riches struggle. There was never a where's-the-next-meal-coming-from or how-do-we-pay-her-school-fees moment in the family as Priyanka was born into what Punjabis proudly call a *khaate-peete ghar* (a family that eats and lives well).

On July 18, 1982, Priyanka Chopra became the tiniest member of the much-respected family of Dr MK Akhouri, her maternal grandfather. Dr Akhouri headed the Congress Committee in Jamshedpur and his wife, Madhu Jyotsna Akhouri (born Mary John in Kerala) was a social activist, MLA and nurse. Women achievers were thus an early phenomenon in the Akhouri-Chopra family.

Baby Priyanka was born at Tata Main Hospital in Jamshedpur to doctor-parents, Madhu and Ashok Chopra. Lieutenant Colonel Ashok Chopra was a surgeon in the Indian Army Medical Corps and Priyanka got everyone's full, undivided affection for the next seven years until her brother Siddharth was born.

She was snugly raised by a large and loving family of Akhouris and Chopras which included grandparents, uncles and aunts. Like a group picture from a Karan Johar film, hers resembled an Indian joint family, and continues to function like one to this day. However, mother Madhu was the big influencer in her life while father Ashok simply doted on his little girl.

"My dad for me is my strength and my weakness," Priyanka had said to me when Dr Chopra was still alive. "Someone I completely adore and look up to. I've always been daddy's little pet."

Her life was marked with such contentment that Priyanka once remarked, "Jealousy is an emotion I've never felt. Envy maybe. Like I'd be envious of say, Rihanna who is so young, so cool, she's done some amazing work. But I've never felt the need to be jealous. Maybe, because I've been lucky enough to have contentment in what I do? Because I've always got the best I could at any point, or because I'm doing the best work I could? Sometimes I feel I've even got maybe more than I've ever thought. So I've never had space for jealousy. Not even as a kid because I've always been really blessed. I've never had the time to give importance to someone else's life because mine has been so consuming."

Proud to call herself an army kid, much of who she grew into was because of the background she came from. She said to me about growing up with the army around her, "Our families (army families) are not conventional. We may be aware of the opposite sex but we don't show it. And we've always learnt how to take care of ourselves. Ever since you're young, your dads are always busy somewhere with their work; you're not with them. Army life is like a close unit. Both my parents were in the army (Madhu left the army prematurely), so we've always been self-sufficient, our survival instinct is very strong. Maybe that's why we're a little more boyish, not damsels in distress, fragile, simpering and feminine. Plus, we're brought up with a lot of discipline, respect for people and people's time. You'll find army kids always well-spoken and polite but at the same time firm enough to call a spade a spade. That makes us very wholesome."

She was such a regular army kid that she didn't stand out as extraordinary.

"Priyanka was a thin little girl, an average student, quite an introvert at the beginning," remembered Pinky Franklin, her 5th Std teacher at La Martiniere, Lucknow. "Ours is not the kind of school where there's bullying but Priyanka was not the sort of girl to bully anybody anyway. She opened up a bit by the time she came to my class and I remember everybody had to participate in the Annual Day dramatics or dance. So she took part in a Hawaiian dance called Agadoo. To be honest," added Ms Franklin, "at that time I didn't see anything special or outstanding in her. She was like any other boarder to us."

She certainly didn't preen like a diva in the making. In fact, those were the days when, like any young, undecided girl, her aspirations changed every day.

"Every year I wanted to be someone else," Priyanka said in one of her many public speeches. "A pilot, a maid. I loved going on all fours and cleaning." Her doctor-parents had not foisted on her a mandatory career in medicine or any other profession. On the contrary, they had instilled in her individual choice and the confidence to see it through by telling her that she could be whoever she aspired to be. Her ambitions thus ranged from wanting to be a criminologist to an aeronautical engineer who'd work at NASA and build planes. Strangely, she never articulated a desire to be an actor even if Sushmita Sen was the idol plastered on her walls and she knew every move and thrust of the '90s heroines. It was either so latent that she herself was unaware of what lay in her heart or she didn't dare voice it for fear of ridicule.

But it was certainly a normal life. Friends from the army remember her parents as "a couple made for each other" with a lot of love and warmth going around.

General Nandwani who was in Bareilly in 1991-92 when Dr Ashok Chopra was posted at the Military Hospital, remembered him as, "a colourful man who loved singing". The genial doctor would often request the General to let him sing at Club events and once he got going, it was sometimes difficult to make him stop.

"On religious days, he would dress up in saffron, come to the unit *dharam sthan* (or a *sarv dharam sthal,* the one place of worship in the army where idols and books of all faith are kept) and sing bhajans and kirtans."

In 1992, during the Ayodhya riots, Priyanka was a sprightly ten-year-old who'd happily flit around at family gatherings. It was the same year when the General and his wife celebrated their twenty-fifth wedding anniversary. They requested Dr Chopra to sing at their party and largely due to his robust, effervescent performance, the evening was a huge success.

What went unnoticed was that the happy child who was prancing around had a curiosity that was way above average.

At age thirteen, she was fearless enough to ask her parents to let her study in the US because the unseen little rebel in her couldn't wait to get out of the school uniform that she had to wear in Indian schools like La Martiniere.

She was vacationing with her aunts and uncles in Massachusetts when she went to see an American high school. "It was the beginning of teenage vanity," as Priyanka put it. She saw that none of the kids had to wear a uniform and it was reason enough for her to want to stay back in

America. She didn't want to miss such a great opportunity to experiment with the untried. Two Fs had kicked in that early – Fearless to test new waters and Feisty in her wanting to shed the uniform.

Father Ashok was protective; mother Madhu completely supportive. Despite the hardships and hurdles that Priyanka had to encounter and cross at every turn of her life, she had a headstart over many others as she had parents who gave her the classic, clichéd combination of roots and wings.

So when she wanted to go to school in America, mother Madhu green-signalled it. Her aunt was fine too with her eager-to-explore niece staying back with her. In the next four years, the gawky but hawk-eyed teenager, ready to soak up a new experience, got a mixture of the good and the bad. In her speeches and in interviews to *People* and *Glamour* magazines, she remarked that school in Cedar Rapids in Iowa, didn't make her feel different from those differently coloured. The only "brown girl" blended in without pressure.

Strange as it may sound but extremely believable was that racism came from a Black American (of African descent) at Newton High in Massachusetts. Being Asian came with a baggage in the way she spoke, the food she ate or her culture. "A bunch of girls who didn't like me, made my life miserable." She was told to go back on the elephant she came on. They called out to the "brownie" and remarked, "Can you smell the curry?" when she'd walk by. One day, twelve girls were waiting for her by the bus.

Priyanka caught the earliest flight out to India. "I didn't want to do it anymore," she said and came back home. But the racism didn't break her, it made her.

The "insecure sixteen-year-old who didn't know what she stood for" returned a different person. Along with a twang in her talk came a little swagger in her walk. A new body language. An adolescent readying herself for the world.

Indians are familiar with the story of an elected Chief Minister who was denied a US visa by the Obama administration. The CM bided his time but when he next stepped into the US, it was as the Prime Minister of his country, as an honoured state guest on the invitation of the same White House resident. The CM/PM didn't change, the perception about him did.

Something similar happened when Priyanka returned to the US many times over but a day came when she stared down New Yorkers from huge hoardings of an ABC television serial called *Quantico*. Nobody could smell the curry anymore.

"When you don't change anything about yourself and still get the world to notice you, that's what's called a success story and that's what I did," she said in her lecture.

"My greatest achievement is the ability to get over my fears, to make my vulnerability my strength. No one's holding a safety net for me. I trust my feet, trust my legs, my instincts. Even if I fall, it's okay, it'll be my mistake."

With no regrets – three words that have been the hallmark of her life, however intense the failure.

There is, on the other hand, a tendency in Priyanka to make her 'falls' fashionably romantic because unlike many other achievers like say, Kangana Ranaut who've had to fend for themselves completely on their own, she always had the emotional support of her family. Even if she went on to becoming the sole earning member of the family as soon as she got out of her teens, and had the courage to take risks in a career where there was nothing to fall back on, it was this net that caught, comforted and cosseted her when she returned to Bareilly and went to the Army School with her manicured etiquette in place. Another mark of one privileged to have parents who educated her and brought her up well.

In a piece titled 'Priyanka Chopra Is Destiny's Child' in *Business Standard* (October 2, 2015), Ranjita Ganesan and Manavi Kapur quoted Shikha Saxena, Vice-principal of the school, who remembered the schoolgirl as "polite, affectionate", often offering a lift to any of the housekeeping staff if she was in her car to school and saw them walking.

But the girl who talked of academics and clinical psychology as a calling actually nursed an inclination for the opposite – an audience and a public platform. In the article published in *Business Standard*, Madhvi Misra, who was in-charge of co-curricular activities at the school, talked of the 16-year-old's perseverance before a performance. Shiv Kumar, the middle-aged, bespectacled music teacher remembered how Priyanka had rehearsed a song and requested him to listen to her. When he pointed out a few flaws in her performance, it was disheartening. But it made her determined to work harder. (It's a comment that many a Hindi film director would soon echo.)

Business Standard also quoted Pushpa Kanyal, in-charge of discipline, who saw the glamour girl peep out of the uniform. "I would see her from a distance and know that she had shortened her skirt again," she laughed. "She was always the one with the most stylish hair and painted nails. She seemed cut out for her profession right from the start."

In 1999, the direction she was headed in became less hazy. For Chandra Pal Singh Rathore of the Bareilly Club, the May Queen Ball of 1999 was memorable. "There were few participants that year, so we went around encouraging young women to participate." Priyanka was not inclined to go up there and flaunt herself because she hadn't prepared for it. "I told her to wash her face and get onto the stage. She hasn't looked back since that evening," said Rathore to *Business Standard*.

Yash Roy, a member of the Bareilly Club who witnessed the May Queen Ball in 1999, told me, "Priyanka was so bubbly. I noticed her when I saw her surrounded by Y.O.s (Young Officers) and wondered who this popular young girl was."

Like any teenager, Priyanka may have basked in the attention but a career as an actor had not visibly loomed on the horizon.

The first turn towards her destiny came when she wanted some photographs for a scholarship programme to become an engineer. The photographer saw her through his lens and said, 'You're so pretty. Can I take some more pictures?'

She was seventeen, she was the May Queen of the Bareilly Club and her mother, "Like every daughter's mom thought I was the prettiest in the room and sent my pictures to Miss India."

"I was inherently competitive" – Priyanka

Would that be enough to reach where she eventually did?

To jump to the crown that changed it all would be shortchanging the person who had more of the "brownie" brand of heartbreak and rejection in store before fame changed her story.

"Priyanka didn't have it easy at any stage," commented Pradeep Guha, former President, *The Times of India* group. It was Guha who spotted, nurtured and watched the girl from Bareilly that the first panel of judges had initially set aside, blossom into the savvy beauty queen who conquered the world.

The best man to track her trek – it wouldn't be out of place to call Pradeep Guha the Columbus who discovered Priyanka Chopra.

"Discovered in the sense yes, in the year 1999, we were looking for contestants for the 2000 beauty pageant. Priyanka came in as a potential candidate from the North Region, actually from Bareilly. I remember the panel of judges didn't think much of her. I mean if I had just left it to the panel, perhaps she would not have come through.

"I think Sathya Saran as the editor of *Femina* was on the panel. I think Lubna Adams (former model) was there. There were four or five people including myself. I kind of found something in her, I don't know what it was, some chutzpah you might call it. So I insisted that we keep her; what was the harm in putting her in the contest? That's how she came into the contest. She was pretty raw at that time.

"It was simply a 'this one is better than that one' kind of scene. Just an opinion that each one had. There was no scientific method except some basic cut-offs and she was well within all of that. On all those parameters (like height, age), she merited being in the contest. But after that, it was a matter of whether you thought she had winning qualities or not. Subsequently, once she was in, I saw her grow in the contest. She was clearly the dark horse."

What also grew was a close friendship between PG (as PC calls him) and the seventeen-year-old he took under his wing. "In fact, she celebrated her eighteenth birthday at my home," he revealed to me.

But when the Miss India pageant was held in Pune, it was a daunting evening for the contestants.

Guha had turned it into a glittering event with entertainment drawn from Africa, and former contestants who'd scored at various international beauty pageants on stage. It included Priyanka's role model Sushmita Sen, Yukta Mookhey, Namrata Shirodkar, Diana Hayden, Manpreet Brar and Madhu Sapre. Miss Universe 1994 Sushmita Sen was the belle of the evening. With tears in her eyes, Sen cheered the contestants and asked the audience to applaud the parents of all the contestants. She also won hearts when she addressed the parents of those who didn't make the cut and asked them not to be disappointed with their daughters. They'll be achievers in some other field, she pointed out, and being a part of that event was itself an achievement.

In this intimidatingly electrifying atmosphere filled with celebrity presence, Priyanka was not even a favourite.

All bets were on Lara Dutta, she was a shoo-in as Miss India. Long before the eliminations began, former journalist and Juhi Chawla's manager KS Sanjay reported that he'd heard the following whisper from a well-connected person in the auditorium:

"Lara is a terrific girl. Though she has no formal training she has been working from an early age. She has bagged quite a few prestigious modelling assignments to date. She had supreme confidence even when she was a novice. She always had this I-know-what-I-want-to-be-and-I-will-achieve-it attitude without a trace of arrogance in it. She is supremely confident.

"Speak to the people with whom she began her career and they will reiterate this statement. Never once was the 'Should-I-or-should-I-not?' attitude visible in her.

"An instance I remember was when we were on a show. We missed the train. There was panic and chaos and confusion galore. Everyone was snapping at each other but Lara stayed cool. Very composed and deep in thought because she had an exam to take the following day. Even under such circumstances, she was composed."

It was that composure that got Lara Dutta the Miss India crown, concluded KS Sanjay in his report.

The only reason to mention the spotlight that was on Lara is to underline how Priyanka was the under-betted underdog, and would continue to be one even after triumphing at the contest in London. But how the tables would turn one day.

For the moment, however, it was Priyanka who came off as second best.

On the high-powered judges' panel sat superstar Shah Rukh Khan and Juhi Chawla, a sought-after celebrity pair at the turn of the millennium. Within a dozen years, equations would change dramatically and the girl from Bareilly would displace Juhi Chawla in Shah Rukh Khan's life and career. But in 2000, it was unsettling, unnerving, certainly formidable for her.

You couldn't tell from her countenance.

Incredibly, Priyanka's first introduction to the man who would one day play a huge part in her life, was that evening when she stood on stage as a seventeen-year-old contestant and he asked her a hypothetical question: "Who would you choose to marry?" He gave her a choice from the judges' panel. A great Indian sportsman like Mohammed Azharuddin, the former captain of the Indian cricket team, or a creative businessman like Marcus Swarovski "who has a difficult name to pronounce" or an Indian actor like him, Shah Rukh Khan?

Even more astoundingly, Priyanka chose Azharuddin over Shah Rukh, explaining that she'd go for a sportsman who'd do the country proud, so she could go home and tell him that she was as proud of him as the country was.

Priyanka became Miss India World, the 1st Runner-up, in a pageant that saw everybody's favourite, fashion model Lara Dutta walk away with the main Miss India sash.

Guha expanded, "In fact, even after Priyanka won the Miss India World title, I remember a lot of my friends in the fashion and glamour industry told me, '*Yeh kaisi kaali kalooti tum logon ne chuni* (Who's this dark girl you guys have chosen)?' Those were the words I'd hear and I'd say, '*Nahin yaar, is mein kuch baat hai* (Not quite true, she's got something in her).' I couldn't put my finger on it and say what it was but it just felt right. It was the year of Lara and she was a sure-shot at the Miss Universe pageant. But that impression of mine about Priyanka became stronger and I became more and more sanguine about her as the days passed. She was definitely impressing us much more as the days went by.

"Lara was clearly a winner. Everybody knew her. By then she was already a model and a biggish one at that. She'd been on the ramp and so on. Whereas Priyanka was an entity nobody really knew. She had done nothing, nothing of consequence. So, in that sense, she was a dark horse. But what one did notice was that she was making a lot of effort right through in whatever way she could. She came into focus the day we had the talent round where she sang an English song and she sang beautifully. That was the day a lot of people sat up, noticed her and remarked, *arre* (wow), she sings wonderfully.

"By the time we got to the talent round, we were well into the contest. Since it was the millennium year, we had a really big powerful jury with Shah Rukh Khan, Subhash Chandra Goel and Carolina Herrera (from the house of perfumes). I'd gone all out to get the best power-packed jury of the day.

"They were good jurors, people who had an understanding of what works and what does not work internationally. At the jury meeting also, Priyanka was a toss-up; she was not like a sure-shot. But she was inching closer and closer, and then in the final round she answered very well and got through. Miss India, the No 1, went to Miss Universe and the 1st Runner-up or the one placed second went to Miss World.

"I can say that one noticed winning qualities and a lot more in Priyanka. In a way, maybe I pushed her a little bit harder because I saw something in her. When she won and was going to be Miss India at Miss World, I said, let me pay a lot more attention to her. Somehow, all of us were confident that Lara would get through. So in terms of time spent, I think we gave more attention to Priyanka than to Lara. Lara became Miss Universe that year, so the pressure on Priyanka Chopra began to build up.

"She was the next one to go for an international pageant in a few months and as the expectations mounted, everybody began to back her and say, let's hope she can do something there. We had all felt that we had a good candidate in Dia Mirza (who won the third place), so she was sent to represent us at the Miss Asia Pacific pageant.

"But it was Priyanka I pushed and she was extremely hard working. She was focused and could take criticism on the chin, at least those days. She knew people were calling her uncomplimentary names like '*kaali kalooti*' (dark-skinned). These things are not said silently and one hears them, *sunayi deta hain na*. There are people who make it known to you in different ways. There are nasty people all over."

The nasty brigade didn't realise that it would work the other way around on her. Priyanka was not the kind one should have pushed against the wall because she does not get pinned down by intimidation or rejection. She is of the breed that recoils and returns with force, rearing to wrest out the best.

Guha noticed that she was not just focused and hard working, "She was a fast learner too and I saw a quality in her that she still has. She's unafraid. She has so much self-confidence that she's not scared. She's not scared to take the next leap into something she doesn't know." Like the thirteen-year-old who went to school in the US.

"She's fearless of the unknown," Guha went on. "It came one after the other at her and she went at it without fear. First was getting into the Miss India pageant where traditionally it was supposed to be familiar ground for models and other glamour girls. Priyanka had none of that background. But she came and she conquered. Then it was Hindi films which was a normal jump from a beauty pageant. But she didn't have it easy there either. But the way she's gone from here to Hollywood, then to film production, you can just see her going from one to the other unafraid. She says, '*Main seekh loongi*', I'll learn. That's her attitude, her spirit. She is willing to take those big leaps."

He sized her up well with the observations he made at close quarters.

"Priyanka was very fond of my eight-year-old son, Sanket," said Guha. "She'd come home almost every second or third day, play with him, she was so comfortable with a little kid. So there was a child in her at that level. And then there was that shrewd exterior. It's quite a deadly combination. Very rarely do you see that mix of qualities. There are people who meet Priyanka and say even after the first time that she's so sweet, but she's very calculating. Yes, she is, and why not?" her *Times of India* mentor demanded. "She realised very early in life that she had to fight her way through and nothing would come easy for her. Nothing has come easy for her," he emphasised.

But fortunately for Priyanka, the right people and the right breaks always showed up at the right time in her life. And she grabbed them.

"Opportunities come few and far between. Our job is to recognise them and make the most of them" – Priyanka

"Miss India, when I was in Army school in Bareilly, Miss World, my first film offer, my music single, my first film production...I recognised them and worked so hard that I squeezed every drop out of these opportunities. It's called drive," she said in 2017.

It's also called destiny. It was fortuitous that Guha was in the seat at *The Times of India* in 2000 because it wasn't a coincidence that so many Indian girls brought home an international crown during his tenure. He was a man who had a clear vision of what he wanted when he picked a winner.

He nodded, "Before I took over, it was Vimla Patil (former editor of *Femina*) who used to run the Miss India pageants. Vimla's perspective was to find a Miss India. Quote, *India*. When I took over, I immediately changed the perspective to finding Miss Universe or Miss World. I was not interested in Miss India because *uska koi matlab nahin banta hai* (that's quite pointless). So the whole orientation changed. What we were looking for changed. We were looking at a global winner. After me, when Vineet Jain (Managing Director, *The Times of India*) started taking charge of it, he changed the orientation once again and began to look for Miss Bollywood. His perspective became Bollywood. In my time too, they went into Bollywood but we didn't look at them from that perspective. I looked at their potential on the international platform. If you look at all of them, they were 5'8" and 5'9". And in those days, the Hindi film industry would be wary of them and say, *itni lambi-lambi* (so tall). But it didn't matter to me because I was not looking for a Bollywood actress."

But it was the *lambi-lambi* girls he chose through an international prism who became some of the biggest celebrities of the Hindi film industry (Aishwarya, Sushmita, Priyanka). As would be proved more than a decade and a half later, he had also unwittingly prepared Priyanka in particular for a global audience far beyond the 2000 pageant.

The making of Miss World 2000 had a team that worked as hard as the contestant herself.

Guha spoke of the high-level coterie of professionals he'd put together for his winners. "Hemant Trivedi did Priyanka's clothes. Lubna Adams was there to guide her through her walk and poise. Dr Jamuna Pai worked on her skin. Priyanka had gummy teeth. So Dr Sandesh Mayekar had to work quite a bit on her teeth, virtually till the last day. Just before she took off for the pageant, he was still working on her. Priyanka didn't need Sabira Merchant (who trained contestants in English speech and diction). She used to spend a lot of time with me because I would tell her what kind of questions were likely to be asked and stuff like that. But most of all, you have to be ready in your mind and she was a winner in her mind the moment she won Miss India. She started telling herself that she'd got the crown on her head. She had won in her mind much before she even left India. And she worked towards it."

Recognise opportunities, grab them, squeeze every drop out of them.

Guha also did something out of character when the contestant he had sent to the Miss World pageant was in London, preparing for the big day.

"I have never been to the Miss World event except much later, after I'd left *The Times*, when I was asked to judge one of the Miss World pageants in China. But while I was at *The Times*, I never went to any of them."

Yet, he was there for Priyanka.

"I had to go to London for something else," he explained. "So I thought, while I am here, I might as well go and say 'Hello' to her. I asked Mr Morley (Eric Morley, Founder of the Miss World pageant) who was alive then, if I could go and see Priyanka. He said, 'Yeah, sure.' You must realise that by that time, Yukta had happened, Diana had happened, Sushmita had happened, Aishwarya had happened and in that year, Lara had also already happened. So the moment the contestant from India would land, people would look at her to see, *arre, yeh kaun hai* (hey, who's this). India had become the land to be feared at that time. It's a different matter today but those were heady days.

"Since India was feared, from that point of view, Priyanka was being watched like a hawk. Not only by the management but also by the other contestants. I had gone just to meet her. What else did I have to do there? But people were already whispering, what's he doing here, how come he's here. I had nothing to do with the pageant. But the other contestants obviously wondered, why should he be here at this time? It meant nothing to me; I was there for half-an-hour or forty-five minutes and then I left.

"But in those thirty to forty-five minutes, I met some management person from the Miss World organisation and he told me that she was giving everybody the shivers. Then I knew that *yeh karegi* (she's going to do it). I realised, *yeh kuch karegi* (she's going to pull it off) because you don't normally hear such comments about any contestant."

Guha paused before making another point.

"You know Priyanka is very close to her parents," he ruminated. "She had a very special relationship with her dad and a lot of what she used to do was, 'This is for my dad' and 'That's for my dad'. The dad thing came up all the time; it still does. It's got nothing to do with him not being here today or with him even having cancer. It was 'Dad this' and 'Dad that' long before. Her dad was central to her life. But," frowned Guha, "I don't think he was totally happy when she joined the contest. I think her father wanted her to be a professional; that's the background they came from. But then the rest is history. Everybody's seen that her mother is like a rock and it's her mother who maintains relations with everybody even today. If Priyanka has to be invited somewhere, it's always with Madhu. It's almost never only PC. I see Madhu even today at so many events. I don't know whether she is doing it because of Priyanka or whether this is now her world. They came from another world – of doctors, Bareilly, the Army, and they adopted Mumbai city as their own. It's fantastic how they've done it. So I think somewhere there is a streak of *karke dikhayenge* (will show you what we can do) in the family.

"When Priyanka is resolute that '*Main dikha doongi* (I'll show the world what I can do)' or '*Main karoongi* (I'll do it)', I think she partly wants to prove it to herself also."

Guha assessed the family equations accurately as Priyanka publicly revealed that after her mother sent her pictures for the Miss India pageant, "Dad wasn't happy about it. He wasn't strict. I went to America at thirteen, returned at sixteen. I wasn't a baby anymore. Dad didn't know how to deal with a teenager. He was freaking out anyway. And suddenly Mom told him I was going to be in a beauty pageant. So he said, 'Make sure Mom's with you.' Mom gave up her practice to be with me for three years. Dad said, 'If your career works out, your mom must be with you.'"

What it really translated into was that the glimmer of a glamour career had taken shape in Priyanka's and in her parents' minds even before she went into the beauty pageant. Let's also not forget that despite seeming wonderstruck at how films happened to her, she had posters of Sushmita Sen and looked up to the Miss Universe of 1994 as a role model.

But she didn't show her hand prematurely at either the Miss India pageant or when she went to London.

In fact, she was introduced at the Miss World contest as a girl who loved salsa dancing and gospel singing. She herself talked of being a girl who'd bungee jumped and wanted to sky dive next. In her interviews, there were still references to wanting to be a clinical psychologist when actually, she'd already tapped the Hindi film industry and had set her sights on an acting career, even before she'd caught that flight to London.

She made it seem unplanned.

"London was where it all started," she said to me. "The Millennium Dome was launched. Ninety-three gorgeous girls from around the world were there. I was eighteen years old. It was the millennium year. I grew up in that one year."

That one year was also when Pradeep Guha spent the maximum time with her as she was contractually obligated to make appearances as Miss World until the crown went to another girl.

It was during this time that he spotted certain qualities in her, including a little-known tendency to be tight-fisted.

"She was a self-confessed *kanjoos* (miser) then," he chuckled. "She would just not spend her money. I think there is a change now that she has so much of it. But I remember we had gone to the Middle East for some event and on our return, we had a stopover in Dubai on Emirates. She was saying, 'I want this' and 'I want that'. I said, 'So, go buy them.' And she said, '*Yaar, paise nikalte nahin hai pocket se* (The money just doesn't come out of my pocket).' So, yeah, she was really a self-confessed *kanjoos* at one time."

But he also saw in her the sterling quality of a girl who wouldn't be flustered by an unexpected complication. "We had gone to make a presentation, I think for the Asian Advertising Congress somewhere in the Middle East, maybe Cairo," remembered Guha. "We went together and when we landed in Cairo, her luggage hadn't reached. She had nothing with her except her handbag. The next day was her appearance at this Advertising Congress and she had no clothes, no crown, nothing with her. She was there as Miss World. Without her crown, she was nobody. She had to step out there with the crown on her head and it was in the baggage that hadn't arrived. But she was completely unfazed. She said, 'Let's just buy some stuff, some lingerie. But you have to pay for it.' All of us were more concerned than she was. All she did was to buy some T-shirts, I think she bought a pair of jeans, she must have picked up a dress, some lingerie, and she said, 'I'm okay, *yaar* (dude).' Anybody else in her place would have been completely rattled or made a scene or got agitated. That too, when you have to make an appearance the next day.

"This happened very early in her life. She had just won the Miss World title. So there was always something in her personality, a winning quality to be able to take things in her stride. Therefore, just like she can handle her success, she can handle her failures. She's able to do that in her professional life and at a personal level too. Like she'd just recently invested six years in a relationship and (when it ended) it was a big loss for her. But she didn't allow it to be a loss."

Gain and loss have always accompanied her. Even in 2000, while there was euphoria over her win, there was also a dark story that emerged which could've clouded her happiness. But she rode out the heartening and the heartbreaking with equanimity.

Press reports published after her win told both stories.

First, the euphoria.

"Miss India was my biggest stepping stone," she once rewound to me. "I was seventeen years old and I was taking a vacation from my pre-Boards. I was studying at the Army school in Bareilly, I'd just come back from America. I went for the contest because I had two months off. I thought I'd come back and study. I was in 12th Std. I never thought I'd win. I won and my life completely changed. *Arre*, how did this happen? The first thing my mother said when I won Miss World six months later was, who's going to study now? I tried to study again but I started working in films and my career just took off."

As always, her family exulted over her victory. Rahul Das from *The Tribune* News Service recorded it in 2000 with this news report:

Talking to The Tribune, *Priyanka Chopra's grandmother, Mrs Champa Chopra said, "I cannot describe how happy*

I felt on learning that Mimi (Priyanka is affectionately called by that name by her family members) has become Miss World."

The phone at Staff Road, Ambala Cantonment, the residence of the Chopras, has not stopped ringing since she became Miss World.

Mrs Champa Chopra said she had wished Priyanka good luck before she left for the Miss World beauty pageant. "I spoke to her on the phone before she was leaving. I told her that from my side, she has already become Miss World. I am so glad that she has achieved it," she said.

Priyanka's uncle, Mr Pawan Chopra, said they watched the Miss World beauty pageant through the night. "When Priyanka's name was announced, it was an out of this world feeling. It is a matter of great pride and joy for us," he said.

He said since childhood, Priyanka had been a confident girl who was active in all spheres of life. "She used to spend her vacations with us in Ambala and she used to love eating pickles prepared by my mother," he said.

Mr Pawan Chopra said he had spoken to Priyanka during the rounds taking place at Maldives. "Priyanka was the youngest contestant and she was under pressure. I spoke to her and reassured her of our complete confidence in her," he said.

Earlier this year in February, talking to The Tribune, *Priyanka Chopra who had come to Ambala to meet her grandparents after winning the Femina Miss India World crown said that although she was never keen on modelling, "I always felt like a princess. Specially after Sushmita Sen was crowned Miss Universe, I had this secret desire to become like her."*

Eighteen-year-old Priyanka Chopra had then said, "I had even made a collage of Sushmita Sen in my room. She was, one could say, a role model for me."

(UNI) — Mrs Madhu Jyotsna Akhouri, maternal grandmother of Priyanka Chopra, finds it hard to believe the little girl who was playing on her lap the other day has become a beauty queen winning the Miss World title.

"I watched the mega event the whole night and felt on top of the world when Mimi was adjudged the winner," she said.

This small town in Rohelkhand region of Uttar Pradesh has woken up to the fact that it is the home town of a beauty queen. Everywhere, people are discussing the mega event.

She credits Priyanka's success to her determination and self-confidence but also lauds the role of her daughter Dr Madhu Chopra behind the success of Priyanka.

The proud "Nani" said it was she who practically brought up Priyanka as both her parents were employed.

The 18-year-old idolises sitar maestro Pandit Ravi Shankar and is greatly influenced by both Indian classical and Western music.

Meanwhile, Bareilly, widely known for its "surma" and "jhumka", is jubilant today over the success of Priyanka and the recognition it has brought to the town.

Simultaneously, there were reports that Miss India had become such an obvious favourite with the bookies in the UK that her winning the crown was, "like match fixing. There was no surprise."

Worse, a thirty-seven-year-old Indian businesswoman based in Dubai, claimed that Miss World's father, Dr

Ashok Chopra had sexually abused her twenty-five years ago when she was twelve years old.

Gulf News reported it on January 23, 2001:

An Indian businesswoman here says she will take court action against Miss World's father, claiming that he sexually abused her when she was 12 years old. The woman, now 37, says seeing Ashok Chopra on television after his daughter, Priyanka, won last year's Miss World pageant brought memories of the alleged 1976 incident flooding back. Chopra, a 51-year-old retired Army officer, denies the allegations and is preparing to countersue for defamation.

The woman said social stigma, love for her parents and uncertainty about the future were the main reasons she had kept silent.

The allegations have stunned Chopra's family, who called them false and incredulous.

His wife, Madhu, told Gulf News *yesterday, "I knew my husband for 10 years before I married him and trust him fully. He would never attempt such a cruel thing on a 12-year-old child. Our whole family is completely shocked by this. This woman should have thought twice before coming out with false stories.*

"What is she ultimately driving at? Selling her reputation and making monetary gains and gaining publicity might be her hobby.

"This woman who is pulling my husband and my family into court should understand that she can never ruin my husband, who is very decent and well respected."

She said that her 18-year-old daughter, who won the Miss World title last November, was equally shocked.

"Priyanka is quite surprised but has full trust in her father," she said. The family lawyer, SK Puri, said he would

file a defamation case against the woman and newspapers which carried the allegations. "We are optimistic about a positive outcome. If proved guilty, under the law of defamation, a person who has made false allegations could face two months' imprisonment."

The family stood together united to weather this unpredicted storm. Like every other reversal, this too was dusted off and got a quiet burial. It was soon a forgotten chapter.

Seventeen years later, four years after Dr Ashok Chopra had passed away, another news report brought the curtain down on the charge that had looked suspect to most right from the beginning. Perhaps it will bring closure to Priyanka and her mother on a subject that should never have reared its ugly head.

On July 21, 2017, a report in *PGurus.com* carried this story:

A Dubai-based businesswoman was arrested by the Enforcement Directorate on July 17 in connection with the kickback distribution in the sensitive Augusta-Westland VVIP helicopter scam. In a bizarre incident in 2000, Shivani had accused the then Miss World Priyanka Chopra's father Dr Ashok Chopra of molesting her 25 years ago. Many saw this as a clear attempt to defame or extort money.

According to Shivani, she was only 12 years old when the incident happened. Many Army doctors who worked in the camp came out accusing Shivani Saxena of blackmail and extortion.

Shivani filed a 25-lakh compensation and damages lawsuit against Priyanka's father. Ashok Chopra vehemently denied all the allegations and accused Shivani

and her husband of blackmailing and attempting to extort
money after his daughter became Miss World. He also
filed a counter suit against Shivani for trying to damage his
reputation and his daughter's. The cases reached nowhere,
and the litigation shuttled from the local court in Bareilly
to Allahabad High Court. Ashok Chopra passed away in
June 2013. Now look who karma has caught at last. Who's
in jail now?

When the Chopras had ridden it out way back in
2000-2001, Priyanka's first boyfriend in Mumbai, Aseem
Merchant had stood by and comforted his girl.

But seventeen years later, he too got a legal notice, this
time from Priyanka. For attempting to make a film titled *67
Days* along with her former secretary Prakash Jaju. For over
a decade, ever since he was shown the door, Jaju had been
on a smear campaign. '67 Days' referred to the number of
days he was jailed for allegedly stalking and attempting to
malign the actress.

Well-spoken and well-maintained, Aseem chose his
words carefully as he confirmed that he had indeed received
a legal notice from his former girlfriend.

"There was a misunderstanding about it," he said. "My
friend and I were looking for interesting subjects, different
biopics to make. Jaju came up with this idea of a celebrity
manager who creates a star and gets arrested. I thought it
was a pretty good concept, so I said, we'll partner it. Before
we knew it, it was in the papers and since we weren't in
touch, she (Priyanka) sent me a legal notice. You know how
a man's ego gets in the way? So we answered it legally and
said, we're going ahead with it. It wasn't her story, it was
the story of this celebrity manager. But a common friend
mediated, cleared the misunderstanding and I understood

that some people had taken advantage of this situation. So, on a public domain, I clarified that I won't be making this film not because of legal pressure but because she's a woman, I respect her. The film was never about her, it was about Prakash Jaju and his journey."

Although the project that never took off could sound like the coming together of an embittered former boyfriend and a malevolent former secretary, Aseem underscored that there was no acrimony between him and her.

Said he, "We have bumped into each other on and off, and we've met quite warmly and sweetly."

Are breakups ever without resentment and rancour?

He shrugged, "We had two different phases in our lives. She was justified in taking the course she took. We moved on and there was no bad blood between us."

Aseem should have made a film on his own life. He's had a tougher life than most and this is not with reference to the exit of a girlfriend from his life. Aseem lost his entire family in what was splashed in the media as a suicide pact.

But before that happened, he was divorced and the father of a little girl when he met Priyanka.

"I was always into business, had an event company even back then. We (Priyanka and he) were both models. Someone introduced me to her and she was so bubbly, had such a lovely nature, we just got along very well. The rest as they say, was chemistry. I loved her spirit, I loved her focus, and most of all, I loved her confidence.

"No, I never felt she was making use of me. There was a lot of love and caring. She was very young but she was mature beyond her years. I should say that she's one of the most mature and focused girls I've met in my life. Her focus was always on work. She always wanted to make something of her life. To do something for her parents.

"When I met her, she was already Miss India and she was going for the Miss World pageant.

"She was very hard working even then. In fact, I was the party animal who'd go to sleep at 5 am while she'd be up at seven in the morning, ready to go for her dance classes. That was a lot of focus for a girl that age."

However, Priyanka's family was not happy about her seeing Aseem at that stage of her life. "They were like any other Indian family. The less said the better," he said curtly but added, "I'm now a single father to a twenty-year-old daughter, so I understand her parents."

He said that the rough cards like the deaths in his family that were dealt to him by life made him value love, family and relationships.

Never once referring to Priyanka by her name, he stuck to "she" and "her" and listed the traits that made Priyanka who she was.

"There are a few things she taught me which I still cite as examples to other girls. At that time, I was doing very well, I was very well connected to the media, and I would tell her to come out more and meet people. And she asked me, 'Aseem, what's the definition of a star?' She said, 'A star is someone who's unreachable.' For a nineteen-year-old to believe that was amazing. So we basically learnt from each other."

He rose to her defence over the wrong answer she gave at the Miss World final round.

"A lot of people don't get it," he chided. "It's not a general knowledge quiz, it's not about the answer. It's about how you speak, how you present yourself and the way you answer it, and she was fabulous at it.

"She was always well spoken. She had studied abroad, she had the exposure. It has a lot to do with upbringing, how much confidence you instil in your child. Her parents never brought her up as a small-town girl.

"Before she left, I threw a party for her and said, go and come back with the crown. When she won and returned, yes, we absolutely celebrated it."

Aseem confirmed that irrespective of how random Priyanka may portray her foray into films, her goal was always an acting career.

When she left for the Miss World contest, he was confident that she'd do well. "I definitely knew she'd do something, knew that she'd succeed. (What she did for one year as) Miss World was because she was in a contract and had to do it. But her focus was always films.

"Films were the next natural step. Initially, it's tough for everybody, they all have their own struggles. But she was so good, so dedicated that I saw her go up very quickly. No, I didn't feel left behind because I had a family tragedy, court cases, and I was very involved with that. I was not involved in her day-to-day work but she was always there for me at that traumatic time and I admire her for it.

"In her work, she's ruthless. It's a jungle out there, if you're nice, you'll get taken for a ride. But with friends and family, she's not," he said, dissecting her nature.

"We were together for about four to five years. We were together when she did The Hero (2003) and her first few films. We didn't grow apart. We had our own commitments and it wouldn't have been fair to trap someone and ask someone to be there when things were working out so well for her."

The quality he saw in her way back then that has taken her this far was, "Focus. It's very important. A lot of girls that age want it all, they lose focus.

"She is a role model. But girls who want to be like her don't see her completely. (They'll say) I want to be like her, f--- the world like her. But that's not the only quality in her. It's about being responsible which she has always been."

What he left unsaid was that once Priyanka got a big break called *Andaaz* (2003), a man called Akshay Kumar entered her life. There was no looking back after that.

"*Andaaz* holds a very special place in my heart because it was my first film" – Priyanka

Although *The Hero* was her first film (in which Preity Zinta had the more substantial part) and *Andaaz* was released a month later, she said, "In terms of achievements and experience, it's been a lot and I'm grateful for it (*Andaaz*)."

Success has many fathers. How many claimed to 'discover' Priyanka, and how many more just knew 'she had it in her' is a testimony to how big a name she made for herself.

But as Pradeep Guha said, nothing came easy for Priyanka. She went through the anguish of having more launches that failed to take off than any other actress.

Senior journalist Jyothi Venkatesh is perhaps the only one around who remembered going to the mahurat of a B-grade film called *Good Night Princess* even before Priyanka left for the Miss World pageant. It was to be made by Atlee Brar, who played a small-time villain in a Dev Anand film, with Pooja Batra as the heroine and Miss India World in 'a good role'.

"The spotlight was on Pooja Batra and I noticed this young girl sitting by herself," said Jyothi. "So I went up to her and asked her her name. She said, 'Priyanka Chopra.' I asked her why she didn't wait for a better debut and she said, 'I'm from Bareilly. Everything's so new for me out here.'"

He wrote a piece on the mahurat and on her in *The Asian Age*. Priyanka and he had exchanged landline numbers and Jyothi was surprised to get a trunk call the next day from Dr Ashok Chopra who thanked him for making Priyanka feel comfortable.

Fortunately for Priyanka, *Good Night Princess* didn't progress beyond the initial flutter and she went on to become Miss World. "We stayed in touch," recalled Jyothi, "and when she finally signed *The Hero*, she called up and told me about it.

"It's true that Priyanka is not the most beautiful girl around," he remarked. "To begin with, she was dark and a little plump too. But her winning trait was her ability to do a reality check on herself. She knew her flaws and worked hard to overcome them. Look at Lara Dutta. She debuted at the same time as Priyanka; it was Advantage Lara at that time. But she faded away while Priyanka grew from strength to strength.

"There are a few more reasons for Priyanka's growth and survival," he counted. "One is that she's so focused on herself, I've never heard her talk against anybody. Not even about Lara who was her competitor then."

In a conversation with me, Priyanka maintained, "I didn't grow up as a film fiend or as someone who watched every movie. I grew up as a very academic child. I wanted to become an engineer, I was studying Science. My world just changed after I came into films. I guess someone up there just wanted me to find my vocation in the movies."

Until she found her vocation, someone up there also made her go through hoops of fire before she emerged strong as steel. For the big break debut was as elusive as a married lover.

One of the many films that she shot for and heartachingly watched as it got shelved was Vijay Galani's untitled film with big-ticket director Mahesh Manjrekar at the helm. The mahurat shot featured her with Bobby Deol, then a busy hero.

"Priyanka and I were friends after she was Miss India," confirmed Vijay Galani. "We used to party together and would meet quite often along with other friends. After she won the Miss World crown, I wanted to make a film with her but she had a one-year contract with the organisers. And she wanted to do my film too. So she spoke to Pradeep Guha about it. When I later had a word with him, he said, 'As long as your film is released one year after the Miss World pageant, I don't have a problem. By then, she'd have finished her contract as Miss World.' She was a go-getter even then because look how she spoke to Pradeep Guha and convinced him into letting her do a film."

What seemed like an impressive project at that time was put together and it was big news that Miss World was being launched. Priyanka had gone to London and she returned to Mumbai on the day of the mahurat when the shooting was also scheduled to begin. She went straight to her make-up room to get ready. Galani was busy overseeing the arrangements for the shooting and hadn't seen her since her return. As long as his heroine had arrived and was getting ready, he had no reason to.

"The media was there in full strength and Prakash Jaju, her secretary, kept asking me to go and meet her," Galani went back in time. "So I went to her room where she was doing her make-up and that's when I realised why Jaju had been egging me to go meet her. She'd just had some nasal surgery done in London where the bridge of her nose had collapsed. I couldn't believe what I was seeing. I had a little bit of shooting here in Film City and then a long schedule planned in London. How could we shoot with the heroine's nose looking the way it did?

"But Priyanka herself wasn't one bit perturbed," remarked Galani. "She was absolutely confident that it was a temporary situation and that the nose would settle down in a month's time, definitely by the time we left for London." The rare conviction that it will turn out just fine, something that Guha had seen at the Cairo airport, showed up again, in the young girl on the verge of making her big debut.

Galani got into a huddle with Mahesh Manjrekar who assured him that he'd manage the first schedule at Film City. "I'll take long shots, don't worry," said the director to the worried producer. Manjrekar instructed cinematographer Vijay Arora not to take close-ups of the heroine during that schedule.

They shot for a few days during which time Priyanka would go to Film City and sit with Galani and the team in an office there to discuss the film.

But a month later, the nose was still a problem.

By then a few other factors also kicked in. Mahesh Manjrekar who had signed a spate of films after *Vaastav*, began to deliver one flop after another. Within weeks his market value crashed.

The Deols too were not comfortable. Bobby was antsy about his heroine's nose and he promised to adjust the money he'd been paid by Galani against another film.

Galani had invested Rs 2 crore in the untitled film before he took a call to shelve it. But Bobby had promised to settle what he'd taken for it by doing another film with him.

What was important to note was that although he didn't make a film with her, Vijay knew she would turn out to be a fine actress. "In those five to six days that she worked with me, we knew that she was a powerful actress. *Bahut achcha kaam kiya* (She put in some excellent work)," applauded Galani who missed the opportunity to be the man who launched Priyanka Chopra.

For Priyanka, it was yet another debut that was distressingly aborted. She was destined to wait until 2003 when *Andaaz* and Akshay Kumar would make a difference to her career.

There are a few landmark films and a television serial that were turning points in her acting career. They either escalated her growth as an actress or hastened her ascent to the top of the glitter heap:

Andaaz (2003) which broke the jinx on her and successfully introduced her as a responsible heroine who could be trusted to do her job well;

Aitraaz (2004) which established Priyanka as a risk-taker who could pull it off on the sheer strength of her performance;

Krrish (2006) which was the first major film that helped her overcome the Akshay Kumar phase, simultaneously catapulting her into the big league;

Fashion (2008) which was her first solo show without a big hero around and won her a National Award for a brave, nuanced performance. Its commercial success also boosted her box-office worth;

Dostana (2008) which was her first foray into the world of high fashion and snob labels. Her most glamorous outing thus far;

Kaminey (2009) and *7 Khoon Maaf* (2011) which took her way beyond glamour into noir cinema, spotlighting her acting chops alone;

Don 2 (2011) which flagged off a six-year relationship with her co-star;

Barfi! (2012) which showed her astounding range as an actor. Playing an autistic, a special child, shorn of glamour and prettiness, and yet so lovable, she was the complete opposite of the diva of *Dostana;*

Mary Kom (2014) which was not only her first power-punched biopic and totally heroine-centric, it also worked at the box-office, proving her to be both saleable and able;

Bajirao Mastani (2015) which did not find her in a title role but as the wife making space for the other woman, she outshone everybody else;

Quantico (2015) which was her big leap Westward, marking her presence in New York, and giving her the opportunity to do a rethink on a relationship that was fraught with more heartache than happiness;

Ventilator (2016) which saw the multi-tasker in her element, working in Hollywood while simultaneously making a foray into film production in India.

The mountaineering began at *Andaaz,* her base camp.

One would think that Priyanka met Akshay during the filming of Suneel Darshan's *Andaaz.* But it was Abbas-Mustan who introduced her to Akshay Kumar when they'd zeroed in on her for their big, glossy film *Humraaz.* This was another film that Priyanka Chopra had finalised before she left for the Miss World pageant.

If Vijay Galani shot with her and shelved the project, big league directors Abbas-Mustan had picked her from a lineup of aspirants to play the female lead in *Humraaz* and had then replaced her with Ameesha Patel.

Dressed in their standard issue white shirt and white pants, Abbas-Mustan acknowledged that Priyanka had indeed been their first choice out of half-a-dozen girls who had auditioned for *Humraaz.*

"We saw her for the first time when we wanted to introduce a new girl in *Humraaz* (2002)," said the two brothers. "She had won Miss India but hadn't become Miss World when we selected her for the film. We were casting at producer Ratan Jain's Venus office. There were five to six other girls too but we liked her best.

"The other girls were all dressed up with full make-up. Priyanka had come wearing non-numbered glasses, looking quite casual and plain. It was when she started talking that we found a fantastic confidence in her. She was not trying to go out of her way to impress us. She was real, natural. That's when we told Ratanji that this was the girl we wanted to launch. It was really very impressive talking to her. But she told us upfront that she'd been selected for the Miss World pageant which was going to take place in two months. She said, 'If I don't win the crown, I'll come back and do the film. If I win the crown, for one year I'll be under contract with them.'

"We told her, 'You go and we want you to come back with the crown. We're going to make this film with you.' She went and she won. All this time, our writing was going on. When she came back as Miss World, half the industry was after her and she signed quite a few films. We were happy for her. But when it came to the shooting of our film, the dates we wanted were clashing with the shooting of another film (Vijay Galani's which was also later shelved). We had already finalised the dates of Akshaye Khanna and Bobby Deol and we had to match Priyanka's dates with theirs. We needed ninety days at a stretch but she was no longer able to give us bulk dates. She had signed many films and didn't want to let go of any of them either. She was in a dilemma wondering how to resolve it. Ratanji also wondered how we could make the film if we got her only for a few days at a time. We were to shoot in Rajasthan and aboard a cruise liner from Singapore to Malaysia. Everything was planned and ready from our side. That's when Rikku (the famous star secretary of the '80s and '90s) came to us with Ameesha Patel. Ameesha was also busy then but somehow Rikku managed to give us the dates we required.

"We had a very amicable parting with Priyanka," they said, a claim that was borne out by the fact that she did *Aitraaz* with them a couple of years later. "We had discussed with her our decision not to do *Humraaz* with her before we got Ameesha on board. And it was mutually understood that we would work together in future. We began planning *Aitraaz* within eighteen months and we were in touch with Priyanka all the while. She used to drop in and see us at this very office in Juhu; there were no ill feelings between her and us. After *Humraaz*, we made *Tarzan The Wonder Car* (2004) and then *Aitraaz* (2004). She did feel bad that she had become so busy that though we were the first to spot her talent and offer her a film, we hadn't worked together."

It was in the period before they dropped her from *Humraaz* that they facilitated her first meeting with Akshay Kumar.

"We were shooting at Hotel Horizon for our thriller *Ajnabee* with Akshay and Bipasha. Priyanka found out where we were shooting and dropped in to see us," they explained. "We congratulated her; she'd just won the Miss World title. Akshay was in his make-up room, so we sent for him and introduced him to Priyanka for the first time. She was at that time going to be working in *Humraaz*, so we told him that this is Miss World and she's going to be in our film."

Destiny works in strange ways. "As it turned out, we couldn't make *Humraaz* with her but her first film as leading lady was with Akshay in *Andaaz,*" they pointed out with some satisfaction. "So when they worked in *Andaaz*, Akshay had already been introduced to her by us."

In casual conversations, her former secretary Prakash Jaju would cast a different perspective on why she'd lost *Humraaz* and other movies. According to him, the filmmakers had conferenced together and conspired to ease her out of their projects after seeing how she looked post surgery.

She lost many films in that period like *Aksar*, *Jaan Ki Baazi*, and *Gandhi* with Sunny Deol. She'd even shot for some of them when she was nosed out of them.

"People in this industry exaggerate limitlessly," observed Jaywant Thakre, the expert who had done the make-up on Priyanka's face on that fateful evening when Vijay Galani and director Mahesh Manjrekar had their mahurat and had been aghast at their heroine's nose. The bridge that had collapsed, costing her seven films from which she was ejected, was not such a big deal, said Thakre. "What are we make-up artistes for if not to camouflage such elements?" he questioned. "When I did the make-up for Shilpa Shetty during *Dhadkan*, there was a cut clearly visible across her nose (after cosmetic surgery). It was my job as the make-up man to take care of it and nobody saw that cut in the film. Between the make-up man and the cameraman, such things can be easily handled. Priyanka's nose was also manageable. It wasn't the kind of disaster that the media and the industry made it out to be."

Jaju had also boasted that when all the producers were dropping her, Anil Sharma too was on the verge of following suit when he (Jaju) pleaded with him to retain Priyanka in his film *The Hero*. The filmmaker had given in but had whittled down her role from the main lead to a secondary one.

"Not true," contradicted Anil Sharma, the director of *The Hero*, Priyanka's undisputed first film.

"When I was almost completing *Gadar: Ek Prem Katha* (2001, one of Hindi cinema's biggest blockbuster hits), I was watching the Miss World pageant on television," said Anil. "As soon as I saw Priyanka Chopra being crowned, something about her face and her smile made me say, 'This girl is very attractive. *Mujhe badi achchi lag rahi hai* (I like her a lot).' Coincidentally, Prakash Jaju was sitting beside me and he reacted. He said, 'You mean if you found her, you'd cast her in your next film?' And I said, 'Yes, I'll cast her.' The next day, Jaju somehow found her and called me up in the evening to say she was out of town but was flying in with her family to meet me. At that time, getting an assurance from the maker of a film like *Gadar* that he would sign up a girl for his next would've made anybody go and find her.

"Priyanka came to meet me with her father. Dr Ashok Chopra was a wonderful man to talk to and we had a very good meeting. She was the first girl I'd signed without an audition. I told my wife, 'It's an auspicious day, keep her cheque in the *mandir* (religious nook in the house).' It was a cheque for five lakh rupees.

"Her father was a very good singer, so one evening we had a big *mehfil* (musical session) at home where top names from the music industry were also present. My wife was fond of singing, Priyanka would also sing, so there was a lot of music and good times."

Demolishing the report that he'd demoted Priyanka from main lead to second, Anil underscored, "That's a fake story. When I signed her for *The Hero*, I didn't have a script ready. We were only sure that Sunny Deol would play the title role, nothing else was finalised. When

Priyanka was signed, it was talked of as a Sunny-Priyanka film. But the script hadn't been written and when it was, it happened to have two girls in it, both opposite Sunny. Preity played one role, Priyanka the other. So I was the one to launch Priyanka, mine was her first film. Those days we didn't have contracts with clauses that stated that this will be your first release and so on. In fact, other filmmakers like Suneel Darshan asked me how she was before signing her.

"The problem with Priyanka was that she had accidentally undergone a nose surgery," Anil said, the nose cropping up once again. "After signing her, I'd gone to the US and Canada for three or four months. When I came back and started working on the script, I began to hear that she'd had some surgery done, that she wanted pouting lips like Julia Roberts. I hadn't met her for a while because after my first few meetings with her, I was confident that she would be a very good actress, I knew that I wouldn't have to slog over her performance. So I wasn't insecure, I didn't have any reasons to feel that she wouldn't deliver. But when I returned, I met Pravinbhai of Time (then a popular production house) and he told me that she'd been dropped from three or four films. He also put a photograph before me. Of a girl in a bathing suit coming out of the pool. I told him, 'This is not Priyanka, this is someone else. This girl is really awful looking while Priyanka is a pretty girl with a beautiful smile.' He insisted that the girl in the photograph was Priyanka. I was shocked, so I called her and she came to meet me with her mother. By then, I'd got a lot of information on what had happened to her. When I looked at her, I burst out angrily and asked her, 'Where was the need to do all this?' Mother and daughter got very emotional at this meeting and they explained that she'd had surgery done, it would take six to seven months for the nose to heal. Since she'd been dropped from three or four other films, they were going back to Bareilly and they returned my cheque to me. Yes, that was a very dignified thing to do. They were very decent, cultured people," he noted appreciatively.

"I was also emotionally moved. So I told them not to return to Bareilly right away. I told them that I'd do a screen test with her. I called Pandhari dada (veteran make-up man), sent for cinematographer Kabir Lalji, decided on her look with short hair and took a screen test. It was in a bungalow near Yari Road. Who would've foreseen that after a successful screen test, one day she would be the owner of a huge bungalow on the same Yari Road?" he asked with a chuckle.

"I sent the results of the screen test to Pravinbhai who asked me who it was. I said, Priyanka Chopra, and he was surprised. I sent it to Sunny Sir; he of course had no objections to working with whoever the director wanted as the heroine. That's how Priyanka came into my film. After that, a lot of people like Subhash Ghai began to ask me about her. By then *Gadar* became a big hit and I would think that to be a part of my next film would've been a big deal for her at that time. It must've benefited her.

"She was determined, *unmein kshamta thi* (she had the ability), that's why she succeeded. As a filmmaker, I had only the small role of presenting her on the screen in the right way. To say that she was shifted from the main to a secondary role is totally false. On the contrary, once Preity was also signed, I was the one who told Pravinbhai that I had given Priyanka my word, so she would be in the film. I was the one who did a screen test to make that possible," he pointed out.

"The first scene I filmed on her featured Priyanka in a long shot with Kabir Bedi. They were playing father and daughter and she gave her shot like a seasoned artiste. *Kamaal ki performer hamesha se thi* (She was always a fantastic performer). I used to tell her that she had very seductive eyes and a lovely husky voice. I knew she'd do very well. *Par kitni door kaun jata hai yeh toh Ishwar hi bata sakta hai* (But how far a person will go is something only god can tell you). By god's grace, her choice of films also turned out well for her.

"But," observed Anil, "she has gone this far in life because of the courteous behaviour and etiquette that she has inherited from her family, her parents. Even more than her knowledge, capabilities and her *kala* (art), according to me, her success story has been possible because of the influence of her family on her, the *sanskar*, the culture she was raised with. The upbringing matters so much that it takes you very far. It teaches you how to interact with people, *vyavahar sikhata hai* (how to behave with people), who to respect and in what measure, who to talk to and how to talk to them. Priyanka has been perfect in the way she behaves with people.

"I remember," he stated as an example. "We shot for *The Hero* in Toronto and in Jungfrau (Switzerland). The production boys wouldn't even get a chair for a new girl. So in minus 20 degrees, mother and daughter used to stand for three and four hours, absolutely uncomplainingly. Since it took three hours to reach Jungfrau, even if her shot was only in the afternoon, she had to come by bus with everybody else in the morning. Only Amrish Puri and Kabir Bedi had a van of their own. So I told them, 'I'm offering you very good company, please start bringing this new girl to the location with you and please have your staff take care of her too.' Those days, the production people never gave a new girl a spotboy or any staff to keep her comfortable. Now they do. But times were different. So Amrish Puri and Kabir Bedi began to take care of Priyanka and keep her comfortable. What I do remember is that she never had any complaints, any grouses. We took her for a two-month shoot. Irrespective of how many days we shot with her, she was always there without complaint. It was a treat to work with her."

Even if they didn't work together after *The Hero*, Anil made an observation common to all those who've worked with her. "Everybody needs a ladder to climb to the top," he remarked. "But the uniqueness of Priyanka is that even after reaching the top, she has never forgotten the people who held that ladder for her. It's another big reason for her astounding success. I haven't worked with her for years," he added. "But just three or four years ago, when I was in the US where my children were studying, I heard that Priyanka was also there. She was shooting for an album or a video. When I called her up, she immediately called me over to the studio and there she made it a point to take my arm and introduce me to each and every member of the team saying, 'This is Anil Sharma, he's my first director.' She doesn't forget those who've walked with her on her journey. She has all these marvellous traits in her."

In 2018, Anil Sharma was poised to launch his own son, Utkarsh Sharma as hero in a film titled *Genius*. "Her mother Madhuji had come to the function we had organised to introduce Utkarsh and Priyanka had also tweeted about him when we'd announced his debut," Anil offered as proof that all of them had maintained good relations to this day.

Farah Khan who would much later choreograph Priyanka as the 'Desi Girl' in *Dostana* was impressed by what she saw of the new girl in a side role in *The Hero*. "She struck me as a very good performer," she mused.

But the abracadabra was really *Andaaz* which opened a whole new world of treasures to Priyanka, breaking the jinx that had dogged her thus far. The success of that film, her packing a wallop in a performance that was a likeable mix of the uninhibited and the vulnerable, and a nose that didn't strike anybody as awkward, had producers looking interested once again.

"Prakash Jaju had tried to introduce Priyanka to me earlier, I think in 2000 or 2001 at the Holiday Inn in Mumbai, when she had just become Miss World," said Suneel Darshan, the producer of *Andaaz*. But she was not his instant choice.

"When I saw her for the first time, I said to myself, 'The whole interpretation of the word 'beauty' needs to be reworked,'" Suneel was candid. "She also came across as quite childish, so I barely met her and moved away. Then I heard she was considered for a few movies, she had also shot for some stuff, and was dropped unceremoniously. I got to know that this girl was actually wanting to pack her bags and move back to where she came from."

That's when cosmic powers stepped in. Darshan had planned *Andaaz* with his then-staple hero Akshay Kumar and two other heroines, Karisma Kapoor and Rani Mukherjee. "Somehow that didn't materialise," he contemplated. "Rani was sweet, very nice and I was very fond of her. Karisma had worked with me before and I always had a great equation with her and her mother, Babitaji. But something didn't quite work out between Babitaji and me for this particular project. At that point of time, she had some financial issues that we couldn't agree on. And I said, 'Okay, maybe in a way this was not destined to happen.' I also began to feel, what's so fresh about casting known faces like Karisma Kapoor and Rani Mukherjee in my film? I'd just moved out of Mehboob Studio where I'd met Babitaji and Karisma when I asked myself, 'What if I don't cast any of the girls who're around?' What flashed through my mind was a *Filmfare* cover where Akshay had done a photo shoot with new girl Lara Dutta.

"Lara was based in Bangalore, her parents lived there and her father was undergoing some surgery. My movie was going to start in seven days when this meeting with Karisma went south. So Lara came and met me. She was an interesting girl, great body, she knew the language well. She was Miss Universe; I had very little time and I signed her on. After she was cast, there were many girls like Isha Koppikar coming to meet me for the other role which was way smaller in the original draft.

"I was still tossing names in my head when Prakash Jaju landed up again at my office with this girl and insisted that I meet her. I'm a man who finds it very difficult to say 'No', so I said, 'Fine, bring her up.' She came in with him; I looked at her and I think success *se zyada defeat aapko bahut kuch sikha deti hai* (more than success, it's defeat that teaches you a great many things). Priyanka Chopra's approach and attitude were very different from what I had seen in that brief, earlier meeting. There was a bit of a bridge on her nose that was being reconstructed at that point of time. In fact, the bridge was actually not there. She had signed a Tamil movie for which she'd already shot a few days. Her pictures were not up to the mark but when I sat with that girl for some time and we talked, I just looked at her eyes and she was amazing. Her eyes and that voice of hers were fabulous. I told her, if you get this movie, you have to give it your best. The other terms and conditions that this would be her first release, were discussed and agreed upon."

Priyanka and Lara were paid a handsome ten lakh rupees each. "I gave them both a decent, respectable figure. I had a contract with Priyanka that she'd do a second film with me for fifteen. She did *Barsaat* for me after *Andaaz* by which time her price had shot up. But she had a contract with me, so she did it for fifteen."

Andaaz, directed by late Raj Kanwar, was destined to be her breakthrough film even though when Jaju took her to Suneel Darshan's office, "There was a problem with the bridge of her nose but she was confident that the correction would happen by the time the film rolled."

What clinched it for Suneel was not her face but Priyanka's personality.

"Her eyes, the voice, her structure and she knew the language. She was fond of singing, she was a ghazal girl and Western at the same time. She had studied abroad, spoke very well. There was a lot to her.

"Although the rest of the team including Akshay always thought Lara Dutta was the real star material out there, I told Akshay, no, this is the dark horse that has got to strike because I think this is how Rekhaji was at one time. I'd seen Rekhaji in 1966 or 1967 when I must have been about seven years old. There was some birthday happening at Hotel Sun-n-Sand and I remember she'd looked like Priyanka, only Rekhaji was plumper. She was not conventionally beautiful but she was attractive with a good voice, lovely eyes and great sensuality. Priyanka was similar, she had something in her. Initially, everyone thought I was joking but I had this strong belief in her. You won't believe it but Manish Malhotra who was the costume designer of all my movies right from the start, found himself so tied up that he couldn't prioritise *Andaaz*. He was prioritising a wedding in (financier and diamond trade businessman) Bharat Shah's family in Antwerp over *Andaaz*."

When Suneel Darshan announced *Andaaz*, he sent out photographs of Akshay flanked by Miss Universe and Miss World.

"That was how we were packaging it," agreed Darshan. "We were going to release the film within six months and we wanted to create a buzz around it right away. I got a very positive reaction to it from the very start; there was something special about these Miss Universes and Miss Worlds. Everything fell into place and happened really fast.

"Priyanka was completely dedicated and focused on what she was doing. She had a secretary (Jaju) who was really pushy and her mother Madhu was always there. That's a very wise woman behind Priyanka. I found Madhu tremendously intelligent. She was always watching, she wanted this career to happen. She didn't want things to go wrong for Priyanka and she was always telling her daughter, *aisa karo*, *waise karo*, do this, do that.

"We went to South Africa where most of Priyanka's portions were shot."

That was where Priyanka's determination to make it showed up. Nothing could come between her and where she was headed, nothing was insurmountable in her quest to be the best. She was, as Pradeep Guha had observed, the *karke dikhaoongi* girl. The tougher the challenge thrown at her, the more she relished springing up and volleying it.

Suneel Darshan called it, "Watching how an artiste evolves." They were shooting the song, 'Allah Kare Dil Na Lage Kisi Se' when he realised that she wasn't very comfortable with Indian dance moves.

"But see how destiny works," he marvelled. "Akshay Kumar's wife was due to deliver their first baby, so we had to abandon that schedule and return to India. That gave Priyanka a long gap before we went back to South Africa to shoot the song. What she did in that time was the blueprint for her success. Mother and daughter went and signed up with Pandit Viru Krishnan who was a very good trainer and the two of them used to be there from 7 am every morning to 10 pm every night, dedicatedly learning Indian dance. After Priyanka, Lara also joined the same class; later Katrina also joined in. These girls were not trained for the Indian film scene. But Priyanka's dedication was unmatched. Not just hers but her mother's too, as Madhu was always there with Priyanka. Priyanka was very attached to her father but her guiding light was Madhu."

Suneel's was a milder spin-off of what happened in South Africa. Priyanka was more brutal when she flashbacked with me, the humiliation an unforgotten memory.

"Dance is a very important aspect of my career," she said, and added with total candour, "I couldn't dance at all. I could dance for like, fun. During *Andaaz*, my first film, I remember I had to do something like thirty-two retakes. It was a jimmy jib shot where all I had to do was run towards the valley, run back, look at Akshay, run into his arms, smile and say my lines. I simply couldn't do it!

"I remember the choreographer threw the mike and said, 'Pack up! Just because you're Miss World, you think you can act? Learn how to dance first and then come into the movies.' That night the schedule was called off because Akshay's baby was going to be born. I went back to Mumbai.

"After that incident, I was very scarred. I started learning kathak the next day. Pandit Viru Krishnan was my guruji. I used to dance almost eight hours a day. I started learning it with a vengeance. Any form of dance will always give you rhythm. When I went back to shoot the song, the same choreographer came and told me, 'I don't know what you've done, there's such a huge difference in you.' So dance plays a very important part in my life. I love dancing. In my movies, the dances and songs are a form of expression for me. And I love stage shows." It was Priyanka proving to herself that nothing was unconquerable by going to the other extreme where she began to love the same kind of dancing that had fetched her a scolding from her first choreographer.

A good word spreads just as swiftly as gossip does and the film industry soon began to hear about this new actress who was dedicated and determined to reach the top of her profession.

During the making of *Andaaz*, Suneel saw a clear difference between Lara and Priyanka. They were two vastly different personalities. "Lara was this," said he, closing his arms over his chest, indicating that she was enclosing everything within herself. "On the other hand, Priyanka was that," he concluded, throwing his arms out to welcome and engulf the world. "Priyanka knew how she had to play her game. I've always defined her as a girl with a man's mind; the ambition glowed in her.

"Even way back, you could see the ambition, the drive and everything. Even if nobody else could see that she would go very far, I for some reason, said, 'This is Rekha in the making.' I know people scoffed at the thought. But she knew the craft of acting. She had been a Miss World, so she knew exactly how the world operated."

By the time the shooting wound up, Suneel could see who was going to be the marathon runner. Perhaps Lara lacked the killer instinct, comforted by the thought that the world had decided she was the winner, stardom was already hers; there was no need to go the extra mile for it. She'd pipped Priyanka to the post at the beauty pageant too.

For Priyanka, it was a case of the underdog having to paw its way up and make it as the top dog.

Suneel analysed, "Lara already had Kelly in her life. Besides, she had this personality where she would take her time, wait for things to come to her. But this girl (Priyanka) knew how to go and snatch what she wanted. Yes, she definitely knew how to do that. But Priyanka had her little *nautanki*s (dramatics) too," he put in.

Suneel expanded on his last remark with an appropriate example of what happened backstage at the music launch of *Andaaz*.

"I had decided to put these two girls with Akshay Kumar on stage for a live item. We had Mr Bachchan coming to release the music, and we had a lot of dignitaries from the film industry and the media as invitees. We'd rehearsed a song from the movie with the three actors and I'd decided that they would be wearing exactly what they'd worn in the movie. About two hours before the show was to start, Akshay came and told me, 'I think we need to change the costume we are putting the girls in.' But the costumes were exactly what they'd worn in the song. Since I was calling the shots at that point of time, we decided to go ahead with the show exactly the way it had been visualised. But I understood that Priyanka was behind it. (Even while shooting) she had done so much *natak* (fuss) about wearing the costume but the film was canned. She was now trying to get to me through the hero by putting him up against me. I had to put my foot down. Anyway, they came on stage in their costumes as planned and that show got a very big response; the media they got was humungous. Immediately after that, I took them to London and did a first-ever kind of an event there where the world paparazzi covered them. The two girls with Akshay were put on covers and there were writeups on how they were being launched. They were all willing to do everything; they were game for that moment of fame and glory.

"What was very surprising however, was that Priyanka was so full of herself. Once the film was complete, she wanted to watch the movie before it was released. So I kept a screening for her and she did go and watch it. I didn't go for the show but I expected her to call me back after she'd seen the film. Surprisingly, she didn't. I checked with her secretary and he said that she couldn't see herself (anywhere) in the movie. I said that was really funny, she was the glamour portion of the movie. And she left a definite impact.

"So I called her to the office in the evening because she lived close by and asked her what had happened. She was so upset, she said, 'I couldn't see myself.' I told her, 'The problem with you is that you were only watching the other girl, that's why you couldn't see yourself.' That was her trait, she was so competitive.

"Once *Andaaz* was released, everything fell into place. Somewhere, she also became the media's darling and by then Akshay Kumar was on the scene. She signed on *Waqt* with Akshay who got her Sajid Nadiadwala's *Mujhse Shaadi Karogi* with Salman and him. So suddenly they started doing a lot of work together."

Interestingly, Preity Zinta with whom Priyanka had to share screen space in *The Hero*, now found the shoe on the other foot. It was reportedly Preity who'd been signed as the heroine of *Mujhse Shaadi Karogi* but it was Priyanka who got to play the girl who's wooed by both Akshay and Salman in the film.

Once she teamed with Akshay, she outgrew boyfriend Aseem who had his own problems and couldn't climb to stardom as dexterously as her. Soon Jaju too would be dispensable.

Becoming a saleable commercial couple with Akshay Kumar gave Priyanka the comfort of having someone in her corner who'd watch out for her. It was a typical box-office story where a lead pair had such scorching chemistry that it spilled over from the set into after-office hours. Akshay Kumar and Twinkle Khanna were married in 2001 and it was during the filming of *Andaaz* that their son Aarav was born. Since Akshay was married and a parent, and Priyanka always relished her privacy, their friendship was never publicly acknowledged by either of them. It's a trademark trait – to this day, Priyanka has never gone public about any of her personal relationships though they become public knowledge pretty soon.

Blissfully, Akshay and Priyanka starred in three more hits – *Mujhse Shaadi Karogi* (2004), *Aitraaz* (2004) and *Waqt* (2005), before his wife Twinkle put a weighty foot down and issued an ultimatum. She succeeded – her husband's ardour for his favourite co-star was doused and she extracted a promise from him that he would never work with Priyanka again. For Priyanka who was just about getting used to stardom, the abrupt exit of Akshay from her life and career was akin to having the safety net yanked from under her.

"I'm completely unapologetic about anything I do in my life" – Priyanka

She fleshed out the thought a little more although this was a general conversation and not particularly about Akshay or anybody else. "I have huge amounts of courage of conviction and I stand even by my mistakes by saying, 'Okay, you may think it's a mistake but I did it. Even if it's a mistake, it's mine.' So whether it's my films, or my decisions, my life, my family or my friends, I'm very unapologetic about anything that I do. I may be tentative about taking a decision, I need everybody's opinion before taking a decision. But once a decision is made, whether it's to go on board a film or to take on something, it's mine. Whether you like it or hate it or abhor it, it's mine. I'm unapologetic."

She owed nobody an apology but was this a costly friendship for Priyanka to have struck? So put it down to life's many experiences. She never claimed to be a paragon or the unflawed diamond.

"I am hugely flawed, and I like it that way. That's the fun of life. You fall, get up, make mistakes, learn from them, be human and be you" – Priyanka

What's vital is that Priyanka was barely twenty-one years old when she worked in *Andaaz,* so put it down as one of life's many experiences. But it was a relationship that brewed right under Suneel's nose during *Andaaz.*

"I thought as much," admitted Suneel, "although I was never involved. I thought it was below my dignity to get into people's personal lives."

By the time *Mujhse Shaadi Karogi* rolled along, it was said that Akshay's wife Twinkle and his mother-in-law Dimple Kapadia had not just sniffed what was happening, they were also devising ways to keep them apart.

Priyanka and Dimple happened to share the same makeup-man at that time and it was believed that he tattled to the latter about the former.

Meanwhile, Jaju is known to have told people that phone calls from Akshay's family had forced him to prevent Akshay from meeting Priyanka, to ensure that they didn't share a vanity van or have make-up rooms next to each other. Reportedly, one morning he switched the nameplates on the doors of the make-up rooms, leaving Akshay next door to Amrish Puri and not to the heroine.

Jaju's moves were suspect and didn't go down well with Priyanka or her family.

By this time, Priyanka's career had taken off, she didn't need Jaju to introduce her around. The view from the Chopra end was that he was getting to be a pain as a secretary who was perhaps imagining that he had a role beyond that in her life. It made her father naturally seethe and turn more protective of her. Dropping him from their lives began to seem more attractive than having him around. It was believed that Akshay too was angered at what he perceived as clear interference and overstepping by a secretary who should've known his place.

The last straw was when journalist Bharti Dubey who was writing for *The Asian Age,* printed Priyanka's telephone bill where her many calls to Akshay's number were recorded. Interestingly, a close friendship with young, eligible Harman Baweja, son of the producer of her film *Karam* (2005), had also started getting reported.

"I made sure about the numbers before I published the phone bill in *The Asian Age*," said Dubey.

Jaju claimed he had nothing to do with it.

Priyanka had discussed with Suneel her growing concern over retaining Jaju as her secretary.

He shared, "One day I got a call from her where she said she was having a lot of problems with her secretary. He was keeping too much of an eye on her life and she said she was somewhere feeling claustrophobic. I told her that it was her decision to make, it would make no difference to me."

What was in no doubt was that the Chopra family was uncomfortable having Jaju around and he had to be left behind. That set off a long and acrimonious battle where Jaju finally landed in jail for 67 days. In Jaju's place came a veteran star secretary called Chand Mishra, a kind, fatherly figure who would pose no personal problems to Priyanka. He minded his own business, did his job well and continued to be on her payroll long after Priyanka got herself a retinue of managers to take care of her professional life.

Personally, when Akshay finally cooled off from Priyanka, they had already begun work on *Barsaat* which Suneel Darshan was producing and directing.

"After *Andaaz*, they were supposed to do *Barsaat* (2005) for me," disclosed Suneel. During *Andaaz* itself, they'd become the couple with chemistry, so signing them up for the next one was almost organic. But it didn't take off immediately.

"*Barsaat* was slightly delayed because I had a bit of a back problem and then Akshay had some other movies on the sets which needed to be completed," explained Suneel. By the time *Barsaat* rolled, Priyanka-Akshay had become a hot-selling box-office twosome, the buzz around them inevitable. Suneel wasn't aware that they'd become so sizzling that plans were afoot to rein the man in and bring him back to home and hearth.

So he continued with his plans for *Barsaat*. "The audio songs of *Barsaat* were recorded, all dates were finalised and the movie was finally launched," he narrated. "We even shot the first schedule, a major song with a big set at Filmistan Studio. The title song was shot on Akshay and Priyanka. After that, I think she was off for a series of stage shows for two-and-a-half months in the US. She was doing very well by then."

Before she left for her stage shows, Suneel recalled that Subhash Ghai's *Aitraaz* with Abbas-Mustan had been offered to Akshay. "Akshay was in two minds," he said. "He wanted to do a movie for them but because it was a very big production house, big directors, the hero would have to compromise on his pay packet. I had insisted that he sign that movie because I thought it was a great way to announce to the world that serious filmmakers were taking him. With Bebo (Kareena Kapoor) also in it, it became an important film for him to do."

Aitraaz was also offered to Priyanka, the interesting new girl on the horizon.

"Take calculated risks" – Priyanka

"People have written me off several times in my career. After *Aitraaz*, I was told I'd remain a vamp. I signed a US TV show at the height of my film career, the stakes were high, the repercussions could've been career-ending. I backed up those risks with my 100 per cent."

Aitraaz was a brave decision but not one taken overnight. As Suneel Darshan remembered it, "Priyanka had initially wanted to be the morally-right heroine of *Aitraaz* and not the vampish wife of Amrish Puri who stalked the hero.

"When Priyanka was narrated the role (which had been inspired by Demi Moore's character in *Disclosure*), she got very disturbed by the fact that she was given a vamp's role and refused to do the movie. She wanted to be the heroine, so she went back home. Because everyone was somewhere connected to me, whether it was Akshay Kumar or it was his secretary Sanjay Bali or Jaju, they asked me to talk to her without the producers or directors of *Aitraaz* knowing about it. So I called her again and she came over. I explained to her how important it was for her to do that movie and that it would be a virtual blunder if she didn't do it. She saw reason, immediately confirmed that she would be doing it, and signed up for *Aitraaz*."

Though they were early days, it was clear that she had a mind of her own – she wasn't going to blindly walk into a big banner offer. She had to be convinced that it would be good for her career.

"Yes, *Aitraaz* was definitely her movie," enthused Suneel. "She knew how to play that role. It was her personality, it was her mind there, and she knew how to carry off this kind of character. She was a woman of the new century. Thereafter, as I told you, she went back to do the big stage shows but stayed in touch with me."

Interestingly, while Priyanka had wanted to play safe and be the hero's virtuous wife in *Aitraaz*, Kareena Kapoor saw the potential in playing Amrish Puri's vampish wife and asked for that role.

"When we were casting for *Aitraaz*, Kareena wanted to do the role which we gave Priyanka," confirmed Abbas-Mustan. "But the role of the wife was also important because she fights for her husband; she's a strong woman too. So we wanted Kareena to play the wife. By then, we were convinced that we had a very strong actress in Priyanka, an actress with great style and we knew she would be the right girl to play Amrish Puri's wife, Sonia.

We'd seen *Andaaz* and other films but we'd been confident of her much earlier just by meeting her. We'd reposed faith in her before anybody else, long before any film of hers was made," they said as a reminder.

The directors were convinced but the actress herself was not. "We narrated the subject of *Aitraaz* to Priyanka. She heard the role and we told her that if she was frightened to do it, she wouldn't be able to pull it off. It was true that the character had been inspired by Demi Moore's in *Disclosure* but only the idea of that character. The screenplay was written completely afresh, we put in a cruise, made it into a musical. When Priyanka finally heard it, she was keen to do it."

Veteran filmmaker Subhash Ghai whose banner Mukta Arts had produced *Aitraaz*, was actually surprised when Priyanka said 'Yes' to their offer.

"I had met Priyanka earlier. After she became Miss World, she'd come to my office. One of my friends had taken her screen test and shown it to me. I'd found her a typical filmy actor," remarked Ghai quite frankly. "You know how youngsters try to act for an audition or show reel. The '*Babuji main aa gayi* (Babuji, I've arrived),' kind of acting," he laughed, enacting the line like an over-the-top '60s actress. "She was trying hard to be there. Pressing hard to impress you. But one trait I could see even from the show reel was her do-or-die attitude. Gauging that comes from experience. I've worked with more than 280 actors so far," he pointed out.

The audition he was shown was not a flesh-and-blood introduction which happened a little later.

"Then I met her at Pradeep Guha's place. She used to come there quite often," said Ghai. "Pradeep Guha told me, you should consider this girl, she's a good actor.

"When I talked to her, I found her very intelligent which was nice. I'd already seen the passion in that audition. But *bewakoofon ko bhi passion hota hai* (even dolts can have passion). So I was impressed that she had passion and was an intelligent, well-spoken girl. You have to gauge people and see if they're dreamy, fake, phoney, intelligent, profound, in-depth. We judge. It's easy for me because I'm good at reading faces."

The filmmaker who walked to a beat of his own wasn't impressed by her Miss World title.

"When I met her again, she told me she was doing a film called *The Hero* and she was very excited about it," he said. "I could see that this was a girl coming from nowhere. Being Miss World could work for you. But it could also go against you. Like I never cast Aishwarya Rai in *Taal* because she was Miss World. In fact, I used to tell Aishwarya that (for me) her being Miss World was the one point that was going against her. I told her, I have to demolish that Miss World right at the beginning. If anything was preventing me from casting her in *Taal*, it was that she was Miss World. An actor is a walkie-talkie person, I always see how a person talks. It's not the same as being a still model."

That's where Priyanka scored.

"I could see that Priyanka spoke well, I liked her voice. An actor's face doesn't have to be pretty; it's how she or he talks that matters. Gradually, the face gets accepted," analysed the voice of experience. "If Shah Rukh, Amitabh, Sunny Deol, Dilip Kumar's faces have been accepted, it's because of their performance, their acting. So how you speak is important." It was a neat way of summing up how Priyanka found acceptance.

"But I knew she'd have to go through a struggle because she didn't have any backing," he added. "*Taal* (1999) had been released and I was busy with *Yaadein* (2001) then. When the subject of *Aitraaz* came to us in 2004, we already had Kareena on board. Mukta Arts had signed her for three films. Then Abbas-Mustan said, 'We want Akshay Kumar to play the hero.' I called Akshay; he came and very nicely agreed to do the film. For the third role, it was Abbas-Mustan who suggested Priyanka."

Before the film went on the floor, it was said that Celina Jaitley had been finalised to play Sonia. But in a surprise move, Priyanka stepped in and Celina was left out of the cast. As the producer of *Aitraaz*, Subhash Ghai explained how the switch from Celina to Priyanka happened.

"For every role, we always have three actors in the nominations. It's called a wish list. If not this one, then that one. For me, when casting, we look at three things. First, the actor must be suitable. Second, must be available. Third, must be saleable. For *Taal*, we had four other heroines as options. There's no drama about it, it's a professional decision. The film isn't going to be stalled because an actor isn't available. We don't wait for stars/actors. That's why we at Mukta Arts have sometimes missed out on stars."

After Abbas-Mustan had put forward Priyanka Chopra's name, Ghai was all for it. "I strongly recommended her for it," he said. "When I met her also, I told her, 'It's a negative role, you must do it.'"

He reasoned that it was the novelty factor that swung the vote in Priyanka's favour. "I told Abbas-Mustan, 'Celina and the other girls who are being considered for the same role have already done negative roles. Priyanka has not. The audience won't be expecting her to be negative. So the shock value you will get from a heroine playing a vamp will be much more than from someone who's done negative roles before.' That was the reason Priyanka was ultimately signed for the role. It was not to humiliate or put down Celina in any way. There was no betrayal here. There was consensus in the team over Priyanka.

"In fact, I was surprised when she agreed to do the role," he commented. "Sometimes," he mused, "an actor accepts an assignment because of the setup. Even today, you'll see a top heroine playing a side character because of the setup, because there's a Khan there or the banner is big. We also understand that Priyanka must've accepted it because of the setup – Mukta Arts was right on top then. But I knew that this girl would do better than the others. When I later saw a few scenes that had been shot, I realised that she was apt for the role."

It wasn't an easy role for Priyanka. The jitters surfaced when it came to actually playing Sonia. But once again, the right people were around at the right time to take care of her. Abbas-Mustan were firm about what they wanted her to do but careful about how they prised a performance out of her.

"She was confident at the time of signing the film but she had her share of nerves, *darti thi* (she was scared), when it came to the actual shooting of certain scenes with Akshay Kumar and to play Amrish Puri's wife. That was understandable because any young heroine would want a young hero opposite her," they remarked.

The real problem arose when they had to film a crucial, pivotal scene with Priyanka and Akshay and she got cold feet.

"When we were shooting in South Africa, there was this crucial scene where she seduces Akshay, grabs him, lies on top of him," the directors recalled. "Priyanka was really scared about doing that particular scene. Her whole worry was, 'Once the film is released, how will people view me?

What'll be their opinion of me?' We assured her that it was an award-winning role."

It was. It was like the anti-hero role that Shah Rukh Khan played in the same director-duo's *Baazigar* (1993). A performance that had ensured his rise as a hero without labelling him a villain.

Her own performance was enhanced because the team worked well. The faith that Priyanka had reposed in the banner and in the directors paid off as Abbas-Mustan described how they finally got her to seduce Akshay for them in the film.

"We sat her down along with Akshay, explained the whole scene to both of them and said that we would shoot the sequence at one go, do only one take. There would be no retakes, no filming it from different angles. But before shooting that scene, her hands were ice cold, she was so anxious. She had to grab him, throw him down, cling to him. We were shooting in a bungalow; the shot was to be taken on the first floor. Before the shooting, we rehearsed thoroughly. She didn't want to rehearse in front of the whole crew, so we went to the basement, only the two of us with Akshay and Priyanka, and rehearsed the entire scene. Every move, every turn, was rehearsed to perfection. Then we went upstairs and did that sequence with just one take. We shot it with multiple cameras to avoid any awkwardness over doing the same scene again and again. The entire sequence of Akshay's phone falling, she grabbing him and seducing him was done in one shot, one take. That way her one big worry was put behind us."

To maintain the same body language, Abbas-Mustan did another 'sequence shot' (the term used for a long take that constitutes an entire sequence) for the same film. It was a challenge for Priyanka to rise to the occasion and do it so early in her career.

"When we were planning the shoot of the song, 'I Want To Make Love To You,' we wanted to picturise it with her looking wild and predatory," the directors said. "We thought that if we shot it in bits and put it together, we wouldn't be able to maintain that same mood throughout, it might look awkward. It was a background song without lip sync; everything was about her facial expressions and body language."

To pull it off, Priyanka had to prepare her mind before putting it into action.

"We'd decided to shoot the full song in one shot. An entire four-minute song was filmed at one go, one shot, no retakes. We did a lot of rehearsals to mark the right movements and spots. Watch that song again and check it out. On the day of the shoot, a four-minute sequence was completed in four minutes. When we checked the monitor, we were astonished that it was a perfect take. So after four minutes of shooting, it was pack up for the day. It was the kind of song we couldn't have shot in parts. Maintaining the mood and the wildness wouldn't have been possible if we'd cut it in between and shot it in parts."

It wouldn't have been possible with an actress who wasn't willing to slog over her work or who didn't have the smarts to understand what she had to do – all the characteristics that combined to make Priyanka the winning woman.

Abbas-Mustan talked of the three best scenes which contributed to marking Priyanka as a suave performer.

"The scene in her house where she comes downstairs, sits, and offers Akshay something to drink. She asks him, 'Will you have something hot?' We wanted her to play with the cell phone in her hand while doing that scene. She prepared herself so well that she did it with unmatched flair and style."

They applauded, "At a global beauty pageant, Priyanka had conquered the world and come home, she had something very special in her – great style. She had everything in her to be a top actress.

"After the film was released and was a big success, many new girls would tell us that they wanted a role like Priyanka's in *Aitraaz*. It was a dream role for any heroine. The credit goes to Priyanka for having carried off a difficult role with such panache. There was a scene where she comes downstairs and goes and sits next to Akshay when her husband Amrish Puri calls. She talks to her husband saying, 'Yes, darling, how are you baby?' but all the while she's playing with Akshay's hair. When we told her about the scene, she said, 'That's very difficult. I have to concentrate on what I'm saying to my husband and also be fondling Akshay's hair simultaneously?' We said, 'Yes, that's what we want in this scene; the audience will enjoy watching this person talking to her husband and flirting with her former boyfriend at the same time.' Priyanka is not the kind of actor who'll say, 'Okay, we'll shoot and see how it goes.' She thinks, she fully prepares herself, rehearses her moves and then shoots. She did an exceptional job in that scene too.

"There was another scene where Kareena as Akshay's wife comes to meet her and asks her to take back the case. We had seen a socialite in South Mumbai with an unbelievable attitude. We had that in our mind and we told Priyanka that when she talks to Kareena, she should keep polishing her nails and not even look up at her. Meaning, she should address Kareena without looking at her. Priyanka grasped it immediately and gave us a shot that was even better than the person who had inspired that scene."

"Be bold. Take risks" – Priyanka

She played Sonia for the camera with all the sincerity she could muster but the question that worried Priyanka was, would the risk label her a vamp and stand in the way of her becoming a top-bracket heroine?

"When we completed the film, we showed it to her. She was still scared, wondering whether a role where a man was suing her for sexual harassment which was unheard of those days, would affect her career in any way," Abbas-Mustan smiled.

She needed reassurance, over and over again. "We told her, 'Times are changing; people will watch your performance and see your acting,' and that's what happened."

Abbas-Mustan relived the excitement of delivering a box-office hit that also allayed Priyanka's fears and, in fact, ushered her into the next level of acceptance.

"When *Aitraaz* was released, a big film like *Veer-Zaara* simultaneously hit the theatres. Priyanka was still very anxious, waiting to catch each person's reaction to her work. She was still worried about what effect it would have on her career. That was one role where we had to keep encouraging her and instilling confidence in her that she would be greatly appreciated for her work.

"But irrespective of her fears, she always had a certain fire in her and she performed with complete *josh* (energy). Whatever we required her to do for the role, she did. Her mother used to be with her on the sets.

"Priyanka got a lot of awards for it, including Best Negative Performance from *Filmfare*. It was definitely a turning point in her career and she began to be taken seriously as an actress," said Abbas-Mustan with justified satisfaction.

What Priyanka never had was casualness. Every filmmaker has talked of the 3Ds that turned an average-looking girl into a stunning success story. The Determination to succeed, the Dedication to pursue success with tunnel vision and the Discipline to do what it takes to succeed.

Abbas-Mustan noted that early in her career. "She's always been very disciplined, very hard working and punctual. She's the kind of actress who wouldn't go and sit in the vanity van after her shot. Even if we were shooting with someone else and we gave her a break, she'd stay on the set. She was so passionate and involved. People don't succeed in such a big way for nothing."

Aitraaz also drew the attention of seasoned journalist Anupama Chopra, currently Founder-Editor, *Film Companion*, who wrote a piece for the *New York Times* in 2005:

Bollywood's Good Girls Learn To Be Bad
By ANUPAMA CHOPRA

Mumbai: Halfway through Aitraaz *(Objection), a Bollywood take on Barry Levinson's* Disclosure, *Sonia grabs hold of Raj. Once upon a time, they were lovers. But when Sonia, an ambitious model, opted for an abortion instead of child and marriage, Raj left her. Now she is his boss. Sonia starts to undress him, whispering, "Show me you are an animal." When he refuses and walks away, she screams: "I'm not asking you to leave your wife. I just want a physical relationship. If I don't have an objection, why should you?"*

The actress Priyanka Chopra had a difficult time playing this scene. A former Miss World, Ms. Chopra was a sophisticated, globally feted celebrity and she had prepared for her role by studying the calculated seductiveness of Sharon Stone in Basic Instinct. *But on the day that scene was shot, Ms. Chopra broke down and cried. The directors, brothers who go by the hyphenate Abbas-Mustan, had to spend a few hours convincing her that she was only playing a character. Filming didn't start until late afternoon.*

Ms. Chopra wasn't just being dramatic. She is a Bollywood actress, and as such, trained to play the role of a virginal glam-doll, not a sexual aggressor.

...But a decade-long cultural churning has overturned stereotypes in India.

...Today, consumerism, globalization, the proliferation of semiclad bodies in print and television, and the emergence of a more worldly audience have redefined the boundaries of what is permissible.

...but as the director Karan Johar, who has made several wholesome, family-centered blockbusters, put it, "In Bollywood, the No. 1 position will always be reserved for the girl you can take home to Mom."

That's why most actresses are hedging their bets. Ms. Chopra got rave reviews and awards for Aitraaz, *but she has followed up with good-girl acts. "I'm not sure I can play such a sexually aggressive character again," she says. "My family and friends were very shocked."*

Anupama was not shocked, she was impressed. Her appreciation marked the beginning of a long work association with Priyanka, dotted with interactions for the print medium, television and the Internet. As part of her professional life, Anupama became an inveterate Priyanka watcher.

"I don't remember my first meeting with her," contemplated Anupama. "I feel like I've known her forever.

I remember doing interviews with her for NDTV, then she had come on my show on Star World. And of course, I went to her house in New York one or two years ago. I remember going to her home and meeting her dad. But the first meeting, my god! I genuinely have no recollection of it.

"I didn't know her when she had become Miss World and all that; I never interviewed her in the Beauty Queen phase. I met her only when she became an actor. You know, the first interview I did with her was probably for the piece I did for the *New York Times*, 'Bollywood's Good Girls Learn To Be Bad'. I started with her story. She told me how when she did *Aitraaz*, and Abbas-Mustan explained the scene where she says, 'Give it to me' or whatever, they are on the floor and all that, 'I was literally weeping, and I was so mortified... I just couldn't bring myself to do it.' So the piece started with that anecdote which was about *Aitraaz*.

"I was blown away by her in *Aitraaz*. First of all, the choice she made, for somebody who was trying to be at that time a mainstream heroine, and they had to be virtuous. This was pre-*Khwaish*, pre-kissing and pre-everything. At that time, you make a choice like *Aitraaz* and do it damn well. The truth is that she was the best thing in the film. I don't remember anything else. I don't remember Kareena, I barely remember Akshay, I just remember her, sort of being this predator. So I was really impressed with the fact that she was willing to go out on a limb and do that."

Aitraaz, released in November 2004, was followed by *Waqt* (2005), another box-office success, five months later. It was her last film with Akshay Kumar. The intoxication of a job well done and well applauded in *Aitraaz* was thus followed by the cold splash of a heady relationship being terminated abruptly. Along with Priyanka, Suneel Darshan's *Barsaat* also suffered.

"I would always advise Akshay on creatives and on professional stuff whenever he asked," Suneel explained. "Otherwise I didn't want to be involved in anybody's personal life because there is a point at which you need to draw the line." But he did get involved, willy-nilly.

"With all the songs recorded, and one already picturised on Akshay and Priyanka before she left for her stage shows abroad, we were on the verge of a sixty-day schedule of *Barsaat*. On the day she returned to Mumbai and we were starting our long and final schedule of shooting, Akshay called me and said, 'I need to meet you very urgently.' I asked him why. Very rarely had I ever gone to meet him. My office was near his house, so he would spend his time there. But he was shooting at Madh Island and he wanted me to go there and meet him. I thought it must be something serious for him to call me over. When we met, I learnt what had transpired in his family – his wife coming up with her reactions, a lot of noise in their family and disturbances cropping up. I thought it was very childish because if the man decides to conduct himself the way he wants to, I don't think just stopping him from doing a movie with Priyanka Chopra was the way out. But he informed me that the pressures were so high that he would have to be eased out of my movie. I was aghast. We'd already done work on it, shot for it, my final schedule was about to start. But I couldn't react much because I thought it would be very undignified. The choice before me was, Akshay or Priyanka? For me it was financially viable to have Akshay Kumar there because somewhere there was chemistry between me and Akshay in the media and in the market. There was marketability about us as a team. We had actually picked him up for *Jaanwar* (1999) when nobody wanted to touch him with a barge pole. And here he was asking me to make a choice. I gave it a thought and said, 'Priyanka has no qualms about working on the movie. She hasn't asked me any questions; her dates are intact. I think I should therefore continue with her. Since you have doubts, you take a call whether you are doing the movie or not.' So it was decided that he would not do this movie but he would do my next one immediately after *Barsaat* and I continued to work with Priyanka.

"Bobby Deol's secretary Mr Bagh Singh was the first to get to know about the development and he immediately saw that Bobby came into the movie. Thereafter, I did make a movie with Akshay called *Dosti* (2005) in which I wanted Priyanka also. But by then, they had decided never to work together again. When Bebo got to know that I was starting *Dosti*, she offered to come in. In five days, the dates were done and in two months we shot with her and finished our work."

Two films made by the same producer had much to do with Priyanka's career: *Andaaz*, the film that set the course for Priyanka's ambitions and introduced the scorching Akshay-Priyanka pair to the market, and *Barsaat*, the film that ended the box-office run of the team.

Suneel Darshan didn't go back to Priyanka for another film. And Priyanka never did a film with Akshay again.

It would've felled a weaker woman.

"I met her at a party immediately after her split from Akshay and she was in tears," recalled journalist Jyothi.

"I hate to fail," said Priyanka to her audience. "Tubs of ice creams, tissues, tears, *dramebaazi* (theatrics), my mother...one thing that's as certain as day and night is that you will fail. But it's what you do after, that'll define where you go. When something I've invested my heart and my soul in, which I do with everything I do, I don't just wallow in self-pity. I roll around in it, I wrap myself around it, self-pity, self-pity, self-pity, it's not a pretty sight… Then I get up, cry a bit, dust myself off and dive straight back into life. The only way to push failure aside is to move ahead. Not ignore it, analyse it. And to get over it. You cannot truly enjoy success unless you've tasted failure. It tastes like shit."

"Fail, fail, fail and then rise like the Phoenix" – Priyanka

Fortuitously, the rise was possible because a film called *Krrish* pulled her out of the emptiness that follows heartbreak and filled it with the happiness that a big break brings in its wake.

Krrish was also the film which ensured that Priyanka's turn as the crotch-grabbing vamp of *Aitraaz* wouldn't stamp her as the next Bindu.

Krrish was her introduction to the big league of A-Listers.

Subhash Ghai's eyes twinkled as he remembered, "One major thing that happened during *Aitraaz* was that Rakesh Roshan who was making *Krrish*, called me home and gave me a nice meal too. He was tossing names around and wondering who to cast in the film when I suggested Priyanka. He asked me if I could show him some of the scenes from *Aitraaz* and I said 'Yes'. So he and Hrithik went to Empire Studio where the mixing of *Aitraaz* was going on and saw some scenes of the film. After two days, Priyanka sent me a big bouquet of flowers with a note that read, 'Thank you very much, it worked and I've signed *Krrish*.' She got established as a heroine from there."

Directors Abbas-Mustan did a vivid recall of it.

"When we were doing the final mixing of *Aitraaz,* Rakesh Roshanji and Hrithik came to see two reels of it at Empire Studio. Priyanka was so nervous that she told us, 'Don't show them *that* scene.' It was the crucial scene of the film but she was anxious and worried about how they'd perceive her if they saw it. We felt differently and told her, 'That's precisely the scene we're going to show them.' We did and they were so impressed by her performance, Rakeshji said, 'What an actress!' and she was signed for *Krrish* the same evening. That night, Priyanka sent us flowers with a lovely note in which she thanked us and said that she had signed *Krrish.*"

A minor sidelight to the celebration was that Pradeep Guha's *kanjoos* eighteen-year-old who found it difficult to open her purse had vanished with a change in her fortunes. Conversations with all those who featured prominently in her story thereafter had references to her gifts, her flowers and her notes. In fact, they became a permanent part of her social skills, as will be evident when the itinerary of her full journey is laid out – with phases that go through tunnels of despair before inevitably breaking into delightful sunlight.

Rakesh Roshan who brought her the much-needed patch of sunlight at that junction, described what he saw in Priyanka to cast her in the role that every leading lady of Mumbai was hankering after.

"When I was making *Krrish,* I wanted to take an upcoming girl because I was myself not sure if I could make this film in the time-frame I'd set for it. I had never before attempted such a subject; it was such an unusual superhero film. Since I was not very confident of how much time I'd need for it, I wanted to take a new girl who would adjust her dates with me and with Hrithik. I had met Priyanka a long time back when she was staying at the Holiday Inn and had won the Miss World title. I had interacted with her and seen potential in her.

"To be certain, I rang up Subhash Ghai. She was working in *Aitraaz* at that time. I asked him if I could see one or two reels and he said, 'Sure'. They were either mixing the film or doing the background score, I don't remember. Hrithik and I both went to Empire. Abbas-Mustan were also there. I didn't know that she was playing a vamp in it but I saw the fire in her and said, 'Yes, she is a very fine actress.'"

Even if she'd initially dithered and struck a Hamlet pose – to do or not to do *Aitraaz* – Roshan was impressed that once she went into it, "She did it with full confidence, with full conviction and courage.

"I thought she was the right girl to cast in *Krrish*, so I called her home. I narrated the whole script to her and I said, 'I'm taking you for my film because one, you are a good actress and two, I want all the dates as per my convenience. You'll have to block your dates for me.' She agreed and that's how we started working together. I dealt with her directly. I gave her the script, I gave her the narration, and I took the dates from her. Financials were also dealt with directly. She had come with her father and we spoke about it. It was very easy and neat, she came from a very dignified family.

"She was very well spoken, very intelligent, and very loving to work with. She was fun on the sets. I never saw her sulking or showing any signs of work pressure."

Observations about Priyanka don't differ from director to director. There's consensus that she's a director's actor but each had his own way of making her grow and deliver, either adding to her repertoire of performances or aiding her in her climb to stardom. Sometimes, it made her famous tear ducts that work overtime, come to the fore as they did while filming one particular sequence of *Krrish*.

Rakesh Roshan smiled, "We were shooting a volleyball sequence where she is playing with her friends and so is Krishna. He is alone with those girls. Priyanka had to hit the ball but while doing that, her one leg used to go up which wasn't looking nice. I told her that, I said, 'It looks very amateur, so don't put your leg up.' I wanted her to hit the ball straight like how a man would but she kept repeating the mistake; she was just not getting it right. I thought the only way she would do it well was if I scolded her. So I said to her firmly, 'Can't you understand what I want? I'm telling you not to put your leg up. Why don't you pay attention?' And she got it right this time but she started crying after that. I went up to her and explained that I only scolded her so that she'd get the shot right. 'I didn't mean anything, and see, you got it right,' I said to her. 'I had to put that fear in you so that you concentrate and do it.' That was the only time I scolded her.

"Otherwise, it was a pleasure working with her. She would do exactly what I would tell her to do," he remarked, as he went on to explain his method of connecting with his actors. "My habit is to enact the whole scene of every character and then tell the actor, this is what I want. Don't copy me but give me what I want in your own way. Having been an actor myself, I'd gone through the frustrating experience of directors being unable to tell you what exactly they were looking for. I've gone through the whole process of them saying, 'Cut, cut, cut, one more, one more,' and my asking them, 'Can you tell me what is it that you want from me?' So with my experience as an actor, I am able to express a scene better than most other directors. I show the actor the expressions I'm looking for. Priyanka was quick on the uptake and very good at following the instructions of the director."

Other than that one solitary time when he scolded her and she cried, "We started the first shoot in Kulu-Manali, we were there for almost fifty-sixty days. I never had a problem with her," he confirmed. "When I called her for the sequel to *Krrish* too, she was very excited and said, 'It's even better than the first *Krrish*.' I've really enjoyed working with her and I'm sure she'll be there in *Krrish 4* but I can't say what the length of her role will be the third time around."

Krrish was the superpower that pulled Priyanka out of the morass that could've demoralised her during this trying period. Otherwise, the hero was its pivot, the heroine couldn't possibly count it as one of her most challenging performances. In fact, there were murmurs that she wasn't satisfied with her make-up and the way she looked in *Krrish*.

"No, no," protested Roshan Senior. "What happened was that we had given her long hair. Who was the stylist or dress designer? I don't remember. For the first three to four days, she was not looking the way I wanted her to look, so we rectified it. She was wearing a wig with long straight hair. *Aitraaz* was on release and she was very stylish in it. But I didn't want that look. I wanted her to be a modern girl but more Indian looking."

What is on recall is that Priyanka was so relieved to have *Krrish* in her kitty as the booster that would ensure she didn't get shunted into the vamp category by *Aitraaz*, that she actually swung to the other extreme. Photographer Rakesh Shreshta's memory is short as he only remembered Jaju bringing the new Miss World to him for a portfolio of the most glamorous pictures of 2001. He had an array of leggy frames that were unabashed in introducing magazine readers to the new tease on the block. They weren't crass. They were classy pictures and tame too compared to the saucy, sophisticated poses she was striking after *Quantico*.

But the day she signed *Krrish* and Rakesh Roshan assured her that his film would change her image, the predator of *Aitraaz* wanted to make the most of it and take no chances with her catapult into the A-List of leading ladies. She therefore turned demure with a vengeance and ordered a ban on the photographer releasing any more of the pictures that had adorned many a magazine cover. As editor of *Movie*, a monthly glossy, I know that a picture from Shreshta's collection that showed her leg on the cover, had her doing a war dance with the photographer who in turn made frantic calls to me. Priyanka wanted to change her image, so there would be no more flashes of leg or cleavage.

It was one more instance of Priyanka wanting to clear a path for herself, being firm about it and being extreme in its implementation.

Rakesh Roshan was convinced that he had nothing to do with her new dictum.

"No, no, I cannot interfere with her personal life," he corrected the impression. "Perhaps when I told her, 'I'm changing your look in this film', she may have carried it into her personal sphere, to what she was doing outside the film too."

Looking at it from Priyanka's point of view, he reasoned, "What happens is that sometimes when you are doing a negative role, you fear that if there's acceptance in a big way, you might not make the grade as a heroine. It happens with newcomers."

But with Priyanka's renowned restlessness, she didn't linger long on preserving herself as the *sati savitri* (literally a devoted Indian wife but commonly used to denote a virtuous Indian woman) of Hindi cinema since her next big attractions were *Fashion* where she played an emotionally-scarred ramp model and a glossy, fun film called *Dostana* where she romped the beaches of Miami in a blingy golden swimsuit, no less. Shreshta's stockpile of smart frames began to resemble a kindergarten album. Priyanka had swung to the other end of the pendulum again, showcasing her versatility, her range as an actor, an actor without an image sticking to her like an annoying label.

Roshan nodded, "She has got tremendous talent, she's very versatile. She is the one girl we can compare with memorable, everlasting yesteryear heroines. And look where she has reached.

"When I worked with her in *Krrish*, I never realised that one day she'd be going to Hollywood. But I always knew that she would hit the top bracket here. It's her professionalism and her acting abilities that have taken her to where she's gone today.

"Once upon a time, there was the feeling that beauty queens can't act because a few of them came (in the early '70s) and couldn't emote at all. But that stamp isn't valid anymore. Today, anybody can become a good actor or an actress; there's no prejudice against anyone. There are so many TV actors too who're very good. But you also need luck to make it. Priyanka has tremendous talent, great discipline and a lot of luck. It's a combination that works for anybody. Even for us," he added, "you get good thoughts and ideas only when the time is right. Otherwise, we're all nobodies. Sometimes when I see my own films, I wonder how I thought of them. But it's because all the great ideas and thoughts are showered on you when you're lucky and when you are extremely hard working like I am."

Priyanka was one such exceptional case where every right element was blended well.

"She was so good in *Mary Kom*. She did *Aitraaz*, she did *Krrish*, all contrasting work. Then she did *Bajirao*

Mastani, she was so good in it, she had the film in her grip. Terrific dialogue delivery and that dance she did ('Pinga' with Deepika), all of it was very high-quality work. She did not have the main role in *Bajirao Mastani* but to have accepted the assignment with a new, younger heroine like Deepika, and then to do justice to it, required exceptional confidence," Roshan observed.

With his vast experience of studying and working with a smorgasbord of actors, Rakesh Roshan also analysed her external appearance to explain why a girl who wasn't a natural stunner had succeeded in her own country and then caught the fancy of the West too.

"Though Priyanka is tall, she still has a certain fragility. She is all-woman, very sensuous. She is like Rekha and Sridevi, she can carry off an Indian and a Western look.

"Her upbringing keeps her rooted. Her parents are (father was) educated and good people to talk to. I know Priyanka's also knowledgeable and a good conversationalist but unfortunately, when I am on set, my interactions are all about work. I don't mix around because I am in my own thought process.

"But I've seen her move from here to Hollywood and I like the way she carries herself with dignity, the way she dresses up. She has really put Bollywood on the world map. I've seen two seasons of *Quantico* and I can see that she has everything it takes to succeed there. There was a lovemaking scene in the car in *Quantico* and she did it so well. There was nothing dirty about it because she did it without fear. It's the way she carries herself that makes everything she does look neither bad nor vulgar."

She may be no born beauty but, said a perceptive Roshan, "She's got some magic in her that comes alive when she's in front of the camera. If you see her personally, you might not find her that attractive but she's beautiful on screen. Now even at the personal level, she's looking very nice because success gives you a certain beauty and glow."

Roshan's own *Krrish* was her first big taste of top-grade commercial success and she gave it the respect that it deserved.

"Commercial success means a lot to me" – Priyanka

"I don't think anybody's career gets set up by one blockbuster alone," she pronounced, "and I want to be consistent in my career. As an actor, you have a very small part to play in a movie which is just the character that you play and of course the brand that you bring along that gets attached to the film. So I want to have box-office successes with credibility in my performances and in the films that I do. That is very important for me.

"There have been so many box-office successes in my career. *Don, Krrish, Fashion, Waqt, Dostana, Aitraaz, Andaaz, Mujhse Shaadi Karogi...*" Add *Mary Kom* and *Bajirao Mastani* to the list for both box-office acceptance and credibility in her performances, and it turns platinum. "I've been blessed with so many films that have worked really well. When a film doesn't work, it breaks my heart because for me, all my films are *Mughal-e-Azams*, each one bigger than the other."

What she didn't ever disclose was how close she came to breaking point in her relentless fight to the top. Her handsome co-star, her first major A-Grade hero, Hrithik Roshan did.

"I have never known her to seek validation or recognition for how hard she works," underlined Hrithik. "Priyanka always came across as a fun person, always cheerful," he stated. "And amazingly spontaneous as an actor. Painfully hard working, without being pretentious about it. She, I assume, was taught by her parents to never allow herself to be seen as needy or dependent or weak. This quality of hers struck me as something out of the ordinary for a girl, hell, even for a guy those days," he chuckled.

"I remember shooting in the hills of Manali, this was way back in 2005 for *Krrish*. It was extremely cold and the air was lacking sufficient oxygen. Some crew members had even fainted. Suddenly we saw Priyanka go limp. She was about to fall but a few people standing close by rushed to lift her up and carry her back to the warmth and comfort of the hotel room. I rushed to make sure she was safe and taken care of but to my surprise, what I saw was an indignant Priyanka, half-conscious but unmistakably furious at being seen as someone who needed help! Even as her body, still limp, showed no signs of co-ordination, she continued shouting at the lifters to put her down. They did that, eventually. It clearly reflected a deep desire in her to always be seen as strong, independent and self-reliant. It was admirable and I was impressed."

Hrithik also remembered watching a few snatches of *Aitraaz* which had firmed up her name as the heroine of *Krrish*. Priyanka's fears of being branded a vamp were unfounded.

"When we saw *Aitraaz,* we were relieved because we found a fresh face which wasn't one bit afraid of the camera," said Hrithik. "She was confident and in *Aitraaz* we saw an actor who could project both sides of the human psyche – goodness and humility plus cunning and vindictiveness – which was rare."

For an actor who himself sought a challenge every time he signed a film, Hrithik was generous in commenting,

"I often compliment Priyanka on her ability to almost mutate into the perfect person to fit any situation, person or environment. Almost like a chameleon. Only in her case, the transformation is of the intellect and is driven by a generous heart to make people around her comfortable. She could just as easily dumb herself down as she could intimidate, depending on the person or situation."

He was also honest enough to initially wonder whether some of the things she did were part of an elaborate off-camera act: "One trait of hers that always stood out was how caring she was of her staff or crew members on set or of her co-actors. She seemed to go so out of her way that sometimes I couldn't help but suspect whether the intention was really genuine or motivated by the preservation of her image. But so consistent was she in her caring that I had to concede it was simply her character. She genuinely cares."

As an actor who's spiritually inward looking, Hrithik had something to add about Priyanka: "She has been unmistakably primed from her childhood to be where she is today." He reviewed her success before cautioning, "Learning from my own experience of worldly success and how little it serves towards genuine happiness, I truly hope and wish Priyanka is putting in as much power and drive towards her own inner fulfilment too."

He added thoughtfully, "I think she is and I am very happy for her."

She was happy too, after *Krrish* took her where she'd always dreamt to be – in the top commercial bracket. But in Priyanka's rules for the ride of a lifetime, there was no space for complacence or stagnation. The peak to conquer was never a constant. It was a range and she had to scale them all. The next daunting daredevilry was to attempt a film in which she was the hero, so to speak. And who better than

National Award-winning director Madhur Bhandarkar for a film that revolved around its central female character? It was time to step into *Fashion*.

"When I was making *Fashion*, I had hardly seen Priyanka's movies. I must've seen only *Don*, I hadn't watched *Aitraaz* or *Andaaz* or any of her other films," was the astonishing revelation that came from Madhur Bhandarkar, the man who would give Priyanka her first taste of acknowledgement from the government itself – a National Award.

"After my film *Corporate,* which was successful, a lot of people told me that I should repeat Bipasha Basu for *Fashion* too," said Bhandarkar. "They felt she would be the natural choice for *Fashion* because she'd been a well-known model and had walked the ramp too. But I was completely convinced that Priyanka Chopra was the girl who should play Meghna Mathur. She was what I'd imagined the character to be, with a certain fragility in her face. While others were advising me about casting a fashion model, I was looking at Meghna more from the character's point of view and the story, and how Priyanka would fit into it.

"Ten years after *Fashion*, Priyanka and I are still very friendly, we talk over the phone and we stay connected. Last year, when she was here, she'd invited me to a party where we had a long conversation. On Diwali too, I spoke to her. We follow each other on Twitter. So I know what's happening in her life and I can say that the one thing I liked about Priyanka when I worked with her and thereafter, to this day, is that she has essentially remained the same person. She was born and brought up as a middle-class girl from Bareilly and she has stayed that way. On the set, she would mingle with everybody, eat junk food like *khakra* (crispy thin Indian cracker) and munchies. I used to go to

Neelam, the food store near my house, and stock up on all the snacks for us to have on the sets. She would say, 'Oh yes, do get this and get that.' She is one actress who eats well. You know how other actresses are, *yeh nahin khana, woh nahin khana* (I won't eat this or that). She's a rare actress who doesn't fuss about eating. I'm a foodie and so is she. So when we'd shoot in five-star hotels, we'd both ask for the menu card and start ordering a whole lot of food. She's someone who'll say, 'Order this and ask for that also. *Dal makhni manga le, chicken manga le, woh bhi manga le* (order dal makhni, chicken and something else too)', and we would both tuck in. I've never heard her say, 'Oh, I can't eat this or I can't touch that.' She doesn't peck at it, she really enjoys her food as much as she enjoys her work. If we were to have a break an hour later, we'd start ordering food right now."

At this juncture, an interesting break from her career would be to talk about Food – another favourite 'F' of hers apart from Films and Family.

"Food is a very important part of my life" – Priyanka

"Where does it all go? I think it goes to my heart!" she said to me. She hates cooking and, "Gourmet food. I'm more of a junk food person. I love Indian food any day. Hyderabadi, Punjabi, South Indian, I love fish curry and rice, love, love, love!"

Almost every person close to Priyanka noted her fascinating capacity to demolish parathas and pizzas and still look the way she does.

Rakesh Roshan: "It's amazing how fond she is of eating but doesn't put on weight. I could never understand how she manages that. I'd be surprised when she would order two big pizzas for lunch and watch her finish both. Not small-sized ones but family ones where there'd be ten or more slices. Then again after four o'clock, she'd be having something else. I always told her, 'You are so very lucky that you can eat like this but not put on weight.'"

Abbas-Mustan: "She eats everything, she's very fond of food. We told her that we're surprised at her because most other girls are always dieting. She told us, 'I love to eat and my metabolism is excellent.'"

Anurag Basu (who directed her in one of the most fascinating roles of her career in *Barfi!*): "I envy PC's metabolism. She can begin the day with four parathas. The first day, she ordered a pizza and I thought, 'She's an actress, she'll probably have one triangle, how much is an actress going to eat?' But she finished the whole 12". She eats a lot, I don't know where it all goes. I keep telling her that her parents or some dietician must've given her a magic pill and to please give it to me too. The only weight she puts on is a little bit on the face (lower jowls). That's when she knows she has to start taking care. Half a day of only water and it all vanishes."

Suneel Darshan: "She's a pizza freak. How she has that pencil-trim figure when she loves pepperoni pizza used to leave me wonderstruck."

Actor Shahid Kapoor who had a love-thy-neighbour relationship with Priyanka when they stayed in the same building, is a vegetarian. Earlier, when he was dating Kareena, he had influenced the girl from the meat-loving Kapoor clan to turn vegetarian. He'd presented Kareena with a book that had changed his life and his eating habits. With that book, Kareena too had become a vegetarian. But his relationship with Priyanka was either not too intense or it was too brief. Or perhaps Priyanka liked her food too much to change for a guy. Whatever the reason, "Priyanka can never turn vegetarian," Shahid had chuckled to me when he was still seeing her, *"woh kabhi nahin hogi vegetarian,"* he'd repeated for emphasis. "She loves her non-veg food too much. Our standing joke is, when we go out, she orders the main course and I end up eating the side order."

After that food break, back to serious work on the sets of *Fashion*.

"A quality that I like about Priyanka is that she made it big in her own capacity without being a part of any coterie or camp," commented Madhur Bhandarkar. "When we made *Fashion*, I found her so hard working that there was never a day when she'd say, 'Let's stop working, *abhi bahut ho gaya*, I'm tired, we've done enough work today.' Or, 'I don't feel like working today.' On the contrary, she was going abroad for twenty days for the shooting of *Dostana* or some other movie. Before leaving, she worked with me for more than twenty-four hours to complete a certain sequence for *Fashion*. I had offered to wind up if she wanted to but she shot and finished that sequence before leaving for the other film. She has that sort of dedication to her work.

"I also admire her willingness to take risks," Madhur went on. "When *Fashion* was being made, a lot of people told her, '*Arre*, why are you doing a film like this so early in your career?' She had until then done typical commercial cinema, so she was being advised to wait for five to six years before attempting a film like *Fashion*. But she took that risk, she wanted to be a part of such a film and *Fashion* became a turning point in her acting career. She had mentioned this in *Time* magazine also that *Fashion* was one movie which changed her graph overnight. She suddenly became the talented actress who not only got all the popular awards but also the National Award."

Fashion was one of the first films where Priyanka Chopra the actress came to the fore in her full glory. A gamut of situations called for the innocence of a new girl, the smugness of success, the headiness of fame, the vanity of beauty, the self-implosion of the famous and the fragility of a breakdown. Madhur who created Meghna Mathur and helped Priyanka navigate her complex story, reminisced about the filming of *Fashion*.

"There were a lot of scenes where her hard work really showed but there were a few that were memorable for me to shoot. There was an important sequence where she's dancing with a black guy. I wanted her to go the whole hog, dance without a care, be *bindaas* (uninhibited). I made her drink real wine before the shoot and I said, 'PC, just go all out.' With her usual *josh*, she just went ahead and did it. She wasn't a smoker but I also made her smoke many times. She'd say, 'My god, smoking *kara raha hai* (god, he's making me smoke)' but she did it all. It was a big chance she was taking. This was Miss World who was doing only commercial films until then and suddenly she was in a role where she had to smoke, drink and more. I've worked with many other actresses but her dedication to her work was on a different level altogether. Priyanka gets into the character completely. After a shot when we say 'cut', I know a lot of actors who switch off after that moment before the camera, and become normal. But Priyanka carries on with the character. My movies are basically heavy in drama, in terms of *rona-dhona* (crying and weeping) and intense emotions. If we were shooting one such heavy scene, she'd be completely immersed in the character, in the zone, in the emotion, maintaining the sub-text too while performing.

"One such intense scene was the one where she wakes up after being with the black guy and realises the extent to which she'd let success go to her head where she's completely destroyed herself. How a girl from a middle-class family has ruined herself. She just had to walk, there was no dialogue. That walk was shot in three different portions. She picks up her clothes and a sandal and leaves. I still get goosebumps when I talk about it. All she's doing is walking, walking down the corridors. Then she's in a rickshaw and finally she comes to her apartment. She's in front of a mirror and the way she removes her kajal, the eye liner, and she throws things... It was not one particular scene but that entire sequence leading up to the realisation, 'My god, what a mistake I've made,' and then completely crashing. That was one really tough sequence for her to shoot with no dialogues to counter anybody, no co-stars to give you a reaction. She had to do it entirely on her own. It was a long introspection, a big mix of regret, anxiety and a lot of other emotions, all going on simultaneously. It wasn't easy to perform this, she had to feel it all within and then convince the audience. So that was very difficult.

"We didn't even shoot it at one go to maintain the momentum. We shot it over three days, that too not three continuous days. We shot one portion in a Juhu hotel – she is walking down a corridor. We shot the next portion in Andheri, then inside a house in Malad. We shot that sequence in three different time zones, different locations and on three different days. But Priyanka nailed it by maintaining the momentum all through. She kept the continuity perfect and the emotions on one level.

"With all my actors, I tell them the beginning of a scene and how it ends and what I want from it. I am not a director who says, 'Oh, *aisa karo, waisa karo* (do it like this, do it like that).' I am a very cool person. I just tell them, *aisa emotion lao* (get this emotion). I have two or three key words that I use which all my actors understand. *Ismein jalwa kar de* (*jalwa* could mean anything from charisma to the divine; Madhur uses it to mean 'make the scene exciting or magical'), *ismein awaaz nahin hai* (there's no voice here), *ismein dard nahin hai* (I'm not getting the emotion of deep hurt). Tabu calls them my Madhurisms. She'll always say, 'Please give me your Madhurism.'

"With Priyanka, once she liked the script, there were no inhibitions about doing whatever the character had to do. I think she liked the script and the thought because the film was completely from her point of view. Of course, it was also a huge risk to do *Fashion*," he agreed.

Like *Aitraaz*, which took her to the next level of stardom, the gamble of doing a heroine-centric film that did not have the support of a saleable hero in the cast didn't just pay off commercially, *Fashion* also fetched her the much-coveted National Award (1999).

The National Award was a big deal for Priyanka. It was best described by her: "The National Award was the turning point of my life," she told me. "I cried when I heard about it. I was shooting *Anjaana Anjaani* (2010) in LA when Madhur called me. It was 4 am there, and he said, 'It's happened, *jalwa ho gaya hai, jalwa* (magic has happened).' And I started crying. Nobody was with me. I was sitting alone in my room. I didn't know who to scream at or who to tell. My nana had passed away ten days before this. Something told me to call my grandparents, my dadi and my nani. When I went to collect my National Award, I took twenty-five people from my family. My *chacha*, *chachi*; I'm very close to my family. We're like a Sooraj Barjatya film," she laughed.

Attending the ceremony in Delhi and watching their "Mimi" get the prestigious National Award from the

President of India was like an emotional gathering of the Chopra-Akhouri family. "Everybody (every winner) was applauded," Priyanka said, relishing the rewind, "but when I got my award, there was the loudest ovation. I ignored it; I pretended it was my popularity and not my family!" It was an illustration of how close she continued to remain with the whole family; her success, their celebration.

Whether one believes in it or not, the blessings of her elders certainly meant a lot to Priyanka. Perhaps their collective *aashirwad* (blessings) manifested itself as luck, the fantastic luck that has always provided her with a helping hand every time she needed one. Having the whole clan participate in her happiness was special, more so when, "My dadi passed away just two weeks after the National Awards. She told me before she passed away that this (being at the National Awards) was the best experience of her life. She cried and held me, so it was a very special moment for me."

There was another off-camera happening that hit Priyanka in a big way in 2009. Tech-savvy and always game to try out a new experience, Priyanka was bitten by the Twitter bug. She hit the ground running by becoming an instant hit. Interestingly, she gave a run to suave politician-writer Shashi Tharoor as they became the two Indians with the highest number of followers, with over a million each. Closely watched by those familiar with social media, it was a friendly match between Priyanka and Shashi as one day, she'd outrace him; another day, his count would go up. When the two finally met at a wedding in Hyderabad, it was big news.

Another savvy celebrity, Shah Rukh Khan who was present there, tweeted about it with trademark flamboyance in June, 2011.

"Met who's who of India in all their glory...and yes saw the meeting of the Twitter champs Shashi and PC

face to face...couple of million followers between them...
ooohhh!!!"

By 2018, Priyanka had left Shashi way behind; he with
under seven million followers and she with over twenty-two.

She'd once talked to me about how she became addicted
to Twitter.

"When I first started with Twitter, nobody else in India
was on it. I'm a bit of a gadget freak, I like anything that's
a little new. When a friend of mine spoke to me about it, the
idea was to do it for a film. I'd been on Facebook and I was
thinking of going on Twitter. So when a friend suggested
it, I said, 'Let's try it.' Once I went on it, I got completely
addicted to it, I just loved it. I spoke to all my friends,
I spoke to everybody about it, I almost became their
brand ambassador in India. And then it really exploded
here. I think it's really cool. I'm very happy with the kind
of followers I've had very consistently. I think I'm one of
the highest in Bollywood. I don't want to use Twitter as a
medium only to promote my films. It's to interact with my
fans. Unfortunately for them, my films are my life, so if I'm
going to be talking about anything, it'll be about my films."

That was then. Today, a more mature Priyanka also
uses Twitter to either chat with her fans, to share a random
thought with them or to make a social comment. On
Valentine's Day in 2018, she asked followers on Twitter to
send in their favourite love songs. She picked 'Fix You' by
Coldplay as one of hers. She got an avalanche of responses
– her way of staying connected with fans.

A random thought showed that she enjoyed a good
chuckle. "#PCRandomThoughts like Why isn't the number
11 pronounced as Onety one?" she wondered in a tweet.

A more serious one came on February 15, 2018
when there was a shooting that killed schoolchildren in

Stoneman, USA. "This has to stop! Children should be able to go to school and come back alive. Heartbroken. #stonemanshooting," she tweeted.

It showed growth as a person – from one obsessed with the film industry to a responsible adult who was aware of her social duties and knew her politics.

In fact, just before *Quantico* happened, Madhur Bhandarkar had attempted a political film titled *Madamji* with Priyanka but had to shelve the idea.

"That's right," he confirmed. "*Madamji* was on but around that time, *Quantico* started, so I shelved the film. I needed sixty days of shooting when *Quantico* started. It was the bigger ladder for her to climb at that point, so we couldn't go ahead with *Madamji*. Once it was put on the back burner, it stayed there. As a filmmaker, the zeal and enthusiasm sometimes change and you start losing interest in a subject. That's what happened to *Madamji*.

"I'm a very restless person, so I lose interest very fast. After shelving *Madamji*, I haven't thought of another film with Priyanka because she's been so busy. We keep talking, so there will be something in the future. But nothing's brewing right now."

However, in typical Priyanka style, she stayed in touch with all the people who mattered to her in India. In this industry, friendships are famously made during filming only to lose steam once they move on to the next project. When new friendships are forged, old ones begin to fade. So yet another guideline that one could take from Priyanka's lifebook of experiences is that she follows a rule of her own. It's a trait that surfaced in conversations with Abbas-Mustan, Madhur Bhandarkar, Tarun Mansukhani and Anurag Basu, apart from a whole range of friends that included certain journalists too.

Meena Iyer, currently Editor, *DNA After Hrs*, and former editor of *Bombay Times*, pointed out that apart from her fine degree of professionalism, what made Priyanka such a winner was, "Her winning nature."

A seasoned journalist and author, Meena has known Priyanka since she won the Miss World title – a friendship of over seventeen years that has mutual respect written all over it.

She gave an example of Priyanka's utter professionalism with the fourth estate too – her meeting a commitment that many others in her place would've cancelled without a second thought.

"I'd gone to meet her at Filmistan Studio where she was shooting for *Aitraaz* and although nobody said anything, there was clearly some tension between her and perhaps Akshay Kumar," recalled Meena. "When I walked into her room, I was self-conscious because of the obvious stress. But she met me because she wanted to keep her commitment. Akshay was sitting outside somewhere on the other side. I'm not sure if he was about to leave but there was tension. I met Priyanka for only about ten minutes because I realised that it wouldn't be fair on my part to be so *dheet* (stubborn), so insensitive. Nothing was put into words, Akshay was not even the subject of conversation but I could see that she was just being polite. Another person in her place would've told me that she wouldn't be able to meet me that day. But she realised that I had gone all the way to meet her and she should respect me for it. Maybe she also got the vibe that I was not the sort of person to mess with her or her circumstances in any way."

Incidentally, Meena is respected in the film industry for being a rare journalist who has a nose for a good story but not at the cost of treading on someone's feelings or making the other person squirm with overt inquisitiveness. Priyanka must've been comforted that she was in company that wouldn't take advantage of her situation. But what followed on that same day of tension in the studio, would've been a journalist's delight. Only, Meena didn't report it at that time.

"Priyanka and I happened to have identical cell phones – the old bulky blue-coloured Nokia," she narrated. "We'd both put our phones on the sofa and when I was leaving, I picked up hers by mistake and walked off. Near the gate, there was a call on my phone and when I looked at it, it was from the co-star. I wasn't particularly friendly with him at that time for him to be calling me. It happened once or twice and that's when it struck me, oh crap, I've picked up the wrong phone. I naturally didn't take his calls but charged back when I met one of her people charging towards me after realising that I had taken her phone."

The matter rested there. The two of them had already met and connected professionally much earlier, so an instinctive trust had been built between them. Meena had met Priyanka when she was with *Filmfare,* and sister-publication *Femina* had hosted the Miss India pageant from where Priyanka was picked to represent India at the Miss World contest. A constant piece of advice that Priyanka gave youngsters who wished to emulate her was to 'Never forget your roots, your background.' She practised what she preached.

"I had met her when she'd become Miss World," Meena recalled. "I'd gone to her house on Yari Road and there was something just so very upfront about her even then. She wasn't a great-looking girl without her make-up and she was obviously not touched by all the luxury that she has today. But there was something just very nice about her, right from telling me how she's called 'Mimi' by her family to her parents being very friendly. Her father Dr Ashok Chopra would always come forth to talk about Mimi. It was such a nice setup. She wasn't trying to hide anything. Over time, I've found that she's very approachable as a person without letting you get familiar. She does draw a line and she keeps her dignity but makes you comfortable in her space which is a wonderful quality. She had retained that quality right up to the last time I met her which was much after *Quantico* – like the time I met her at Mehboob Studio when she was here on one of her fleeting trips from New York."

Priyanka was being featured in one of those paid interviews that *Bombay Times* specialised in. So what had to go into it had already been decided; there was no need for anyone to go and interview her again. But to make it look more organic and natural, Priyanka insisted that Meena meet her. "I told her, since what we're going to say in it has already been decided, it looks too much like a sham," said Meena. "But she said, 'No, why're you saying that? Come and see me.'"

Priyanka was shooting a commercial that day for a toothpaste with director Siddharth Anand and Meena ended up doing something she'd never done – she took a selfie with the star. There were lots of people around discussing *Quantico* and clicking selfies with her. "Her team itself is so big. She walked in with an entourage of eleven to twelve people," commented Meena. "I was the only one sitting by myself when she asked me, 'Don't you want a selfie as well?' I told her, 'I don't even know how to click one', and she said, 'Shame on you, come, I'll click it.' And she clicked the selfie.

"I was leaving for the US the next day and she said, 'What a pity that you're going there when I'm here.' But a standard with her has always been to say, 'Whenever you're in my side of the world, give me a shout.' Once, I was in Florida when she asked me to come to New York and I said, 'That's the other coast, Priyanka.' But she asked me to come and see the shooting of *Quantico* on the streets of New York. She said, 'Come and see the real thing.' I couldn't make it but her invitation is always there and you know she means it."

It's an echo of what most of her friends say about her – that she cares. Meena experienced it when on three or four occasions, she was in an emotional state and Priyanka stepped in to practically be her therapist. On one particular instance, Meena was at her own home in Mumbai distraught over her mother (she'd just lost her) when Priyanka spoke to her from America.

"She actually acted as my therapist," recalled Meena. "She asked me where I was sitting; I told her I was in my hall and she said, 'I suggest you take a walk.' I told her that mine was a *chhotu,* small little place. She said, 'No, no, no, just get up, go into the next room and try sitting there.' All this long distance, from America. 'Change where you're sitting, it'll help,' she urged. I told her, 'You're acting like my shrink,' and she said, 'No, darling, I'm just trying to get you out of your blue mood.' She does little things like that which are so very sweet and thoughtful. I think she'd also just lost her father, so she understood. I ended up actually crying that day because the way she was talking, it was like experiencing a catharsis. I've told her that she could double up as a Hollywood shrink if nothing else!

"On three or four occasions, she has sent me Godiva chocolates. Really nice ones picked up from the airport at London or wherever. She'd tell me that she couldn't come and see me personally, so she was sending chocolates with

Natasha Pal, her manager, who'd come home and give them to me, and not send them randomly with some driver. It's all about adding that little personal touch to whatever she does."

Following her usual rule of never discussing her personal life, no Akshay, Shahid or Shah Rukh Khan figured directly in Priyanka's conversations with Meena. But sometimes, something would slip in. There was one time when the actress almost let the cat out of the bag.

"After my retirement, when I was changing jobs and I told her about it, she trilled, 'I already know,' and I wondered how she knew. She said, 'Somebody told me all about it.' I scratched my head wondering who. Could it have been the one person I'd had a conversation with on this? I won't mention him but there was only one common friend – let's just say a superstar we both knew! Maybe they had talked about me? That kind of awed me. Do they really discuss us?

"Another day, she was shooting for a soap commercial made by Dharma Productions which Tarun Mansukhani was directing. I'd gone all the way to Madh Island to meet her; Natasha had fetched me and taken me to meet her. You know, I have this habit of getting up as soon as my work is over. Priyanka saw me do that and said, 'You will sit yourself down there and not go till I tell you. You must learn to sit down and talk to people. What's this, *kaam ho gaya* (the work's over), so you want to leave?' She was dressed up as a Maharashtrian housewife for this commercial, wearing a *mangalsutra* (chain Indian married women wear). Without taking names, I teased her about the *mangalsutra* and she was laughing. So even though she's never discussed her personal life, and I've never been comfortable discussing it either, she's not closed about these little jokes."

It's her caring and showing it in tiny little ways that have stayed with Meena. "They say that a star is one who, if you ain't talking about him, he ain't listening. But with Priyanka that's not true. I don't know from where she's picked up this quality but she definitely encourages you to speak about yourself; she's genuinely interested. She wants to know all about you and she's always trying to include you in something. Like when my mother was alive, she'd always enquire about her. When she sends a Diwali gift, she does it thoughtfully with a personal touch. She once sent this lovely *puja thali* (decorative platter used on religious occasions) with a Lakshmi and a Ganesh and two small *diya*s (mud lamps) on it which came with a *shlok* (prayer) that's chanted to Goddess Lakshmi on Diwali. I take out the *shlok* religiously every Diwali and read it. You can see that she doesn't do something or send something across only because it has to be done. It's always thoughtful."

On the wonderful manner in which Priyanka has survived severe setbacks like Akshay not working with her at a time when it mattered to her or Shah Rukh Khan avoiding films with her, Meena perceptively reviewed, "She took it as a challenge and moved on. Unlike actresses who have come in much after her and are already jaded and labelled as an Ajay or Akshay heroine and younger actors won't touch them with a barge pole, Priyanka has always reinvented herself to fit into the next slot. She has made herself relevant right up to Ranbir Kapoor and Ranveer Singh. After a film like *Bajirao Mastani* where she didn't have the title role, she was proud that Kashibai (the wife that she played) had her moments in the film. She can be paired to this day with all these younger actors. It's only Priyanka who has managed to do this with herself."

The Diwali gift with the *shlok* wouldn't have come as a surprise to anybody who knew her well, like Madhur Bhandarkar who had gone to a puja at her place and watched a Priyanka very different from the diva in the studio. She personally served lunch to the priest and waited at the door to see him off.

"Yes, she's very religious," nodded Madhur. "She was wearing a *salwar-kameez* (loose pants with long shirt) and sitting with the priest. She touched his feet, and performed the *aarti* (a religious ritual). She's got extremely traditional, middle-class values." To this day, Priyanka travels with a little *mandir* wherever she goes; her gods go with her all over the world.

"There's a saying in Tamil," pointed out journalist Jyothi Venkatesh, "*Enda idathukku porayo andha idathukku ethapadi.* In English that would translate into, 'Wherever you go, you adapt the features of that place and make it your own.' It's a saying that aptly applies to Priyanka."

That's precisely how Priyanka would like to see herself. As she put it, "I want to be like water...put me anywhere and I take the shape..."

Her breaking into the West with an album didn't astonish those who knew about her singing prowess.

Madhur had an amusing story about her singing. "I have to tell you this," he said. "Since everybody told me, Priyanka *gaati achcha hai* (she sings very well), I always thought that she had sung the song 'Tinka Tinka' for her film *Karam*. So one day, I told her that she sang really beautifully and that I loved the way she'd sung 'Tinka Tinka'. That's when she told me, 'Sir, I haven't sung that song. It was sung by Alisha Chinai but I don't know why many people think I did.' But she does have a flair for singing, so it was entirely believable when she went abroad and cut a single before taking another huge step towards acting in the West."

His assessment was that Priyanka will survive anywhere because, "She's strong, she is a fighter. A lot of people have tried to put her down in the film fraternity itself; many were against her for different reasons. But she always believed in herself. When I travel abroad, I feel proud to see her photographs and interviews, watch her on the best of shows, at the Grammys and the Oscars. She's the one actor who has truly put us on the global entertainment map.

"She's someone who's abreast of current affairs, she is very active on Twitter. She was one of the first to go on Twitter when nobody else from here was on that platform. The phenomenal success she's seeing in LA and New York couldn't have been easy. People from here have tried time and again to make a name out there but nobody could take off like Priyanka did. Apart from all the high-end events, she's a brand ambassador for UNICEF. It means she's really in the big league, in the league that matters. As I said earlier, she's a fighter. I know for certain that you can put Priyanka Chopra in any part of the world and she'll survive because she's a tiger. She's strong, she doesn't give up easily."

It's incredulous to learn that the Priyanka Chopra who adorns the covers of *Vogue*, *Harper's Bazaar* and *Elle* as a high priestess of fashion and is wooed by designers and brands in the East and the West, was unaware of the Valentino-Prada world of style and chic dressing until a film called *Dostana* (2008), and men called Tarun Mansukhani (director) and Manish Malhotra (sought-after Indian designer), entered her life and changed her wardrobe forever.

But for a team that finally hit it off well enough to forge lifelong friendships, it took off rather shakily.

"It was Karan (Johar) who suggested Priyanka for *Dostana*," recalled the director of the film. Karan's Dharma Productions had produced it. "He made a call to her. I went over and gave her a narration and by the time I was back in the office, she'd called Karan to say she really liked the script. But she thought I was the wrong person to make it, that I was too serious to be directing a fun film."

Karan had stifled a giggle, and told her cheerfully, "I don't know who you met because he's quite a wacko, you don't worry about that part of it," and got her on board. *Dostana* was a stylish film shot in Miami, the story of Kunal and Sam, two straight testosterone guys pretending to be gay to share an apartment with stunner Neha, while each secretly lusts after her. It was comic, it was chic, it was contemporary and it was high-end classy for a Hindi film.

If Priyanka thought her director was too staid for a film that brimmed over with funniness, his first thought on meeting her was, 'So okay, I'll have to do a lot of styling out here.'

"She had no fashion sense at all," said Tarun spiritedly. And to think together, they made a stylish *Dostana* with Priyanka in a golden swimsuit on Miami beach as the visual highlight.

The making of *Dostana* was a picnic in picturesque spots. The only initial creases that needed to be ironed out were over the clothes that Priyanka had to wear.

"Like when we were shooting in Miami, as soon as I'd come into the room, the first thing I'd hear from her would be, 'Yuck, it looks like I'm going to a funeral.' And I'd say, 'Okay, just leave your fashion sense out of this, I will handle it.' I had Manish Malhotra there, I had Mickey Contractor for the make-up, so I had all the top guns around to back me up."

Her 'brand knowledge' and his sharp comebacks on it were a constant. His exasperation then was something he could laugh about now.

"She didn't know Gucci from Prada and she'd be questioning things," he exclaimed with an eye-roll. "For me it was like, 'Listen, you don't know anything about fashion, you let it be.'

"To be frank, when she came into *Dostana*, she didn't know Prada. She knew Gucci because they had a store here. So we had to actually sit her down and tell her about brands."

Mumbaikars would know all about the great divide between SoBo (South Bombay, considered tony and upper crust with snob value) and the suburbs. Tarun was a SoBo boy (as was Karan Johar until a few years ago); Priyanka lived in the North Mumbai suburb of Andheri West, miles away from him.

"And she was questioning the costume every morning," he reported. Sacrilege! "It was irritating me actually because she just didn't have a fashion sense. I'm South Bombay and classist about it. I used to keep telling her, 'You're like Lokhandwala (Andheri W), just let it be.'"

Read that with a huge smile to understand the tone of the banter.

But he conceded like a true friend, "Within a matter of three months, she knew her brands. She's very hard working, very intelligent. So she learnt very quickly. She would ask me questions like, 'Why did you give me this and not that kind of dress?' I'd explain to her about her body type. I'd say, 'This suits you, that doesn't, it accentuates the wrong body parts.' Like giving her really tiny shorts, tight fitted ones, doesn't flatter her. Give her slightly ballooned ones, looks better. Give her attitude rather than sex appeal and she'll bring the sex appeal. Like the gold-coloured swimsuit, it's how you stand in it, the carriage, what curves we want to show, what we don't want to show. Like I'd tell her how to place her legs while standing so I don't have to see her fork; a back can be way more exciting than the cleavage, it's how you shoot. When she was standing, I'd go, 'Suck your stomach in, suck your stomach in', and she'd scream, 'How much more can I suck it? I'm barely breathing over here.' I get that from Jacqueline (Fernandes who stars in his next film *Drive*) even today," he said wickedly. "I keep saying, 'Suck your stomach in', and Jacqueline says, 'But I don't even have a stomach.'"

Actually, Tarun and Priyanka spoke the same language – young, urban Indian with irreverent humour.

This was Tarun's debut film as director while Priyanka was already a celebrity. But what helped was that having assisted Karan Johar on some of the biggest blockbusters of Hindi cinema, Tarun was not intimidated by her star status and Priyanka didn't bring any airs in her vanity case.

"What I loved about having her there was, she asks a million questions about everything," he remarked. "So you have to be on your toes. You have to correct everything and have it all ready before you go to her. As a first-time director, that was great for me. I've known Abhishek Bachchan since he was sixteen, so he was already a friend. John was fabulous once he came on board. He'd done a little part as a DJ in *Kabhi Alvida Naa Kehna*, so there'd been a little bit of an interaction with him. And he'd done *Kaal* with us. He also happened to know my brother from college. So there were connections with him, a few strands here and there. With Priyanka, there were none. With her, we needed to build a friendship. There had to be the start of a completely new friendship on a clean slate with her. But having someone around who constantly asked questions so that you had to think everything through and be sure, was great.

"Her being a big star didn't ever bother me because I'd been an assistant on films with stars who were so huge and so normal that a star's stature never intimidated me," he confirmed. "When you've worked with Mr Bachchan and Shah Rukh Khan and they've been so normal that you no longer look at them as stars but as people you're working with, you can't be intimidated by anybody else."

It didn't take too long to make that new friendship.

"Priyanka started having a certain amount of faith in me pretty soon," he recalled. "She realised that he's not shooting anything badly, it's all being done aesthetically."

Still, she had her initial inhibitions over wearing a swimsuit. "But once she saw the swimsuit, she saw that it covered all that had to be covered, she saw it was a glamourised version of a swimsuit, it's not the sort you go into the water in, she kind of understood where I was coming from and why I was asking her to wear it," Tarun explained. "I wasn't using it as a shot, I was treating it as a moment with the two boys; it was story-related and not something like, I need to put a girl in a swimsuit, so let's put her in one. So there were no inhibitions at all on the day of the shoot. If an actor is not comfortable wearing something, you can't get a great shot," he put in.

For all his brashness over her style quotient, Tarun handled her with gentlemanly sensitivity, especially when it came to the swimsuit shot. He provided an elaborate behind-the-scenes peep into the filming of *Dostana:* "I'd told her about the swimsuit shot and she said, 'It would all depend on the swimsuit, I should be comfortable in it.' So Manish, she and I went shopping together in Miami and we picked the golden swimsuit together." The key word was 'together', to ensure that she was comfortable. "She tried it on, made all the adjustments, and till she was comfortable in it, we didn't even schedule the shoot. Till she was fine with keeping it on, we didn't shoot the scene."

Priyanka was also assured of the fine aesthetics of Tarun and Manish.

"When she saw the shots and how we were shooting the scene, she knew that this was not going to be sleazy, it wasn't that kind of film anyway," Tarun shrugged. "That built a lot of faith. So after a while, the questions over should I wear it or not would stop. She felt, he knows what he's doing, so move ahead with it. Because I had answers to her million questions, it helped to build a rapport with her."

For all her morning rounds of tantrums over her clothes, ultimately, she wore all that the director wanted her to.

"There was nothing that I had to cancel or do a rethink over. I gave her nothing that was awkward," he asserted. "We didn't have to go out and buy clothes again. But there were moments like the scene where she goes out on a dinner date with Bobby Deol and she said, 'It looks like I'm going to a funeral.' I was like, an LBD (Little Black Dress) is the most popular thing that all girls have and you have a problem with it? So there were those little arguments, silly ones. Mickey would go out for a cigarette break, thinking, this is going to take at least twenty minutes and he would be like, at the end of twenty minutes, 'You're still going to wear it, so why are you irritating all of us?' But that's what I liked about her. As an actor, you have to convince her before she does something. You can't just say, 'This is what I want, therefore.' She'll question, 'As a character, you tell me why I'm doing this,' and you have to give her a reason. It helps you as the director too, to constantly think of the character and stop thinking of it as, 'This is how my actor must look.' You get rid of the star-space and hold on to the character. She makes you do that.

"Ultimately PC received a lot of accolades for *Dostana*. Everybody talked of how gorgeous she was looking; the golden swimsuit became a big thing," he pointed out triumphantly. The film too was an instant and universal hit, the cherry on top, with everybody sure that he'd roll out a chuckling sequel soon.

Dostana also gave Priyanka the permanent tag of the 'Desi Girl', a chartbusting number that had her swaying sensuously in a saree that Manish had designed for her.

But 'Desi Girl' was not an instant hit with anybody else in the unit.

"I remember," said Tarun, "when I first made her hear 'Desi Girl'. I took the music, we sat in her car in the open space at Mehboob Studio and I put it on for her. I told her before she heard it, 'Whatever else you may achieve, for the rest of your life, you're going to be called by this name.' When she heard it, she felt it was okay, the usual. To which I as always said, 'You don't know anything.' I got that reaction from Karan, John, Abhishek, everyone thought it was a mediocre song when they heard the scratch version."

Farah Khan who choreographed 'Desi Girl' had her own experiences with Priyanka that few knew about. For instance, how many would remember an ad for a defunct company called Home Trade that had Priyanka playing a star-struck fan who holds her palm out to Shah Rukh Khan in pouring rain for an autograph? It was directed by Farah way back in 2002, even before *Andaaz* happened to her.

"That's true," confirmed Farah. "I had directed one of the first ads that Priyanka did. She'd won the Miss World title by then. She was not polished at that time though she was Miss World. She's looking her best right now. She knows what to wear, how to do her make-up, hair. She has the best people taking care of her.

"For the Home Trade ad, we were shooting in Australia and that's where I first met her. In the ad, she was supposed to be this big fan of Shah Rukh's, standing in the rain and watching him. She was very quiet and nervous. Very much in awe that she was working with Shah Rukh Khan."

But that was not Farah's first meeting with Priyanka as she herself remembered a little later.

"We were shooting with Shah Rukh and Juhi for *Phir Bhi Dil Hai Hindustani* (2000) near Film City. There's a hotel there with a golf course where a lot of shootings take place. Some round of the Miss India pageant was going on at that time and the contestants were staying in that hotel. Now I recall that all of them had come to meet Shah Rukh and Juhi. Lara, Priyanka, Dia, all of them were there. At that point, you'd never have thought that Priyanka would go this far, farther than all the others. It was Dia who had the typical good looks. But Priyanka's the better actress and has the drive," Farah analysed.

"The first time I liked her was in *The Hero*. Even though she had a small role in it, she was wearing strange clothes, bad hair and make-up, I said, 'This girl acts well. And she has a great voice.' But her breakthrough was *Aitraaz*."

Soon, Farah choreographed her in *Mujhse Shaadi Karogi*. And then came 'Desi Girl'.

Naturally forthright, Farah observed, "She's not a dancer; she may not know the technique but she's a good filmy dancer. She has that *namak* (a certain sauciness) in her, she's the *chhammak chhallo* (flashy) kind of dancer, very sexy. She's got rhythm."

The world at her feet – after beginning as the underdog at the Miss India contest back home, Priyanka won the Miss World 2000 title at the Millennium Dome in London. "I won and my life completely changed. Arre, how did this happen?" she exclaimed. It was soon studios and shoots instead of studies and books

Nani and Mummy for Daddy's li'l girl – with protective father Dr (Lt Col) Ashok Chopra and supportive mother Dr Madhu (Akhouri) Chopra as her parents, Priyanka grew up surrounded by a large and loving clan of Chopras and Akhouris. "We're like a Barjatya family to this day," is how Priyanka likes to put it. There were fun trips with Dad and Mum and much of her early years were spent with her Nani (maternal grandmother) Madhu Jyotsna Akhouri in Jamshedpur (above). Nani, incidentally, was born Mary John and hailed from Kerala

Army, family and school, the three familiar institutions that her early life revolved around. Academically inclined in school, proud to be an army kid and always close to a host of uncles, aunts, grandparents and cousins, Priyanka had a new career choice every few years but never articulated the latent desire to become an actress. What she did reveal was politeness towards all, especially elders, an army trait, she says, and the spirit to explore the untried. "Army kids are self-sufficient, our survival instinct is very strong. And we're not damsels in distress," says she

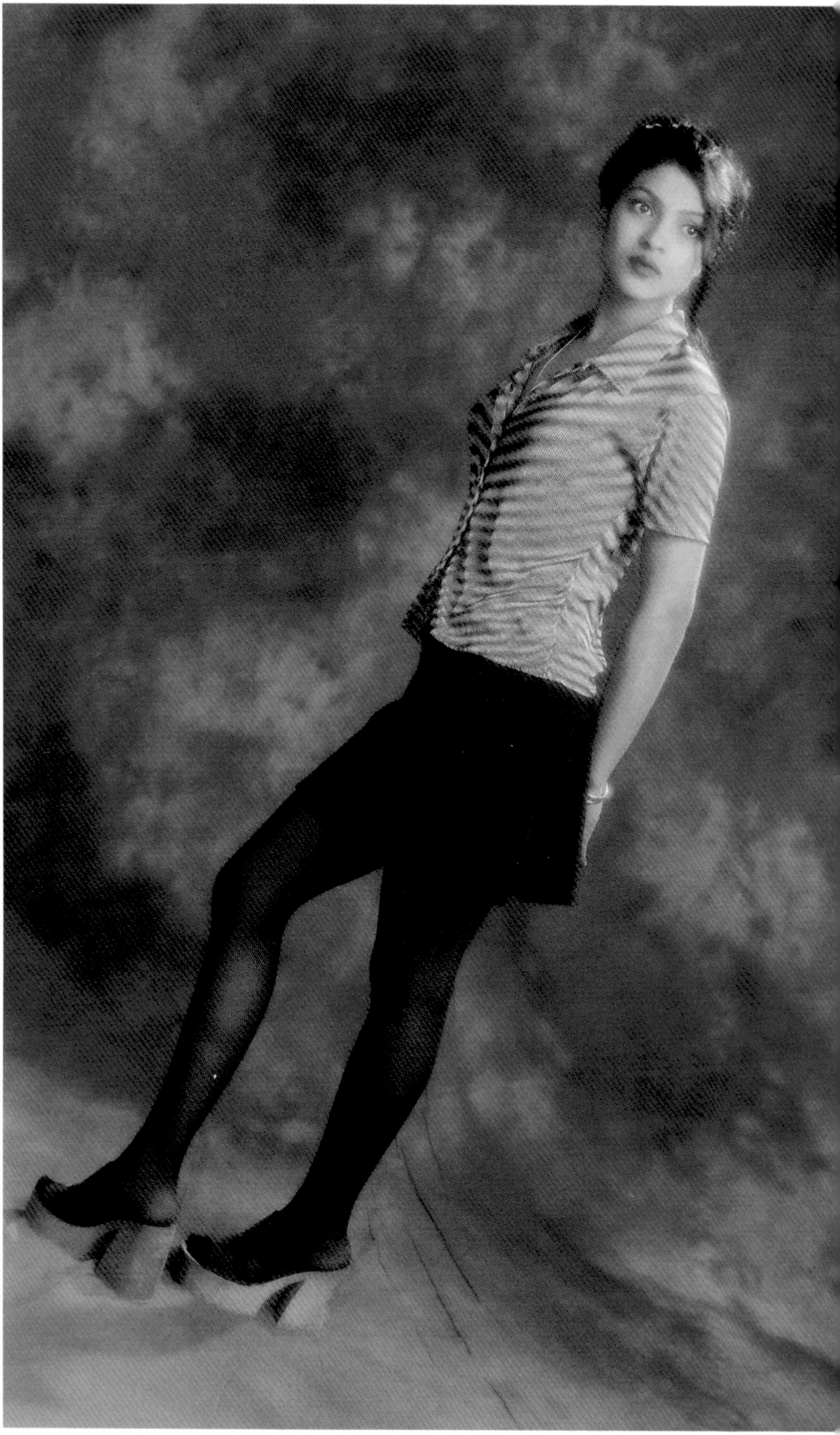

Courtesy: Dainik Bhaskar

This is how it all began – Priyanka's first photo shoot in Bareilly with photographer Rajeev Suri. The pretty face caught the eye of the photographer and his pictures set mother Madhu's mind ticking. Off she sent her daughter's pictures to the Miss India beauty pageant and the Bareilly ki ladki *went on to create history*

Her first mentor – Pradeep Guha of The Times Of India *was the Columbus who chose her for the Miss India beauty pageant in 2000. Pradeep at the homecoming party for triumphant trio Lara, Priyanka and Dia with Aishwarya Nair of The Leela*

(Left, middle) It was in Pradeep's house in Mumbai that Priyanka celebrated her 18th birthday. Here she is with his son Sanket when he was eight years old and (above) that's Pradeep visiting PC, the international celebrity in her Manhattan apartment

(Left) Along with global fame came Diana, her new doggy in New York

What they have in common – Sushmita Sen, Lara Dutta and Priyanka Chopra won international beauty titles, all three have a defence background (Sushmita's and Lara's fathers were in the Indian Air Force and Priyanka's in the Indian Army) and the trio headed towards Hindi cinema for fame and fortune. For Priyanka, Sushmita was the role model she secretly aspired to follow while Lara was the contemporary with whom she shared the Miss India stage and her debut film Andaaz

Family first – no celebration or function is complete without near and dear ones by her side. (Left to right) Brother Siddharth, mother Madhu, late Nani and late father at one of Priyanka's events

My time or yours? Aseem Merchant, her first steady boyfriend in Mumbai. He was with her when she went through the highs and sighs of the world beauty pageant. And she stood by him when he faced tragedy at home

Surviving setbacks – huge ones. The big debut that packed up within days over her botched-up nasal surgery was producer Vijay Galani's (2nd from left) film co-starring Bobby Deol and Suniel Shetty (2nd from right) which Mahesh Manjrekar (centre) was to direct. Pahlaj Nihalani (far left), then a big-time producer, gave the mahurat clap

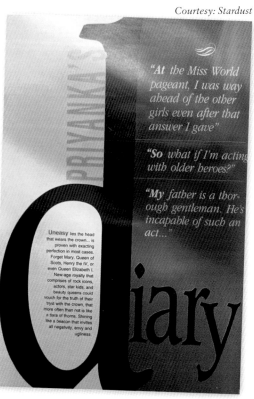

It didn't make a splash – (top left) the photo that lost her half-a-dozen films. The Chopras had packed their bags to return to Bareilly

The Hero to the rescue – Anil Sharma (above) retained her in his film with Sunny Deol (top right, centre)

Trying times – Stardust, July 2001 (right) where she talked about her wrong answer at the Miss World contest and also defended her father against a molestation charge on him

PRIYANKA'S diary

Uneasy lies the head that wears the crown... is proven with exacting perfection in most cases. Forget Mary, Queen of Scots, Henry the IV, or even Queen Elizabeth I. New-age royalty that comprises of rock icons, actors, star kids, and beauty queens could vouch for the truth of their tryst with the crown, that more often than not is like a tiara of thorns. Shining like a beacon that invites all negativity, envy and ugliness.

"At the Miss World pageant, I was way ahead of the other girls even after that answer I gave"

"So what if I'm acting with older heroes?"

"My father is a thorough gentleman. He's incapable of such an act..."

Scorching chemistry – Suneel Darshan's Andaaz, *directed by late Raj Kanwar, threw Akshay Kumar and Priyanka together and they hit it off so well that they went on to become a very saleable box-office couple. It was* Andaaz *that gave Priyanka her first taste of commercial success in the Hindi film industry*

A tale of two beauties – Akshay Kumar was the man caught between Miss Universe Lara Dutta and Miss World Priyanka Chopra in Andaaz. *Amazingly, all bets were on Lara and not on Priyanka. But very soon it was PC who zoomed far ahead, leaving Ms Dutta far behind*

Bobby stepped in – when Akshay Kumar had to step out of Suneel Darshan's (left) Barsaat *due to pressure from home. Bobby Deol (centre), the same actor who'd once been apprehensive about Vijay Galani's film with Priyanka, was now happy to co-star with her*

Courtesy: Mukta Arts

The seductress at work – Priyanka took the risk of playing a man-stalking vamp in Mukta Arts' Aitraaz which turned out to be a winner on all fronts. Apart from being a commercial success, it marked the arrival of a very competent actress who was unafraid to experiment with her roles. Aitraaz played a huge part in fetching her the lead role in Krrish, a plum assignment opposite heartthrob Hrithik Roshan. Interestingly, Aitraaz was directed by Abbas-Mustan who had once replaced Priyanka with Ameesha Patel in their film Humraaz

The 3 'D's – which took her places. Filmmaker Rakesh Roshan and his actor-son Hrithik who made Krrish with her, were delighted to find a heroine who was Determined, Dedicated and Daring

Hrithik recalled the day Priyanka slumped on location but was furious to be seen as somebody who needed help

Rakesh Roshan observed from a male perch, "Though she's tall, Priyanka has a certain fragility, she's all-woman, very sensuous." But he did make her cry one day

Dry run for Baywatch? *Director Tarun Mansukhani (opposite page, below) would certainly like to think it was his golden swimsuit in* Dostana *that taught Priyanka how to carry off beachwear with style*

The 'Desi Girl' tag stuck to her after she did that swinging number in Dostana. 'Desi Girl' was her calling card when she went West with her single 'Exotic' with Pitbull

Brand value – Tarun Mansukhani initially found her clueless about high fashion

(Above) The right moves – Farah Khan who choreographed her in 'Desi Girl' recalled that she had also directed Priyanka way back when she was Miss World in a commercial where she was a starstruck fan standing in the rain to catch a glimpse of superstar Shah Rukh Khan

(Top) From sour to sweet – ace designer Manish Malhotra's equation with Priyanka started off on a rocky note. How she turned it into a warm friendship could rival Dale Carnegie's mantras on how to win friends

(Above) It's all about carriage – Manish picks Ralph Lauren's beige trenchcoat which she wore to the MET Gala and Zuhair Murad's outfit in which Priyanka walked the red carpet at the Oscars (right) as samples of how well she carried off her clothes

" 'Love Story' has been a very difficult film for everyone it's a massive massive budget" Priyanka declares, "The budget's gone beyond anyone expected it to be and also looking also beyond anyone's expectations. It's certainly a dark horse for next year. When I went into the film I never expected it to look the way it is now. It's going to be the first of its kind and I can say this with utmost confidence. And you know me; I wouldn't ever praise my own films to the sky..."

Let's keep it discreet – running true to nature, Priyanka and Harman Baweja never went public about their relationship. Not even when promoting the two films in which she co-starred with him. But in an interview to Stardust *(Jan 2008), she did go uncharacteristically overboard with her praise for his film* Love Story 2050 *which eventually turned out to be a dud*

A gamut of expressions and situations – the film that proved she was able and saleable

Food and Films – that's what National Award-winning director Madhur Bhandarkar and Priyanka bonded over when he made Fashion *with her. Winning the National Award for her work in it was one of the high points of her life*

Fashion trio – (left to far right) Kangana Ranaut, Mugdha Godse and Priyanka with the filmmaker

Jai Maharashtra – Priyanka's first turn as a Maharashtrian was in Vishal Bhardwaj's Kaminey *in which she had a short but effective role*

Love thy neighbour – a friendship with Shahid Kapoor that was typically kept under the radar

The 7 Lives of Susanna – Priyanka picked up the challenge of playing a woman who murders seven husbands in 7 Khoon Maaf, a film in which she aged and turned downright ugly too. "Every actor must work at least once with Vishal," she enthused about her director

Her fearless foray into downplaying her glamour to be in character won her the admiration of co-star Neil Nitin Mukesh who played one of her seven husbands in the film

Very special – playing a challenged girl in Barfi! *wasn't a cakewalk, especially since Priyanka was simultaneously shooting for* Jai Gangaajal *in which she played the diametrically opposite character of a tough female cop*

Time out for partying – despite a taxing assignment, the Barfi! *team of (left to right) Ranbir, Priyanka, Anurag Basu and Ileana had crazy times too*

The multi-tasker – she stayed in character, she partied and she practised her singing with a coach she'd carried along to the shooting of Barfi!. She also became a family friend (top: with Anurag's daughter Ishaana) and went incognito with Anurag and Ileana to the Mahakal Temple on Mahashivratri (top, middle)

storyboard of his film Mary Kom

Courtesy: Omung Kumar

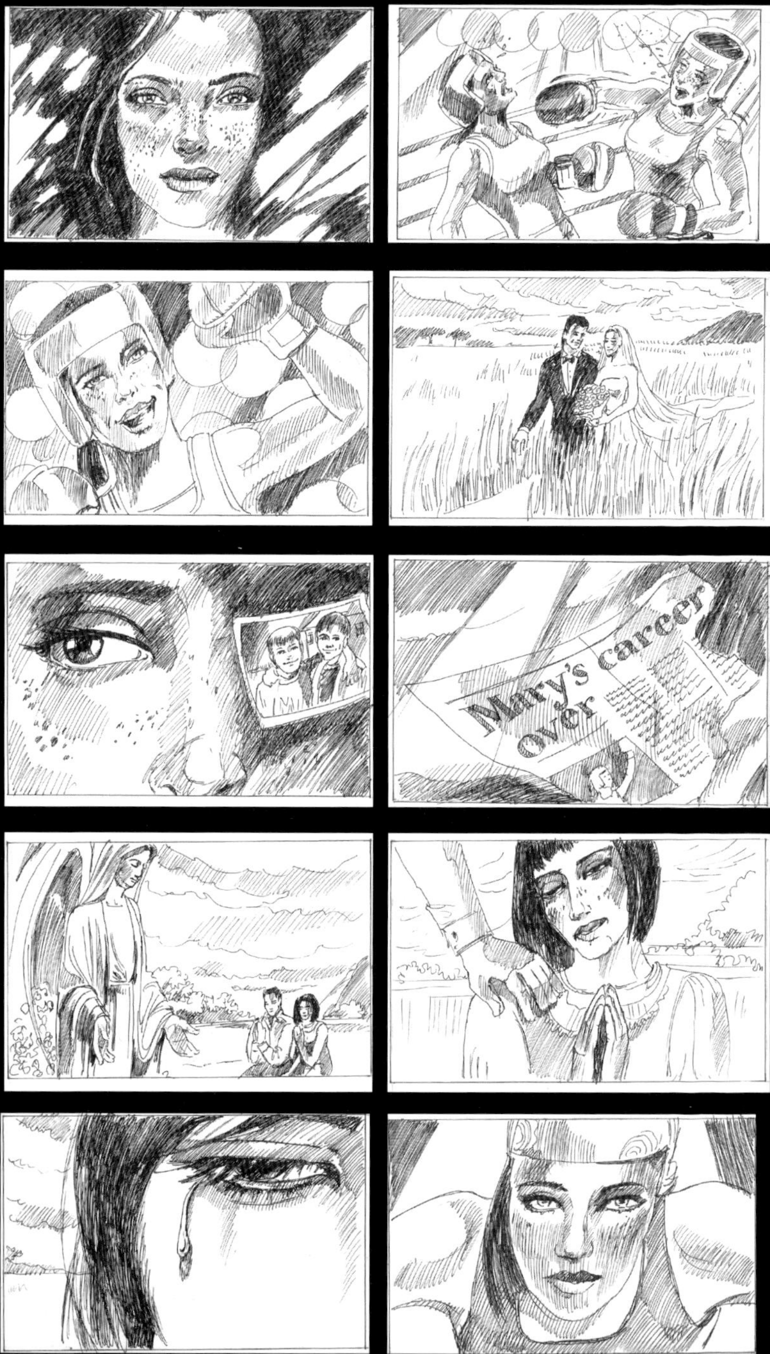

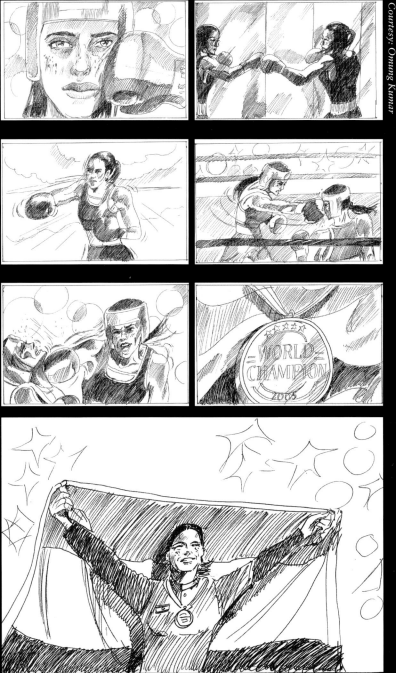

A sprinkle of freckles – the real Mary Kom didn't have them but Omung's sketches did. And they helped when prosthetics couldn't be used for Priyanka's eyes in the film. Playing Mary not only called for fitness of a very high order and boxing skills but also asked the impossible from a heroine – to build muscle and to take blows

Ergo no ego – when Priyanka came on board to work in the first Hindi biopic on a sportswoman, it marked the end of her cold war with producer Sanjay Leela Bhansali (right) who was impressed that she could shed ego to accept the challenge of playing Mary. CEO Sandeep Singh (below) of Bhansali Productions played the go-between. Priyanka soon did the raunchy item 'Ram Chahe' in Ram-Leela *and walked away with applause as Kashibai in an eleven-minute role in* Bajirao Mastani

(Bottom) Matching steps with Deepika Padukone in the pulsating 'Pinga' folk dance of Maharashtra

A stage whisper – her six-year relationship with Shah Rukh Khan was clandestine as expected and never publicly acknowledged. It was rumoured to have begun with Don 2, *the sequel to their commercially successful* Don *which was a new spin on the eponymous 1978 Amitabh Bachchan-starrer. When the tumultuous relationship ended, it was such a wrench that Priyanka admitted, "Heartbreak is a bitch"*

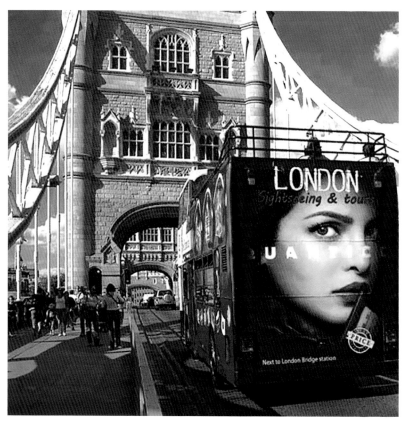

The big leap – kickass agent Alex Parrish announced her arrival in Quantico *with billboards and posters on the back of buses all over New York and London*

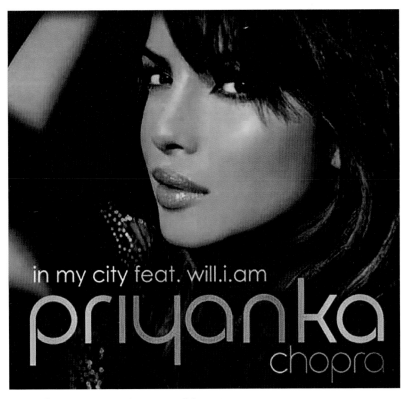

Watch it – her debut film in Hollywood, Baywatch, *tanked but she filmed two more –* Isn't It Romantic *and* A Kid Like Jake *– and wrapped up a third season of* Quantico

Musical entry – wooing the West with her voice

*Starting anew in New York – once
more rising above the need to keep
reminding herself that she was
a celebrity back home, Priyanka
had the gumption and humility to
walk into auditions and introduce
herself all over again. It paid off
as reputed journalist Anupama
Chopra watched her settle down
to a new work ambience in New
York. Anupama was one of several
friends who visited Priyanka in her
swank Manhattan apartment*

Gifted in many ways – a beautiful puja thali *and a* shlok *for Diwali arrived with a
handwritten note, reveals journalist Meena Iyer. PC even acted as therapist when
Meena went through a low spell after losing her mother*

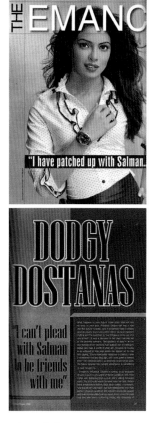

THE **EMANC**

"I have patched up with Salman."

DODGY DOSTANAS

"I can't plead with Salman to be friends with me"

Khan't help it – for a variety of reasons, Priyanka's resumé could never boast of films with all the three reigning Khans. No project with Aamir (above) ever fructified and in interviews to Stardust *in Jan 2008 and Aug 2008, her uneasy equation with Salman was apparent. But 2018 is when they teamed up in Salman's lavish home production* Bharat

Mee Marathi – after she lost her father to cancer, Priyanka and her mother Madhu set up a film production house, Purple Pebble Pictures, in Mumbai, with the actress calling the shots long distance from the US. Straddling two continents, she astonished her colleagues by backing small-budget regional cinema in a big way. She came up trumps with the Marathi film Ventilator *which Rajesh Mapuskar (below) wrote and directed for her company. Priyanka also had a coach in New York to teach her to pronounce the lyrics of 'Baba', a song she sang in Marathi (right) and dedicated to her late father*

In high places – among the many honours that have come her way, Priyanka was the proud recipient of a National Award for *Fashion* from President Pratibha Patil (left), and the Padma Shri, the third highest civilian award (below)

Meeting ground – Priyanka and Prime Minister Narendra Modi are both outsiders who've risen from the ranks to the top

Wearing Daddy on my arm – Priyanka was always so close to her father that when he succumbed to cancer, it broke her heart. She got 'Daddy's lil girl' in his handwriting tattooed on her wrist. Meanwhile, Madhu Chopra had her own way of showing how much she missed Dr Ashok Chopra

Farah has directed a few ads with Priyanka, including one for a washing soap for utensils and another for a luxury soap.

"She's wonderful to work with. She's completely a team person," said Farah. "I've worked with heroines where it's all about them, how they are looking, how comfortable they are. Anybody who's worked with Priyanka will tell you that she's one of the hardest-working heroines here. Okay, she was new during *Mujhse Shaadi Karogi* and would be punctual – on the sets at 8 am. But when we did *Dostana*, she had become a huge star. She was punctual and hard working then too."

It was typical of Farah to not walk onto the set of 'Desi Girl' and think she was creating an iconic dance number.

"I never feel anything is iconic till it becomes one," she said crisply. But she was naturally thrilled when it did become one. "It was a hit song, shot nicely. Till now, when Priyanka is called anywhere, she does that 'Desi Girl' step," she commented, repeating the movement where Priyanka shrugs with her hands.

It was during the filming of 'Desi Girl' that Priyanka proved she could teach Dale Carnegie a lesson or two on how to really make friends. It was on the set of this number that she turned a misunderstanding that could've become bitterly ugly into a lifelong friendship – a masterclass worth following for anybody.

Today, Manish Malhotra is such a close friend of hers that he visited her in New York and went with her for dinner to an Italian restaurant opposite her apartment. And when an American couple at the next table recognised her and told her they really admired her, he came out beaming. He also threw a party at his lovely Pali Hill house specially for her when she was in India after becoming a brand in the West.

But it was a friendship that didn't get off on the right foot.

Suneel Darshan had earlier observed that Manish, who designed the clothes for *Andaaz*, had not even prioritised the film at that time.

As is habitual for a man whose day dawns and sets with clothes, Manish's first glimpse of Priyanka was about what she wore. "She was at the Filmfare Awards when she was Miss World and she was wearing a black saree."

He turned out to be doing the costumes for her first film, *Andaaz* which also he remembered. "My friend Suneel Darshan told me that he was making a film with Lara Dutta and Priyanka. That was the phase of my life when I was running from film to film. It was really hectic. Those were the days when films were not planned like they are today. Filmmakers would tell you at the last moment what they required and you'd be running all over for the clothes. It was just me without the infrastructure I have today. I sent across lots of shorts and shirts for Priyanka; I couldn't be at the shoot personally.

"Then I would see her on the set of *Aitraaz* more as Kareena's designer. I didn't do Priyanka's clothes for that film. Priyanka was the upcoming star then, in the same space as Kareena. I hardly did much work with Priyanka."

It was, therefore, entirely imaginable that when Karan told Priyanka he wanted Manish to do her clothes for *Dostana*, she raised an eyebrow and said, "Absolutely. But will he be able to give me that much time when he's so busy with Kareena and other actresses?"

When Karan Johar wants someone on board, few question it or disapprove of it. And so *Dostana* had Priyanka and Manish working together and it didn't go off well. Tarun has already detailed all those morning queries about the clothes she was being given to wear. It was topped by an incident which put Manish off completely.

"While shooting in South Africa, one day she said, 'Where are the clothes?' and I thought she tapped her finger towards me." Manish described what had happened ten years ago like it happened recently. Because he took it to heart.

"I quietly finished my work on the film and we were on to shooting that last saree song 'Desi Girl' at Film City," he spoke up. "I was on my way to the shooting when I texted my nephew Puneet and said, 'Karan's insisting that I come to the shooting and see the set. Thank god, it's the last day of Priyanka Chopra for me.'"

Here comes the fun part that could've seen them parting ways forever. Manish naturally had Puneet's and Priyanka's numbers stored on his phone and when he sent that message, by mistake he sent it to Priyanka instead of Puneet.

On the set was now a Weepy Girl instead of the Desi Girl.

"Karan called me up immediately and said, 'What've you done? You sent that message to Priyanka!' And I panicked," recalled Manish.

Going across and facing her was the most gentlemanly thing for Manish to do. "I walked into the set and went straight to her," said Manish. "She was teary-eyed and she asked me, 'What was the problem?' I told her, 'I'm really sorry, it was a message for Puneet and wasn't meant for you.' But she said, 'Where was the problem? I really like you and I like your work. What was the problem?'

"So I told her that perhaps I'd misunderstood the way she'd tapped her finger towards me in South Africa and she said, 'I wish you'd told me then because I didn't even realise it. And you completed the film as if nothing had happened.'

"I said, 'I didn't want to let a personal issue come in the way of the work.'

"Priyanka handled it brilliantly," he ended. "She laughed, all of us laughed, everybody laughed and it was fine. On the set were Mickey Contractor, Farah Khan, Tarun Mansukhani, and they were all watching her tearing up before I got there."

Tarun who was witness to the lack of warmth between them that led to Manish's message and the face-off on the set, put it pithily. "They had their silly misunderstandings," he said. "Manish is also emotional, and when he gets the feeling that you don't like what he's doing, he kind of takes it very personally."

The gifted designer was used to his ladies showering compliments on him for his creations. He couldn't fathom the lack of reaction from Priyanka to what he was putting together as a wow wardrobe for her.

"They didn't have too many conversations about it but he was peeved that he wasn't getting the expected reaction from her (to his clothes and styling) and she didn't know that she was meant to gush," Tarun said judiciously. "The truth was, she just didn't know how nice she was looking; when she arrived in *Dostana*, she didn't know anything about fashion and clothes. I don't expect someone who doesn't know anything about the fashion world to be able to say, 'Thank you for this, Manish.' Manish didn't have any idea. He didn't get it that she didn't even know she was looking good. I don't blame her either because she didn't know she had to gush. She didn't even realise how well she was being groomed."

But instead of throwing a tantrum and cutting ties with the designer who'd sent her the message, 'Thank god, it's the last day of Priyanka Chopra for me', she handled it with elan.

"She's also extremely emotional and she didn't understand where she'd gone wrong," Tarun emphasised. But by telling Manish that she liked him and to tell her where they'd gone wrong, and then laughing it off with the others when the air was clearing, she made a new friend. Tantrums and tempers would've ended the relationship sourly. "But it was fun for all of us," Tarun added cheekily. "To this day, we rib both of them about it and laugh. We won't be letting them forget it too soon."

Tarun also found that initially, Priyanka felt, "A little isolated by the fact that there was me, Manish, Mickey, Bose (cinematographer), Abhishek, John, Bobby, all boys, and she was the only girl in the group." She did the best thing in those circumstances. "Midway through it, she became one of us; she became one of the boys," grinned Tarun. It's a shout-out to what Priyanka had said about being an Army girl, "…our survival instinct is very strong. Maybe that's why we're a little more boyish, not damsels in distress, fragile, simpering and feminine." The Army girl became one of the *Dostana* boys. And then she ganged up with them to sometimes bully the director.

"Abhishek is 6'2", John's 6', Bobby's 6', Priyanka is 5'6" and wears 6" heels, so she towers above me. I'm 5'6". They'd all purposely stand in a circle around me, look down and make me feel like a dwarf," he said with a light laugh. "*Dostana* was tons of fun. Shot six days a week from ten to five. Chill out. Go to the gym. Even the camera attendant would be in the gym, take beach breaks. It was wonderful."

And the work itself got a boost from Priyanka's presence.

"There was a scene where she's crying and Kirron Kher comes there, sits and talks to her about her own sons.

When Karan read it, he said, 'It's a bit of a funny scene, right?' And I said, 'No, it's an emotional one.' He was a little confused about a mother and daughter talking about gay men with a reference to god in it and felt I must take it into a funny zone. I didn't. When we came on set and I gave them the scene, which they'd read earlier of course, in the first take itself, both the women just got it. After that first take, I still remember going up and kissing Priyanka on the forehead and giving Kirron Kher a big hug because they were the first two people who'd understood the tonality. The rest of them didn't; they kept feeling it was a funny scene – from my DOP to everybody. It was a great moment for a first-time director that they'd understood what I'd written and got it bang on."

Priyanka did something else that every filmmaker would want from his actor – she made it all about the film and not about herself alone.

Tarun talked about it and also contrasted her approach with that of other actors he'd worked with. "I didn't anticipate her becoming a global icon, a global star," he ruminated. "But when you work with her, you know she's got so much more in her, there's so much talent, she has a great adaptability. In the same year as *Dostana*, she was making films like *God Tussi Great Ho* and *Love Story 2050*. She'd never been in the *Dostana* space before but she adapted to it wonderfully. She understood that this guy's running behind characters; she studied that character, asked me all those questions, and you realise, 'My god, this mind really works.' That's when you know she's got so much more. And we've worked with so many. All Karan's films have strong roles for women.

"Kajol was a natural. Others gave him what he told them to. But here was this girl who asked you questions and who understood the character. I was so glad to be working with someone so involved. She was never about wanting to steal a scene. If I was ever in a space where I was even a little confused about a scene, I'd put it across as a debate, involve all the main people and discuss it. None of them ever said, 'It won't be good from the point of view of my character.' They all thought about the film. And I think she was the lead cause of that because she would always say, 'Neha, Sam and Kunal wouldn't have done it that way.' It was never about Neha alone. So for all of them, it became a trio that they talked of and not individuals. All the conversations became about Neha, Sam and Kunal for which I have to thank Priyanka."

There was also the famous going-beyond-the-call-of-duty that Madhur too had referred to.

"I have seen her with a fever of 103 degrees and still shooting," he said, still touched by the act. "It was the set we'd erected in Mumbai which was supposed to be their house. She just took a shot (an injection) and continued shooting. At that point, she was also promoting *Love Story 2050*, so after 9 pm, she'd be doing interviews till twelve midnight and be back on set at nine in the morning for my shoot. So even with a temperature, cough, cold, that machine keeps working. She'd quietly go to the hospital, get a shot and move to the next location. She's unbelievable that way, utterly inspiring. She never gets complacent. Even before she achieves something, she moves her goalpost which is the great part."

But for a hard-nosed professional, Priyanka is known as the girl whose water-taps flow easily. Like all those who've worked with her and known her, Tarun too had witnessed it on numerous occasions.

"She cries very easily," affirmed Tarun. "If you shout at her, she'll cry. Of course, I've shouted at her many times.

And of course, she's cried. More so, in the friendship zone than in the work space because I never scream at my actors."

Once, the tears actually sprang up because of a hoodie.

"She's cried for silly things," Tarun said. "Like, she'll come home from an event, would want to be comfortable, so change out of some gown she was wearing, wear my track pants and disappear. I've lost my hoodies to her, my track pants to her. One of my favourite hoodies also went with half my wardrobe, so I screamed at her and she started crying. I'm like, 'It's only a hoodie, calm down. Aren't I allowed to scream at my friends?' If a random person shouted at her, said something nasty, it wouldn't bother her. But if the people closest to her have said something that's not nice, like that hoodie, she has the 'I have a right to everything in this house' logic. What's one hoodie, what's the big deal? That's her logic."

He added quietly, "She also cries if she has a father moment. Those are the times that really get to her. She's always been Daddy's li'l girl. She was extremely emotional when he passed away (in June 2013 of cancer). I was there when she lost him and I know how emotional it was for her. Those triggers will always be there. For a girl to lose her father is a big thing; for her it was that much more. Father is a big trigger for her because he's not around. Otherwise she's utterly strong and incredibly smart."

And she's got the knack of making friends.

"It's a great, great friendship that has stood the test of time," he acknowledged. "Now we don't speak to each other for six months because she's busy and she's there; I'm busy with my work and I'm here. But it doesn't matter. Nothing changes; it's not like you have to be in touch all the time to be friends. It's like school friends. You don't meet for years but you just pick up the phone and you're back in school. With her, it's like that.

"The friendship has lasted and only grown stronger. Most friendships last only till the film is over." Which made the *Dostana* team special because even though it's been ten years, Tarun's friendship with Neha, Kunal and Sam has outlasted the film.

"My friendship with Abhishek has lasted because we've been friends forever. I worked in his mother's company, Saraswati Audio Visual; it was my first job. At that time, Jayaji would berate him saying, 'Look at him and look at you.' I was working eighteen hours a day and he was sixteen and would be playing basketball. That's how our friendship has lasted.

"The friendship with John also lasted. He's more Bawa (Parsee) than filmy, so he's casual, informal; he'd come home for Sindhi *khaana* (food).

"But it's a deeper friendship with PC," he underscored. "I'm very protective of her and she's more than protective, motherly about me. As in when I didn't make another film for the longest time (there was a ten-year gap between *Dostana* which was made in 2008 and his next film *Drive*, a 2018 release), I would get the longest lectures from her on why I wasn't making another film. I still get fired. When my film *Drive* got delayed, I got fired by her over why I couldn't get my film ready on time. Karan didn't scream at me but she did."

In her playbook on life, staying connected was a priority and it wasn't equated with buying equity to be cast in the next film. At one time, Tarun had even started *Dostana 2* with Katrina Kaif. They did not do a repeat act with Priyanka but that had no effect on their friendship.

"For the first two years, all three were continuously gung ho about wanting me to make *Dostana 2*. But Priyanka was never in the space of telling me to write *Dostana 2* so that she could be in it. She knew very well that in *Dostana 2*, something would change and since she'd ended up with Bobby Deol in the original, it was logical that the element that would change in the sequel would be her. She knew we'd signed Katrina for it. The casting had happened, the set was going up. But when I came back to the office and read my script again, a voice at the back of my head became louder. I called up Karan that night. We were just nineteen days away from starting the shooting when I told him that I didn't want to do the film. I was in Andheri and he was in his house in Bandra but it seemed like he was sitting next to me when he screamed, 'WHAT?' But at the end of the day he understood.

"I gave the script of *Dostana 2* five years of my life," Tarun rued. "But I was just not happy with it. It was funny but it didn't have a soul. It was forced. At the back of my head, I just didn't want to make the film, but I wasn't willing to say it out aloud. It's taken me ten years to make my next film but at least I'm convinced about what I'm making and that's what matters to me."

Through it all, it was Priyanka who was agitated that he hadn't started another film; it didn't matter that she wasn't going to be a part of the cast.

"Priyanka's only concern was, why wasn't I making another film? She had this huge amount of faith in me; she still has," he said, touched that she watched out for him. "She was never one to tell me, 'Write another film because I'll be in it.' Which is where the friendship bloomed because she was not selfish about it. It was concern for me."

It changed the way Tarun looked at actors.

"Initially, I always chose not to become friends with actors because there was this boundary – each one has to think of their own lives. It started changing when I became friends with this girl who was genuinely caring of me rather than about how we can work together.

"It just went more and more into the friendship zone. Chilling out at home, going out for dinners. She wasn't a star-friend, she was a friend. One of the pluses after *Dostana* was that she got groomed in all ways but she didn't change as an individual."

The fact was, *Dostana* was eventful. It was a cheeky commercial film that gave Karan Johar the courage to keep introducing new directors from his stable. It also lived up to its title and gave Priyanka and Tarun a friendship that seemed unlikely after their first meeting. And it turned Priyanka into a glamorous fashion plate.

Her satisfied director agreed, "*Aitraaz* had its own version of glamour. Times had changed; a good six years had gone by. So I would think *Dostana* was her most glamorous role. It did take her into another league."

It also turned out to be a dry run for her later romp on the beach in 2017 with Dwayne Johnson, the biggest star of Hollywood.

"Pretty much," averred Tarun, pleased as punch. "She was supposed to wear a red swimsuit because it was *Baywatch* and she knew exactly how to stand in it. She told me, 'Thanks for all the preparation.' It was being shot in Miami too. So each element added to the comfort level."

In fact, it was an ode to *Dostana* when she cut her single, 'Exotic' with Pitbull, where she packaged herself as 'Desi Girl' (it's part of the lyrics) and pranced with confidence in a skin-coloured swimsuit. It was her passport to the West.

One more quality that could be lifted from her playbook and implemented by those who want to be another Priyanka Chopra would be to focus on yourself with a distinct disinclination for commenting on anyone else. Whatever the snide little swipes at her from many a colleague, Priyanka is, to quote Tarun, "Not a comeback bitch."

As already seen, her work ethic and her people ethic bowled over Manish Malhotra, after a surprise twist to his *faux pas* handed him a new friend.

When *Dostana* was behind them, Aditya Chopra and his brother Uday wanted their best buddy Manish to do the clothes for *Pyaar Impossible* (2010) which co-starred Priyanka. Her only query to them was, "I'm fine with it but would he want to do it?"

"I got close to her and her mother in Bangkok when we were doing *Pyaar Impossible*," stated Manish.

"It was from that film onwards that I began to see her as a progressive, forward-thinking, very cool person. She didn't bring a star tantrum into it that he did this to me. She put that incident behind her and I took that from her," Manish said, learning from her to let bygones be bygones.

"Thereafter, we did a lot of work, a lot of shows. Wherever she is, I've been with her in NY, on *Quantico*, in a restaurant, Bangkok, Miami, MIDC in Mumbai, Film City, shows, shoots, awards functions, and she's the same everywhere. She makes the most of every situation she's in.

"In earlier days, I used to say, 'Oh my, she's trying to do too much together.' But now I see she's managed to do it all.

"Last year, I went over to her apartment in New York and we stepped out for dinner. I met up with Anna Kournikova and her for dinner, I went to her *Quantico* set. What warmth that girl has. And I've seen her slog it out there too. She had three managers around her; someone showing her the cut of an ad, another discussing an event she was doing. She was personally involved in everything with full gusto, complete focus. I like that because I'm also a workaholic.

"Another thing I have noticed and really admire in Priyanka is that the film industry has a lot of people who don't move with time. She's one actor who's moved ahead of time; she's put herself out there and done it. I remember she tweeted quite early, 'Just finished the look test (or the pilot) for *Quantico*.' She wasn't afraid that what if it didn't work? That confidence and positiveness is something to be admired. She doesn't fear failure."

Being essentially a man who was obsessive about how a girl was presented and how she looked, Manish assessed her through his professional glasses.

"She has a great smile which she gets from her mother and she has a great body," he began to size her up. "I remember we were doing this film called *Anjaana Anjaani*. I'd shopped for a lot of cool stuff in Dubai, lots of shorts and stuff. But by the time we went to New York, it was freezing, it was snowing. So we had to really layer her up by adding tights, boots and sweaters. But when we were shooting for the title song back in Mumbai, I didn't want to add the layers and told her, 'Let's keep it very simple.' She understood and said to me, 'I know you're trying to tell me I've put on a bit of weight, right?' So she's intelligent, she's fun."

The man who had impeccable brand knowledge and knew just what made a woman stand out, finally came to the fore as he commented, "Most importantly, she's got a great carriage. Clothes, fashion and style are not about colour, weight, height and all of that. It's about carriage. What you wear, you wear with confidence. And that confidence, Priyanka Chopra has. I think more than anybody else here."

He reeled off the clothes she'd carried with rare flair.

"Look at that classic Ralph Lauren beige trench coat she wore with a trail," he drooled at her appearance at the Met Gala in 2017. "I thought it was a great idea, very different and she carried it off. Or the Zuhair Murad dress she wore to the 2016 Oscar. She was so good on the red carpet. And that golden swimsuit we did in *Dostana*. It was my idea to try a grey saree with silver lining for 'Desi Girl'. We went on to make so many of those sarees because of all the shows she was doing. We've enjoyed working together and we've come up with some good work together."

He finally provided an unexpected endorsement by remarking, "I would think if you had to write a book on an actress which is all about achievement and beyond, my first pick would also be Priyanka Chopra. Because she's not only achieved so much in India but has gone ahead and made a place out there too. So I would have also told you that the person to write on would be Priyanka Chopra."

Thank you, Manish.

During *Dostana*, the man in her life was Harman, the man who to this day, has never spoken about his relationship with her, not even when promoting their film together. Two years older than her, Harman Baweja, the good-looking son of producer Harry Baweja, was eligible in every way. As reticent as Priyanka to go public with their relationship, Harman managed to stay under the radar for quite a while, although, with her rising popularity, it became increasingly difficult to keep it a family secret. Once, at a fashion show choreographed and directed by Farah Khan, after the lights had dimmed, a young couple slipped in and sat in the row behind me. It was Priyanka and Harman who'd avoided the flashbulbs and the front row.

Characteristically, Priyanka struck up a close friendship with his sister Rowena, indeed with the whole family, a friendship that outlived the PC-Harman relationship.

Harman not seeking attention for the equation he had with her suited Priyanka because she was always protective of her personal life and he was cut from the same cloth. In fact, he stepped out with her officially only as the co-star of two of her films, *Love Story 2050* (2008) and *What's Your Raashee?* (2009). Disappointingly, the sizzle of Priyanka couldn't be matched by the hero and both films were failures. It buried Harman Baweja's dream of becoming a star while Priyanka's life continued to look up. It wasn't long before the distance between them grew and Priyanka-Harman as a couple faded out of focus.

With her stars on the ascendant, Priyanka was excited to be introduced to noir cinema which she hadn't tried before. When Vishal Bhardwaj cast her as a perky Maharashtrian girl opposite Shahid Kapoor in *Kaminey* (2009), a lineup of fresh experiences followed. She filmed her first screen smooch with Shahid who in turn was reportedly ecstatic at who he was getting to kiss on screen.

Priyanka and Shahid also happened to stay in the same building, Raj Classic. True to nature, she didn't divulge any details of the neighbourly romance that brewed between them and would, in fact, be indignant about it. The more easy-going Shahid, or Sasha as friends know him, who had been very forthcoming when he was dating Kareena Kapoor, played ball this time by not going on record. But he would say with a twinkle in the eye, "I've learnt from my mistakes. I'm a wiser man now."

Of all the things, it was an income-tax raid on Priyanka's properties in 2011 that opened the door to their being more than just neighbours. The news that made headlines was, when the I-T team raided Priyanka's house, it was Shahid Kapoor who opened the door in his boxers.

"Why would anybody open somebody else's door in their boxers. Why?" Shahid muttered to me. But officially Shahid said, "Yes, I was there (during the raid) with her for quite a while. I think she did quite well for herself. She was balanced and calm, she was waiting for her mother. Initially (when you're raided), you're surprised, you don't know what's expected of you. So I went over to help." It was another way of saying, it wasn't he who opened the door.

Priyanka herself had said at that time, when you're raided by the I-T, "You feel like a really big star! As far as I was concerned, they (the I-T people) were just doing their job and it was absolutely fine with me. I was one of the highest taxpayers of Bollywood last year (2010) and this year as well, I think. I really respect the country that I live in. They haven't found anything but if they ever did, I would be the first person to go and make a payment. I would never say, 'It's a lie', or run away from it. They were very kind to me when they came to my home, very well spoken. There was always a lady with me. They always asked me before they opened anything. When they first came, I thought it would be traumatic but it was absolutely not. I think they also expected to find a lot more than what they did."

They did find 'Shahid opening the door in his boxers'.

"I was so upset with that!" she exclaimed. "I'm a girl; I have a father, a family who reads papers. What proof did they have when they published something like that?" she questioned. "Obviously, wouldn't my maid have opened the door? And they had the cheap mentality to actually put as front page news that he was sitting in his boxers? It was disgusting, revolting, I was livid.

"Shahid is my neighbour. I called him and the I-T people were very kind to actually let him come in and be there."

As was customary with PC, more than bringing the bachelor boy from her building into her life, the gush was over the adrenaline rush that working with Vishal in two films gave her. They did nothing at the box-office but gave her great pleasure as an actor.

"*Kaminey* was a very special film for me," she said. "I had to play a Maharashtrian girl which I knew nothing about, that too a lower middle-class Maharashtrian. I've lived in Mumbai but I didn't know the language. And I had to play the part convincingly. Plus, it was just about eight scenes and I had to make an impact in an all-boys' film. It was an important film for me."

A few years later, she did a repeat of the Maharashtrian in *Agneepath* (2012) but went into a different strata of society as Kashibai in *Bajirao Mastani* where she didn't even get to play the title role of Mastani. Yet, she left an impression as the wife who was wronged, and for someone who was yelled at by her choreographer during *Andaaz*, Priyanka matched Mastani Deepika step-for-step during the confrontational dance number 'Pinga'.

Her short but saucy-strong appearance in *Kaminey* was followed by *7 Khoon Maaf* (2011), another film with Vishal Bhardwaj that had her go from a coy bride to downright ugly. It was a film that consummate actress Vidya Balan had turned down because, apart from featuring her in the role of Susanna, a murderous wife who goes through seven husbands, through a range of situations, and startling changes in her character and appearance, she didn't think the story itself had much cinematic merit. Priyanka accepted it for just that reason – for the challenge it threw at her as an actress.

"I don't think I'm the most beautiful person on earth. That's not my USP" – Priyanka

While she and I had sat and chatted outside the YRF Studio where a trial show of *7 Khoon Maaf* was going on, she'd enthused over her director.

"Vishal Sir is one of the few with whom I share a tremendous director-actor relationship. We have an unsaid understanding of each other where if he's cut a shot, I know why exactly he's done it, he doesn't have to come and tell me. Or if I'm doing something and I say, 'Vishal Sir, just watch,' he'll know why I'm doing it. We don't have to explain anything to each other. On *7 Khoon Maaf* and even on *Kaminey*, he just put me on the set and said, 'Do it.' There was no direction whatsoever. I'd go by my natural instincts as an actor. I'd do what I thought Susanna should do. He'd, of course, tweak it after the first take was over. But he sort of just throws you into it. That's why I've come out with my best performances in his films. I've always said that every actor should in his lifetime work at least once with Vishal Bhardwaj. He's someone who'll teach you so much more about yourself as an actor because he just throws you there. Most directors will tell you what to do. Vishal Sir doesn't direct because he believes that your instincts as a human will come out when you're on set. He's someone who makes the kind of cinema that he completely believes in. He doesn't at all feel, 'I must change my film or tweak my story because people may feel this way or that way about it.' He has the courage of conviction about his own product. Whether people like it or hate it, you'll never be able to ignore a Vishal Bhardwaj film."

Whether or not the films fared well commercially, Priyanka's work in both films stood out as exceptional in her repertoire of performances.

Unafraid to look her worst in a scene, as long as she stayed true to the character she was portraying, Priyanka mirthfully agreed, "I look almost scary in some scenes (of *7 Khoon Maaf*). I was supposed to. In any case, I don't think I'm the most beautiful person on earth. That's not my USP. I don't think I'm beautiful. I'm a decent-looking girl, I'm easy on the eye, that's about it. I'm not arrogant about the way I look. As a matter of fact, I don't think much of it. For me, I'm an actor. As an actor, even if I have to look almost ugly or repulsive at some point, I will. Because I know I have the ability to look like I did in *Dostana*. I can do a *Dostana* and a *7 Khoon Maaf* where I'm a sixty-five-year-old. That's my USP. I can play any character you want me to play. As an actor, I don't want to restrict myself to anything. If you ask me to play a man, I'll play a man!"

She deliberated, "Like my acting, my career is my school. I didn't know the 'A' of acting in my first film. I just followed instructions. I can't be objective about myself but I'm enjoying the process of creating. Like I've created Susanna. I know how much I've put in, I know how much of her I've discovered along the way because I was willing to."

As always, she went into it ready to learn and didn't walk in smug about her skills.

"As a film, *7 Khoon Maaf* initially scared me when I took it on," she said. "I didn't know if I could pull it off – as a heroine to do a film that's entirely on my shoulders, if it would be accepted, if it would get the kind of opening it should. These days, they say the opening should be good and heroine-oriented films they say don't get an opening. But it happened to me with *Fashion*. People were like,

'Opening *lag gayi* (it's got decent opening collections).' *Fashion* and *7 Khoon Maaf* have been films that didn't have a lead pair. The main protagonist was just one person and that was me. I was nervous about the fact that *7 Khoon Maaf* was in a genre of its own, a film with the ability to transcend safe cinema." It didn't fare well at the box-office.

But, "The very fact that a filmmaker had the confidence to mount a film on a female actor in the main role with seven male protagonists around her, that a filmmaker cast an actress who had played herself very beautifully in commercial films, speaks very highly of her," saluted Neil Nitin Mukesh, one of the seven husbands in *7 Khoon Maaf*.

He was relatively new and she was already the National Award winner when he went into *7 Khoon Maaf* to play an injured ex-army man who wore a false leg and had a streak of sadism in him. In this film, he was the student and there was much he learnt from his co-star.

"Brand Priyanka is so smart and solid, she's moulded herself, her career very gracefully. *7 Khoon Maaf* was definitely one of her finest performances. To stand tall with seven heroes around you – I may have been new at that time but to get into the skin of your character with men like John Abraham and Irrfan Khan around – and to make it your own, is so commendable.

"I observed her very minutely even when I was watching the film later and, in commercial cinema where looks and clothes matter, here was this actress not at all intimidated that she would have to age, have grey hair, not be glamorous, or worry about what people would think. It took 'wow' to another level. She was just the character."

7 Khoon Maaf was noir cinema and being sadistic with Priyanka who was his senior in the industry didn't come easily to Neil.

"There were certain grim, very dark scenes," he affirmed. "I'm an extremely shy person though I've done my share of dark, intense roles. There was this scene where she takes out my leg. It's been amputated and I had this fake leg which was caressing her body, going up to her chin, touching her face. An actor who's that gorgeous could feel, 'What if my fans get freaked out.' I was so nervous. I kept hoping I don't demean her in any way, her character, her stature by doing something like this. But her conviction in the character and the director's conviction in her as an actor, made each element fall beautifully into place. The scene just stood out in the film.

"Even now when people talk of my best performances, they mention 7 *Khoon Maaf*. But I know that ninety per cent of the credit for my performance goes to Priyanka. If I didn't have a co-star who reacted to my menace so well, it wouldn't have come through so effectively.

"We shot for quite some time," he reminisced. "The first section had a full song sequence and quite a few scenes that we shot in Coorg. There was a sequence which we shot very late at night. It was the climax of my character in the film where I had to shoot a panther. We shot that part in the jungles of Coorg. A small platform-like structure *(machan)* was erected in the tree for just the two of us to sit between shots. We had to plonk ourselves there for the entire night. It was high up and just about enough for the two of us. At the most, a bucket could go down a rope for us to get something to eat. It wasn't sturdy enough for a make-up man or hairdresser to join us. There were mosquitoes; it was not the most comfortable place to shoot in. But not once did she, being a heroine, have any complaint during the entire shoot.

"I also saw her depth of understanding of a scene. Sometimes I would wonder in my head why she said a particular dialogue in the way she did. Probably because I'd prepared myself to react differently. But you realise later that the depth with which she creates the character is very layered. Not many people catch on to the layering that she does which later translates into magic on the screen. You might not see it in person on set. A film is shot non-linear and stitched together later on the edit table. It's then that you realise how this character has consistently managed to retain her character graph."

Perhaps Priyanka herself was unaware that she was making an impression, impacting her colleague.

"Another take-away I got from her was, it's not about looks, not about what clothes you're wearing, which designer is dressing you up," said Neil. "Those are perks you get with a certain film. She has also balanced her career so remarkably. She does completely commercial films and off-beat ones simultaneously. She'll do a *Bajirao Mastani* and a *Barfi!* where she's playing a special child. I fell in love with her in that film. Priyanka's special ability is to make you fall in love with her even when she's not looking her best, as in *Barfi!*

"From the time she won the crown to this day, there has only been growth. There's been a constant upswing not just stature-wise but also as a person. We've learnt from the greats that as you become bigger, you become humbler. Well, I've experienced that with Priyanka first-hand.

"*7 Khoon Maaf* was my fourth or fifth film, so I was new and she was already Priyanka Chopra. Multi-talented, singer, actor, entrepreneur, she's made herself a global icon, and trust me, it's not easy. Most of us are struggling to keep ourselves afloat even now. We struggle to sustain ourselves as long as we can in the same place where we are. And here is a girl who's levitated to another plane. Her transition from Bollywood to Hollywood has been so smooth, so graceful. At the same time, she's staying true to her roots, her culture, she hasn't got an attitude or cut herself off from here. Her upbringing is so strong, it comes across in her as a person. She's Daddy's li'l girl. If I ever had to get a tattoo done, I'd probably get one done like that – yeah, Mamma's boy or whatever," he smiled.

Priyanka herself divulged that certain latent qualities perhaps surface when she's before a camera. She posited, "I have a very wicked streak in me, maybe that's what came out in 7 Khoon Maaf (and later in Baywatch). I've always been very naughty since I was a kid. Over the years, naughty has turned into wicked but in a fun way. I'm not a witch, I'm never evil. I wouldn't deliberately hurt anybody, it would kill me if I did. I do things for fun because I'm not malicious. I do things from the heart, I don't do wicked things seriously. I don't do rubbish things to people. I get away with it because my intentions are always right. Most people let me get away with murder!"

Watching her with Natasha, her manager, and that famous entourage around her was a little like watching Meryl Streep in The Devil Wears Prada. Like the scene where Streep got the name and a quick briefing on the person approaching her, Priyanka would mutter, "Who's that? Have I met him/her?" She'd get her brief even before that person has reached her, so that her response would be appropriate – warm if required, lukewarm otherwise.

"No matter what I do, I do everything with tremendous passion" – Priyanka

"It's like I have blinkers on," she said to me. "If I'm tying a shoelace, it has to be the best shoelace ever, the bow must be just correct. Not OCD, but I have this huge passion and intensity in everything I take on. Like I want this to be your best interview. I'm very excited about it. I'm very passionate about every moment I live. So my films also show that. When I get angry, I get angry with passion. When I love, I love with passion. When I hate, I hate with passion. So everything is extreme in my life. It gets magnified tremendously."

Every film is an emotional investment for her. Thus Priyanka will be passionate about everything related to it. She'll be like a watchful *chowkidar* (watchman) when there's a special screening of her film, pulling up latecomers with, "It's not fair to the film."

Priyanka's involvement with her films can go into three categories – it can be very welcome for a team that benefits from her inputs; it can be overbearing for a team that finds her wanting to organise screenings and promotions a bit like she's taking over the film; and it can be terribly embarrassing if she's standing outside when the film you've just seen is going to get a no-show from the audience and a low rating from the critics.

Anupama Chopra had the last-mentioned experience, although she has otherwise hugely admired the actress.

"She's been very consistent," Anupam said, scanning her work mentally. "Like for all the problems I had with something like *Mary Kom*, her performance was amazing. For me, the real show of strength was something like *Bajirao Mastani*, where she had eleven-and-a-half minutes. And you walk away thinking about Kashibai and what that situation was like for her."

A critic who also has interactions and interviews with actors, can often be put in a spot. Anupama recollected one such moment where Priyanka's response could serve as an example to many of her less-sporting colleagues.

"I'll tell you one instance that's always stayed with me," said Anupama. "It was about that terrible film she made with Ranbir, *Anjaana Anjaani*. Right after my review was posted, I was scheduled to do an interview with her. It was literally that Friday afternoon after I had just posted it and I was like, 'What was I thinking, I should have scheduled this with her for another time.' But she picked up the phone and said, 'You really didn't like my film, did you?' And she started laughing. For me, that really spoke volumes on how sorted a person was. To be able to say, '*Theek hai, tumko nahi achchi lagi* (It's okay if you didn't like it)', was brilliant because I have had such extreme reactions from people when I review a film negatively. To be able to take it on that same afternoon, is a bit rough. It's a big release, Ranbir is a big star, but she was just great. She didn't even bring it up. After that first line, she just let it go."

But there was also that moment of embarrassment when Priyanka's enthusiasm over a film made her go to a press screening where every critic spilling out couldn't avoid meeting her.

"I remember the preview of *What's Your Raashee?* (2009) which was just dead," chuckled Anupama. "Dead, dead," she repeated. "I remember seeing it at Famous Studio, and Priyanka was outside, and we literally ran. I remember trying to look somewhere else, not knowing what to say. I remember her standing there and I was feeling so terrible, oh Jesus, but what can you say? I have no ability to lie. I was like, 'I can't do this', and I just ran away. That was spectacularly bad."

But more often than not, she came up with something brilliant where all her reviewer-friends could look her in the eye and shake hands with her.

One such film was *Barfi!* (2012).

The man who got Priyanka to uglify herself as Jhilmil, a special child (autistic) and still win hearts was Anurag Basu, the maker of films as diverse and delightful as *Gangster* (2006) and *Life In A Metro* (2007) before *Barfi!*.

Interestingly, it took a long while for Anurag to be convinced that Priyanka was the right actress to play Jhilmil. It was his wife and partner in the work space, Tani who thought Priyanka would make a perfect fit.

"It's to Tani's credit that she thought of Priyanka as Jhilmil," acknowledged Anurag. "I didn't picture her as Jhilmil. But the next day, I saw Tani drawing some pictures of Priyanka to look like Jhilmil and I thought, maybe she would be good. So I went to narrate the script to her."

They'd met and known each other before.

"We'd also got along very well," he confirmed. "She'd once dropped in to meet Duggu (Hrithik Roshan) at Filmistan Studio where I was shooting *Kites*. She had a large wound on her foot and while everybody was going, 'What happened, what happened?' around her, she saw that I was dying to say something else. So she asked me, 'Dada, what's on your mind? Say it.' And I said, 'It looks like a messed-up pizza.'

"I have a dark sense of humour and so does she, so we hit it off really well. We connected on our politically incorrect dark humour which she can't come out with publicly. So when I went to narrate *Barfi!* to her, we already knew each other. I'd also seen her work and loved her in *Kaminey*."

But the narration was no clincher.

"It was really odd," recollected Anurag, "because I thought I'd give her a short narration of about twenty minutes. But even while I was doing that, the thought playing in my mind was, 'She's the wrong person to play

Jhilmil.' She was sitting before me like the front page of a fashion magazine, looking so fabulous, I couldn't imagine her as Jhilmil. With that on my mind, I was mixing up things in my narration, getting it wrong. Then I told her outright that maybe she was not the right person for the role."

It was a role that fetched her awards and applause but her response to Anurag was a cool, "Dada, I'm also in two minds, I don't know if I'll be Jhilmil or not."

It was Anurag who came up with a solution.

"I told her," said he, "if you have the time, give me two or three days for a workshop. Let's see how that goes and then make up our minds. I was asking for something no established actress would ever agree to. You didn't have workshops those days. Today too, they happen after casting takes place. Here I was asking for a workshop to see if we could cast her, like it was an audition. You don't do that with someone as big as Priyanka Chopra. But she got my point."

Another little-big lesson here – do not let ego come in the way of trying out something that seems intriguing and challenging. She not just agreed to do the audition-like workshop, she also came prepared for it. Not that it helped.

"I had a small little office in Aram Nagar and we started there the next day. It was a disaster," he laughed.

"Priyanka is so articulate, she's all, 'Sir, these are the books I've read, this is how the character should be.' There was just no personal connection between her and me. I felt a big wall between her and me, a wall between the actor and the director. I had to break it."

The unconventional director did something that was his wont.

"I asked her to step out into the compound outside the office. There I told her, as the first step of the workshop, catch hold of my collar and give me the filthiest, dirtiest abuses that you can in Hindi. *Hindiwali, gandiwali* (in Hindi and really dirty). She was hesitant but then she did it. She abused me, eyes popping, she screamed her lungs out at me. My assistants came running out to find out what was happening. But by abusing her director, the ice was broken. She was fantastic after that. Otherwise, she was someone who wanted to do everything right, be propah, address her director as 'Sir'," he shook his head and chuckled.

The second step was to call a few special kids. "Tani and I are closely associated with an NGO called Soul Star and we called for some kids from there. Coincidentally, Soul Star school for special kids was at the same place where I had the workshop," he documented.

Here's the making of *Barfi!* with Priyanka Chopra in the award-winning, heart-stealing role of Jhilmil, in the words of the director.

"Rukhsana was the first girl who came in. I wanted Priyanka to follow her walk and the way she looked. I wanted her to observe these special children, not follow any character or any mannerism but to get into their head. I wanted her to internalise these kids. It went on for three days. Then PC and I started conversing like two special kids. By this time, she'd got Jhilmil into her system. She understood how they see life, how they see light, how they feel. These kids don't feel the ground like we do. They feel it differently. They're sensitive to the feel of the floor and the ground, so they won't put their full foot on it; the heel will be lifted to the side. PC observed all these little things and understood it. It was a cakewalk after that.

"After watching *Barfi!* people were talking of method acting and tons of homework done on it," he chuckled. "But we did nothing of the sort. This basic workshop was the whole homework. PC just took it from there."

He had his own way of breaking in his actors before getting them to perform the most complex of roles.

"She never got stuck in any scene," he said in her praise. "She got stuck only on the first day of the shoot. I'd told her, 'PC, we'll catch the bull by its horns, we'll do the most difficult scene on the first day.' We shot for a few days in Mumbai on a set for everybody to get used to their characters before heading out to Darjeeling. I told PC, 'We'll do some rehearsals and then shoot.' She was in her van and wouldn't come out of it. I called her once, twice, she didn't come out. I'd told her, we'll do rehearsals, you go back and relax, then we'll shoot. She didn't come out even for the rehearsals. I went into her van and found her crying. This confident Priyanka Chopra that we all know was actually crying. She said, 'Dada, I don't know if I can pull it off.' Along with her confidence, she has this unsure side because she wants to do everything better and better. This unsure, vulnerable side of hers is what has taken her far ahead of others to where she is today.

"She's confident, not cocky. She's shaky. It is like an adventure of getting into a dark tunnel without a flashlight. I had the whole scene clear in my head, so I explained it to her. And she got the character. Jhilmil came out on that first day itself. I had Jhilmil and Barfi (Ranbir's character) on the set for five days. I wanted them to do the difficult scene first and then head for Darjeeling."

It was Darjeeling in North East India where *Barfi!* was shot. But it wasn't as if Anurag had the luxury of uninterrupted, start-to-finish shooting.

"We didn't do the film at one stretch," he detailed. "PC did so many other films and had so many other commitments while *Barfi!* was going on. I've never seen anyone multitasking with so much focus and without any chaos. A singing teacher would come along with us on every schedule because she was also working on her album simultaneously. Her father was ill, so the whole family front was also on her mind. She was shooting *Barfi!* at the same time. I wondered how she managed to do it all. Post-shooting too, she wasn't shutting herself up in her room to do her thing but enjoying herself with everybody. If fifty of us were going out for dinner, PC was very much a part of it and having fun."

Anurag's ways of keeping her in character were also laudatory.

"Every time she'd come back to do *Barfi!* after shooting for some other film, I'd keep whispering, 'Jhilmil, Jhilmil, Jhilmil' to her over the phone and I'd talk to her like a special child just to psyche her," he disclosed. "I think she was shooting for Prakash Jha's *Jai Gangaajal* (2016) at that time where she was playing a tough woman cop. From there, she'd come to be Jhilmil. So I'd have to psyche her. But that was only for the first shot on the first day after she returned. Then she'd be fine.

"Although they were doing other work in between *Barfi!* and this film wasn't shot at one stretch, it wasn't difficult because the actors trusted me a lot," he accepted. "They didn't question my decisions while shooting and we went with the flow. I found her a complete director's actor. Some days she'd ask, 'Dada, show me what to do.' Other days she'd say, 'You want me to show you? I've got it.' She knew when to be in the driver's seat and when not to be.

"There's another point about Priyanka that I cite to a lot of actors who must learn from her," he said, veering off from on-camera ethic to off-camera conduct.

"We were shooting in Polachi (a town in the Coimbatore district of Tamil Nadu). We cheated by showing Polachi as North Bengal," he unabashedly added. "So we landed in Coimbatore where the main stars were booked into the Taj. The location was one-and-a-half hours away where there was nothing, no bungalow that could be hired, no big hotel. Only one very small dingy hotel at the bus-stop, with very basic rooms like a lodge. I was staying there with the whole unit, including the cameraman, everybody. When Ranbir and Priyanka asked me where I was, I told them, 'I won't be staying with you there. But both of you leave quickly because it's a one-and-a-half hour drive each way.' Both of them insisted that I stay with them. I thought it wouldn't be nice for me to check into a five-star hotel far away, it would be better to stay with the unit.

"Surprisingly," he noted, "the two of them drove down and insisted on staying with all of us in that *chhotu* little hotel with no facilities. We're used to stars who want AC, bedsheets and bathrooms. But they came and stayed with us. I don't see this happening with other people from our fraternity. Most of their energies go into where they're staying, which car they're travelling in and all such trappings of stardom. As producers, we also fall into the trap because we want to look after them well," he admitted.

He went on, "Once Ranbir and she wore their costumes, they became Barfi and Jhilmil. When PC would get out of her car, she'd be Priyanka Chopra. Once she'd come out of her make-up van, she'd be a different person, she'd come out as Jhilmil. So the chemistry was between the characters."

Once more, Priyanka's strength in being the character irrespective of how she looked was noted by Anurag.

"She has no problems with not looking nice and glamorous. Actually, I wanted to make her even uglier with stuff coming out of her nose and she was all right with it. As I said, once she came out of the van, she was willing to do anything to be Jhilmil. On set, the way she'd be playing, sitting and behaving even when the camera was not on, she was Jhilmil all the way."

In Anurag's armour was his clarity of where the story was heading and the blind faith reposed in him by his lead actors who were introduced to their respective characters but not to their sequential journey.

He submitted, "During the making of *Barfi!* Ranbir and PC didn't have a clue where the film was going. It was only after they saw the film that they understood the story. So Priyanka would ask me on the set, 'What does Jhilmil do after this scene?' And I would say, 'Jhilmil shouldn't know what's going to happen to her in the next scene. If you know, Jhilmil will know. Better let her be clueless.' That's the trust they had. The *glamvali baat* (being glamorous) never came up. Everybody knew it was an unsafe path before they came on board. Like Ranbir knew it was a risk before he came aboard *Jagga Jasoos* too," he pointed out.

It was risky enough for even the team to be unsure of how it would turn out and perform at the box-office.

"Before the release, everybody thought it was a good film but wouldn't work, won't do numbers," he said, with disarming frankness. "We were ourselves very surprised that it got such a good box-office response. We had no hopes. When we were doing the trailer, I remember they (Disney) wanted to put in a song and so on. And I said, Ronnie (Screwvala, then big boss, UTV-Disney), let's be true to the film and keep it silent in the trailer. He agreed; he had the guts."

But the general uncertainty over its acceptance was so pronounced that Anurag was alarmed to see it in his actors during the pre-release promotions.

"They'd gone to London and from there, they were going to Dubai to promote the film. But when I watched the promotions they did in London, I told them to come back to Mumbai because they looked so underconfident about the film," he shared. "They were saying things like, 'I hope it turns out the way it was narrated to us.'

"So I called them back and showed them the film. They hadn't seen it until then. And after the show, they both gave me such a warm hug; it was genuine.

"After the release, we sent PC and Ranbir to Busan, Morocco, to so many festivals everywhere. We divided all the festivals we were called to between us. We got the Golden Shisha Award in Osaka, Japan. Jury head Joel Schumacher (director of *Batman Forever*, *Phantom Of The Opera*) had some great things to say about Jhilmil, not about Priyanka – he didn't know her name then. And to think we had no hopes of getting the award with *Beasts of The Southern Wild* which had two Oscar nominations in competition with *Barfi!*. But Priyanka won, she got a lot of recognition internationally also.

"But the best of PC is still to come," he conveyed. "She has the potential and doesn't know it. She can be moulded into anything. The range she's capable of hasn't been explored so far."

What has been explored so far by Priyanka herself is her propensity to find a new raison d'être every few seasons.

"She showed signs that she was headed for the international scene," he voiced. "What I can say for her is, she knew where she was going. She always knows where she's going. She talks to herself every day about where she's headed. She doesn't talk to others about it but she gives little hints to people she trusts. She's a little superstitious about talking prematurely about what she's going to do.

"I didn't really see her moving to the West like this," he admitted, "though I knew she had the ambition. But I thought it would be at the level of all the other actors from here who've achieved (something) in the West and then come back to Hindi cinema. I didn't think she'd go way beyond that.

"The first time I realised she was doing something really big out there was when she made me hear her first two songs before they were released, which was much earlier than *Quantico*. That was when I knew it was serious business for her and that she was going to crack it big out there.

"Pitbull sings with others but when she got me to hear the single ('In My City') she made with will.i.am who doesn't easily feature with other singers, I wondered, how did she crack this? *Yeh kuch chhota-mota nahin kar rahi* (She's not doing something small and insignificant)."

Anurag evaluated her ambitions, her adroitness at finding a new target each time and her hitting it with resolve, topped with the willingness to footslog it.

"She knows what she's doing, she's an inspiration," he laid out his assessment. "She's focused, she doesn't judge people too much. But at the same time, she knows what to say when. She's so smart. What people learn after three years of corporate training, comes naturally to her."

Her move to the West was not just cleverly strategised, she left plenty of elbow room back home for her to return. There are enough Hindi filmmakers who're ready with scripts for her and that includes Anurag.

"I'm working on three scripts right now out of which, there's one with Priyanka which I have discussed with her," he revealed. "She's excited about it, wants to do it, but we've to figure out if she has the time for an Indian director," he added pragmatically.

"One more dangerous thing with PC is," he laughed, cannily understanding his friend, "she'll give you the feeling that she's doing your film. Like right now, she's given me the feeling that she'll be doing my next one. But I also know for sure that she's given the same feeling to twenty other filmmakers.

"She has a good girl complex, doesn't want to disappoint anybody. So when PC says, 'Yes', you shouldn't take it as a 'Yes' until the film goes on the floor."

Whether she does his next film or not, Priyanka has stayed connected with Anurag.

"With so many actors – like Kangana was my best friend during *Gangster* and *Life In A Metro* – once the film is over, there's a detachment," he said. "It's not like that with PC; she keeps in touch and becomes a friend for life. Just one film and I've grown very close to her and her family."

Close enough for her to quieten him when he famously says more than he should.

"She corrects you when you go wrong," he grinned. "I'm a great one for putting my foot in my mouth. I say wrong things at the wrong time. Quite often, she has nudged me under the table and made me stop, made me keep quiet and not talk too much."

It's a friendship that was possible because he saw dimensions to her personality that few were privy to. And she managed to break whatever reservations he had about actors.

"There's a spiritual side to her," he let out. "When we were in Darjeeling, it was Mahashivratri (Hindu festival celebrated in honour of Lord Shiva) and people were going up the hill to the Mahakal Temple. PC told me, 'Dada, I want to go there for *darshan* (seeking blessings of the Lord).' I passed it off as an actor who wants to go places where they can wave out to crowds. So I rejected it and said, '*Chhod na* (Forget it), why would we want to go into that crowd?' I've seen actors do these crowd-pleasing things. But she really wanted to go. So we went and I kept feeling, 'At any moment, her scarf will come out, her glasses will be off and I'm going to be caught in a mess.' Only three of us, PC, Ileana (D'cruz, actress who co-starred in *Barfi!*) and I had gone to the *mandir*. You can imagine the crowd in Darjeeling on Mahashivratri. We walked up and did our *darshan*. And the scarf and glasses did come off but only very briefly and quietly before the pandit where we took photos. So only he noticed that she was there. And then we were out. So I was wrong there; she really wanted to go to the temple for *darshan*. Imagine, Priyanka Chopra with *tilak* (holy coloured spot on the forehead) and *prasad* (symbolic religious food) on Mahashivratri. People would say, '*Kya baat kar rahe ho* (What are you saying)?'" he laughed. "But she genuinely wanted to do it and she has proven me wrong like this quite a few times."

In direct contrast would be crazy times where all of them would let their hair down.

"After non-stop shooting, we'd be tired and we'd hang out in her room. One evening, during promotions, all of us were high. Right through the shooting of *Barfi!*, I was sober. So they wanted me to get drunk and all of were in high spirits. That night, PC performed. She danced to all the hit numbers of the '90s. Raveena, Madhuri, Bhagyashree, she knew all their songs and dance moves. She knew precisely where Bhagyashree had turned her head in a song, which line, where her hair went. She's a fully filmy kid," he cheered.

"We've done our share of childish pranks too. Once, we were returning to our hotel after a really boring day's shoot. There were some huge frames in the hotel, some four or five of them. It had been such a boring day. So I quietly took one off the wall, PC picked up another; we took out all of them, and put them in the lift. (Actor) Saurabh Shukla who got into the lift didn't know what was happening. Then she and I got off on one floor, left one frame outside each room, rang the bell and ran off. We've been up to some really childish, stupid pranks."

They've shared distressing times too. Anurag Basu is a cancer survivor. Right after *Gangster* which was a very successful film, he was diagnosed with leukaemia. But to his good fortune and that of his wife and two small daughters, he recovered and is in remission.

So he understood the trauma more than anybody else when Priyanka's father was battling cancer (he was diagnosed in 2008) in its last stage. "I was there with her and her family at Kokilaben Ambani Hospital on the fourth floor. Those were hard times. It was slow and long, he suffered a lot. So I was relieved (when the suffering came to an end). She didn't turn to me for advice as such. They were doctors themselves, they had the best medical attention for him. But she became caring about my eating. She'd seen her father suffer, so she was concerned about me."

But they had their fights too, as friends always do.

"Once, after we fought, she presented me with a laptop. She was angry that I don't use a Mac, so that was my first MacBook. Any other actress would've stopped talking to me for two days," he said with charming candour, "because I was at fault.

"PC likes to discuss things. It's a very man-woman thing. Men don't like to talk and discuss things; women do. So it was a 'Men are from Mars and Women are from Venus' kind of fight. And I shouted at her, saying something like, 'Stop talking and do the job.' I said it very rudely, so I was the guilty party. I should've been the one to give her a gift but she gave me one. It was very smart of her. It made me realise that I was wrong."

Instead of a long sulk that could have sent the friendship into a cold phase, Priyanka's natural gift of being able to steer it into warmer waters, saved the day again.

"I'm always in love" – Priyanka

"I love the idea of love. I love doing this interview with you. I love the fact that people are watching my film. I'm a die-hard romantic. Everything for me stems from love," said Priyanka.

By the time *Barfi!* was released, there was the unexpected entry of a Khan in her life in 2011-12. The whisper was that he swept her off her feet and after they shot together in Germany for *Don 2,* it became serious enough to create a storm in his marriage.

She worked as Shah Rukh's heroine for the first time in *Don* (2006), a slickly-made crime thriller that did very well commercially. It was director Farhan Akhtar's spin on the 1978 Amitabh Bachchan starrer *Don* which had been scripted by his father Javed Akhtar and his partner Salim Khan (who called themselves Salim-Javed until they split in 1982). Priyanka who reprised Zeenat Aman's role in it, did an impeccable turn as a wildcat matching her wits with a ruthlessly wily criminal, and the box-office acceptance of the lead pair made it inevitable that they would top-line its sequel too.

An accepted green flag that an actress had arrived on the scene was for her to own a resumé that ticked off a film with each of the three Khans of Hindi cinema – Aamir, Shah Rukh and Salman – who had been ruling at the top for over two decades. Senior leading ladies like Madhuri Dixit and Kajol had done it in their heyday, so had those who came in later like Kareena Kapoor, Katrina Kaif and Anushka Sharma.

Priyanka was one of the rare exceptions who took her own circuitous route to the peak without the support of the trio. With Aamir, it was just one of those unfortunate coincidences that every time a film with Priyanka was considered, it fell through and not because Aamir had anything against her. In fact, after all these years, one film had officially fructified in 2017 when a biopic on Indian astronaut Rakesh Sharma tentatively titled *Salute* was announced. Aamir and Priyanka were to head the cast when the Khan pulled out of it. Once again, it had little to do with the heroine as he himself told her about his stepping down from the project. He had decided to put all other work aside to dedicate the next ten years of his career to the ambitious cinematic re-telling of the *Mahabharata*, the Indian epic, which, it is said, will be rolled out in five parts. With Aamir out of the picture, another Khan had to be tapped for the film to remain commercially attractive. But when Shah Rukh Khan stepped in to play the astronaut, it meant that the chances of Priyanka continuing to be a part of *Salute* were bleak. After all the rumblings at home, Shah Rukh was not doing films with her anymore.

The intensity of this friendship surprised those close to them. Shah Rukh Khan revelled in his image as a family man and was not known to be an off-screen Casanova. But this seemed no passing fancy. There were whispers about their trysts where discretion was of primary importance – from his fetching up in a nondescript car to avoid recognition to backdoor dates at his workplace. There was also the inevitable 'taking sides' as friends like Karan Johar stood by wife Gauri Khan against 'the other woman'. For the first time, Priyanka was entangled with a man who matched her in every way – sharp, witty, knowledgeable and well-travelled with friends in high places outside their little film circle, Shah Rukh could dance at a wedding with as much charm as he could deliver a sensible lecture at Yale University.

'Aag donon taraf se lagi hai (The fire's on both sides)' – a common cliché in the film industry – was used to describe how close they'd become and how passionate the mutual attraction was. At one time, there was a strong rumour that they had even gone through a quiet nikah in the UAE. It remained an unconfirmed rumour but hinted at the depth of the attachment. Perhaps to make up for not being able to flaunt her openly, it is believed that the man did everything he could do to please the lady and prove to her how much she meant to him. One friend said that because he would get her anything she wanted, she'd wittily nicknamed him Khan-cierge.

This time, more than Priyanka who always protected her privacy, it was the man who desired that it remain a secret liaison. He was married, he had an image he wasn't about to sully and they ended up having more lovers' tiffs than romantic evenings.

One incident that had the media circles abuzz involved the daily newspaper that broke the story of a surrogate baby for Shah Rukh and wife Gauri in May 2013. When the paper carried the story, a livid Shah Rukh Khan went after the entertainment editor of the paper and the correspondent who'd filed the story, insisting on a post-midnight meeting with them on the road. This was the impetuous Shah Rukh of the early '90s when he'd pick up the phone and abuse or go snorting to a journalist's house or office if he didn't like a story. It was not the media-savvy star Shah Rukh had become over the years. Why a story that was soon confirmed should have set off such an over-reaction from the actor bemused many. While one speculation was that the story had been leaked by sources close to his ladylove and there'd been hell in the actor's home over it, another explanation was that this wasn't the way he wanted the lady to know about the new baby.

But whatever the fights that ensued between them, it's a relationship that lasted six long years though the outcome – that he would not and could not make it official – was apparent to all but her. He couldn't even cast her in his Red Chillies' films where his wife was a partner. Those with an ear to the ground knew that when he produced *Happy New Year* (2014), the heroine in mind was Priyanka. But try as he might, he couldn't bring her aboard his production – wife Gauri who was its Executive Producer wouldn't hear of it; there was no way she would share title credits with the actress. Deepika Padukone who had made her debut with Shah Rukh and Farah, had to be brought in for the film to finally take off.

And so Priyanka continuing to be a part of the Rakesh Sharma biopic opposite Shah Rukh Khan was a moot question.

Salman, the third Khan, had his issues with Priyanka and he was vocal about it to all his colleagues. He had watched Priyanka and Akshay at the peak of their association at the long outdoor shoot of *Mujhse Shaadi Karogi* in Mauritius. Like the others on set, he'd watched them and also noted with amusement how the man swiftly put much distance between him and his heroine as soon as his wife and young son arrived to meet him.

He did agree to do a film titled *Salaam-e-Ishq* (2007) for young director Nikhil Advani and *God Tussi Great Ho* (2008) for his friend Rumi Jaffrey, both co-starring Priyanka. But on set, he was unabashed in letting people know how indifferent he was to her.

Most people said that Salman's coldness developed into icicles when Priyanka turned down his brother Sohail's film *Mr & Mrs Khanna* (2009). He found it unforgivable.

However, Priyanka had a very special equation with Salman's sister, Arpita. They were close friends and even after *Quantico* and *Baywatch*, every time Priyanka flew into Mumbai be it for the shortest of visits, there was no question of going back without meeting Arpita at least once. It was a girl date that had to be scheduled, however busy the diary.

In 2012, she also drove to Salman's apartment after midnight for a long meeting with him. When she stepped out after 4 am and Salman went to see her off, he was surprised to find tabloid flashbulbs popping off and wasn't too pleased. An offshoot of this visit was the speculation that it upset the other Khan down the road.

Although it took him four years, Priyanka's olive branch to Salman finally thawed him. After wrapping up the third and last season of *Quantico,* and her two Hollywood films *Isn't It Romantic* and *A Kid Like Jake*, Priyanka is scheduled to return to Hindi cinema in 2018 for *Bharat* which will be Salman's next big Eid release in June 2019. It took a while but Priyanka's skills at making friends worked again.

But four years before that, she had to develop not just skills of a different kind but build muscle too as the most physically gruelling role of her life came her way.

Mary Kom.

How *Mary Kom*, Hindi cinema's first female-oriented biopic, was conceived is a story that must be told.

'Nothing worth having comes easy' was painted on a beam on the roof of the artistically-overloaded office of Omung Kumar, director of *Mary Kom*. An actor by intention, an artist by natural inclination, a television show host by profession and one of the most successful art directors of the film, television and theatre industries, Omung found his ultimate calling in filmmaking a few years ago. But you can't get the art director out of him – his office looked like one elaborate and imaginatively designed set, every inch of wall space seeking attention.

When Omung would visit the many sets he visualised, designed and erected for filmmakers across the board, and watched directors at work, he told himself, 'I can do that. I can direct actors since I'm an actor myself.'

He began to write and dreamt of making a huge and glitzy *Moulin Rouge* kind of film, with all the heroes that he was close to. He soon discovered that they were friends as long as he designed great sets for their performances at glitzy awards shows. When it came to parting with dates for a film, they'd say, hey, he hadn't assisted anybody.

"I was so frustrated that I finally told my writer Saiwyn Quadras (who also wrote the much-lauded *Neerja* in 2016), 'Let's make a female-oriented film.' At that time, women-centric cinema was not in the picture and biopics were not in vogue. Neither *Bhaag Milkha Bhaag* nor *Paan Singh Tomar* had been released. I thought of female-oriented cinema because I thought

I could at least influence the heroines to do a film for me," he laughed.

After considering and rejecting the stories of many women, including Princess Diana, Jhansi Ki Rani and Durga, Omung was at his wits' end when Saiwyn suggested, 'How about Mary Kom?'

"I said, '*Suna toh hai* (I've heard of her), but why would I want to make a film on boxing?'" he smiled at his naïveté. It was Saiwyn who urged him to at least read her story and when he did, Omung was bowled over. 'My god, five-time world champion from India and we don't know about her?' he questioned himself. If he wasn't aware of her, most others wouldn't be either. It was time to introduce Mary Kom to the world.

The first step was to sign her. "My wife, Saiwyn and I took a flight to Manipur, met Mary Kom, sat with her for fifteen minutes, and when I said, 'We want to make a film on you,' she laughed, 'Why would you want to make a film on me? Are you mad or something?' Luckily, she didn't know anything about Bollywood, so she didn't know anything about me, which was good," he smiled broadly. "We clicked as people and within fifteen minutes she started showing us her house and other places. We signed her, we paid her and we had two years to make it.

"We came back and started writing it. Just when the script was ready, the Olympics happened (apart from being an Olympics boxer, Mary Kom also won a bronze at the Summer Olympics). Suddenly everybody woke up to Mary Kom and started asking, who's got the film rights to her story? Many producers started showing an interest in it. At that time, I was making the sets for *Shireen Farhad Ki Toh Nikal Padi* for Sanjay Leela Bhansali's sister Bela. I was in his office when he asked me what I was doing and

I told him I was making a film but it wasn't his kind of film. At that time, his *Rowdy Rathore* (a commercial potboiler with a macho hero that did extremely well) had just been released. But when he came to the lift to see me off, Sanjay asked me again, 'Tell me, what is it?' I told him that it was on Mary Kom and he said, 'Send it to me, let me read it.' I sent it and he said, 'I'll take ten days to read it.' But much after ten days, there was no word from him. Other producers were making enquiries about it, so I told Sanjay that and he said, 'How can you give it to anyone else? I'm producing it.'"

That was how a big backer like Bhansali stepped in to produce *Mary Kom* with first-time director Omung Kumar.

The next call to make was, who would play Mary Kom?

Omung knew, "There were only a few actresses we could count on who would give their life to something like this." An actress' mastery over acting was the last item on the impossible wish list. It was about finding the one actress who would give her sweat to the role.

"First, it was about building muscles which was very difficult for a female," Omung enumerated. "Second, it was about learning to box. Competence in acting was a far thought at that time. To play Mary Kom, the actress had to be fit, learn boxing and build muscle. Paan Singh Tomar had to only run, Milkha had to only run. *Chalo*, you had to be fit and build your body to play Milkha or Paan Singh. But as Mary Kom, *maar khaana hai* (you have to take blows), you have to take hard punches. You have to think of a technique you've never done before."

His not having assisted anybody else was no longer an obstacle because such a film had never been made before in Hindi cinema. So it would've been a first time for anybody.

"I was in a good place because anyway nobody had shot a boxing film before," he emphasised. "If I was unaware, so was everybody else."

A producer as accomplished a filmmaker as Sanjay Leela Bhansali who understood cinematic drama boosted the project as he also stepped in to help cinematise Mary Kom's life story.

"When I direct, I think like an actor," Omung described his style of calling the shots. "I don't direct, I act it out. For me the easiest character to film was Onler, Mary Kom's husband, as I based his personality on myself. When Mary Kom's husband saw the film, he said, '*Arre* (Hey), I should've kissed like this.' So they moulded themselves to the idea that this was their story. We took their stories but we took cinematic liberties with it," he said frankly.

But who would play Mary Kom?

"Priyanka was on the shortlist," he said, "and I told Sanjay that I wanted her for it. He asked me if I was sure about it and when I said, 'Of course', he said that he also felt confident she was the right person for it. Priyanka was the one actress whose dedication would be unrivalled. So a meeting was fixed by Sandeep Singh (former CEO, Bhansali Productions, now Omung's partner in film production)."

But there was a twist in the tale and a serious one at that. Something had happened and Priyanka and Sanjay Leela Bhansali were not on talking terms.

Before *Mary Kom* took off, Bhansali had begun filming the large and lavish *Goliyon Ki Rasleela Ram-Leela* (2013), a film that had originally been planned with Ranveer Singh and Kareena Kapoor in the lead. But at the last minute, Kareena had walked out of it, leaving Bhansali in a dilemma. With his set erected and a shooting schedule all planned and ready, who could he get to step in and play the lead opposite Ranveer? He had to finalise an alternate heroine double quick. He turned to Priyanka Chopra and even though she knew she was a replacement, she agreed to do *Ram-Leela*. However, just before filming started, Bhansali did an unbelievable switch and brought Deepika in as the heroine.

His CEO, Sandeep Singh talked about it.

"Kareena had walked out. PC with due respect for Sanjay immediately agreed and gave her dates," confirmed Sandeep. "Then for some reason, Deepika was brought in. Any human being would've been upset with Bhansali and me, and Priyanka was," he accepted. "It was her desire to work with Bhansali and I believe that to this day, no film has fully tapped her talent. Anyway, shooting started with Deepika. PC was understandably no longer on talking terms with us."

And Omung wanted Priyanka as Mary Kom.

Sandeep went on, "When we wanted to produce *Mary Kom*, we were wondering who to cast, who could perform it perfectly and hold the budget at twenty-five crore rupees. We couldn't think beyond Deepika again, and I was scared to approach Priyanka."

Sandeep had known Priyanka for a long time, ever since he'd interviewed her as a journalist during *Aitraaz*. "She'd called me then into her make-up room and said, 'Start.' She was getting her make-up done, answering my questions and going through her scenes, all simultaneously. That was seventeen years ago. I kept meeting her after that and we became friends. I'd meet her with Harman also. And she always offered me her car to drop me home."

There was, therefore, an equation that didn't exist only because he was the CEO of Bhansali Productions. So although there was the initial hesitation to approach her when she was clearly angry with them, Sandeep did the tricky work of contacting her on behalf of the company he represented.

"To her credit, she called me over," Sandeep breathed with relief. "To her credit again, she gave importance to the subject and not to what had happened in the past."

This was the classic Priyanka at work, living out another lesson worthy of noting and emulating. It was: be pragmatic. If you want your career to move ahead, don't hold on to grudges.

It happened with Manish Malhotra, it happened with Bhansali. And everybody benefited from it.

At that moment, it was Sandeep who was relieved. "PC met Omung, heard the narration and after that, because she was upset with Bhansali and me, she didn't call him or me, she called up Omung and told him, 'I'm doing this film. How do we take it forward? Let me know.' Once she agreed to do *Mary Kom* with us, I started meeting her again but for a very long time, even after she started working for *Mary Kom*, she never met Bhansali," disclosed Sandeep. The ice wasn't broken until much later when she consented to do a raunchy item dance in *Ram-Leela*, the very film in which she was to have played the lead. By then, she had started work as Mary Kom.

Bhansali had a more elaborate way of describing how Priyanka agreed to come into *Mary Kom* the film, after the unpleasantness of *Ram-Leela*, and topped it with 'Ram Chahe Leela', the item song into which she infused rustic sensuality.

"When creative people get together, it's important they realise that what they're creating is more important than you or me," Sanjay wove his words intricately. "Therefore, if I had cast an actor that may not be absolutely apt for that character, it would have been an injustice to the actor as well as to the film, to myself and to all of us working in it," he said, conjuring a creative justification for the change he made in the lead cast of *Ram-Leela*.

"Priyanka is a very big star and a very good actor. So if one were to work with her for the first time it would have to be something where I'm convinced that it is right for the film, it is right for her and right for me," he elaborated. "When Kareena Kapoor walked out of *Ram-Leela*, it was in complete shambles. The set had been erected. We met a few people (to step into Kareena's role) and one of them was Priyanka. But I felt it would be nicer if I did something more correct that suited her. She also understood very beautifully that it was important I be satisfied with what I was casting," he maintained.

"Then came *Mary Kom* and I realised that this was a film she should do and must do but (given the strained circumstances) whether she would or not..." he shrugged. "But she also understood that this was a separate film, an independent idea, not linked with the other film."

He threw up a few home truths that were like a scan of Priyanka's mindset.

He analysed, "Once an actor is focused only on acting, on playing a character that you like a lot, the rest of the paraphernalia which has ego, pride, all of that has to be shed. How do you take on another character if you don't shed your own personality, if you hold on to me, to me the star, to me the actor?

"I think for a person like Priyanka, acting is what matters most. She felt Mary Kom was a wonderful idea, a wonderful character. It was a very inspiring tale, something she hadn't done before. She had to learn boxing, she had to play an athlete. It was very challenging for her. She has this wonderful spirit of taking challenges.

"Till you venture into the unknown, how do you arrive anywhere?" he contemplated pertinently. "You have to take up roles that you haven't done before, or you think you cannot do, or that which makes you ask, 'Will I be able to do full justice to it?' All these things bring out your inner potential, make you give your best to it.

"Priyanka's always in search of something that stimulates her. The tried-and-tested is *theek hai*, all right, something you're very good at, so big deal, you're doing it every day. When you've reached that level of stardom where you can take on different things, you've been there, done that, she's done it all, then she's in that liberated position where she can do what she wants to do or not do what she doesn't want to.

"When an actor continues to have the spirit to become another character, without being bothered about things like, 'What'll the world say? He didn't take me in *Ram-Leela*. How can I do his film?' such trivial feelings won't really matter."

If she transcended the common human reaction to a hurt which would have been to switch off and not entertain Bhansali's new offer, it was because, "She doesn't let go of opportunities," remarked Bhansali. "What's very important is that opportunities come rarely. There are those who snap them up, never let them go while there are a lot of people with great potential who let opportunities pass them by. They're laidback or lazy, *hua toh hua* (if it happens, it happens). Far too much importance is given to unnecessary things – to discussing other people, their work, anything but your own career, where your career is going, what you have to create, what you want to leave behind, what you can look up to when you pick that one DVD from your shelf and say, 'This is a film I liked, I enjoyed doing it.'

"You have to be ambitious in a creative way and not in a greedy way to achieve all that you want to, to fulfil your dreams, to never let them go.

"Priyanka is that person who enjoys an opportunity, who gives her all to an opportunity, so they never stop coming to her; they keep coming to her. Once you give, you're ready to receive everything that comes your way. People all over the world have realised that this is an actor who gives to a role, everything. Directors, story writers, they all want to give her more stories to tell. It's a very nice give-and-take that an actor should do after reaching that position. Priyanka does that."

Midway through *Mary Kom*, Sandeep approached her, very tentatively again, with what would've seemed an outrageous offer – to do an item number in *Ram-Leela*. That's when he brought Priyanka and Bhansali together for a meeting in her house to sort out their issues.

Sandeep recorded, "We had an item song for which it was ideal to bring two great talents, Bhansali and Priyanka together. They were not on talking terms only because of a situation. Priyanka had been replaced by Deepika in *Ram-Leela* because Bhansali was coming from (surfacing from) *Guzaarish* (a financial and box-office setback), and he had to go for the saleable Deepika-Ranveer combination. Anyway, when it came to the item song, I contacted Priyanka and said, 'Mr Bhansali would like to meet you.' She said, 'It's okay, I'm doing *Mary Kom*. You're producing it, I'm fine with it.' But we went to meet her at her house and in half-an-hour, she said, 'When I was doing the film, why wouldn't I do a song?' After that Bhansali and she became the best of friends."

Bhansali added, "She was very sporting to have said, 'You want me to do 'Ram Chahe Leela', fine, I'll do it.' And she did it with such flamboyance, I enjoyed working with her those seven days."

But for first-timer Omung Kumar, the wait for a miffed heroine to come around and say 'Yes' to *Mary Kom*, was a nail-biting mix of anxiety and suspense.

"I was waiting down while Sandeep went up to do a bit of fielding," he went back in time. "She wanted to know who was directing the film and when he mentioned my name, she said, 'Ah.' She knew me, we'd met umpteen number of times. At all awards shows, I've made those huge, larger-than-life sets for every actor. Every actor wants to be in your good books then because they want the best for their act. I'd also done *Love Story 2050* (the Priyanka-Harman starrer). So I'd worked with her before.

"When I went to her, she questioned, 'Are you sure you see me in the role?' I was sure. We narrated the first half to her. She loved it. We'd barely left, when she called me. 'Omung, are you sure I can do this?' she asked me again. I said, '100 per cent, you can.' 'But boxing?' she wondered. I said, 'If anybody can, it's you.' I said that because she's so very dedicated about everything she does. She told me, 'Fine, I'm doing it,' and I was over the moon."

With Bhansali as producer and Priyanka Chopra in the lead, Omung couldn't have asked for a better debut. But when Priyanka was announced as Mary Kom, there was censure from some quarters.

"I got a lot of flak for not casting someone from the North East as Mary Kom," Omung nodded. "But I wanted the movie to have legs; I wanted the movie to go everywhere. That's why I wanted a star. Sanjay Leela Bhansali is a big producer but I was new, I needed a big actress to bank on."

Getting the 'big actress' on board was the first baby step.

"It wasn't a smooth ride," he recalled. "As said earlier, it wasn't about acting at all. It was about fitting into the mould, understanding this character, what her childhood was like, how she built muscle, how she became a boxer. To top it all, I came to know that Priyanka had never been to a gym. So the first step was to make her go to one. Building muscles is something no actress will do. This wasn't about just going to the gym and training because I needed to see the muscles – she would be wearing sleeveless shirts. If you see Mary Kom, she's short but she's absolutely taut and tough. That was our first hurdle.

"We got in Mary Kom's trainer. Some things just worked out miraculously for us. For instance, Shiamak Davar brought us someone to assist us on the film and coincidentally, he turned out to be Mary Kom's trainer's son. It was like all the favourable elements were coming together. So all of us in the unit, including I, ended up getting trained in boxing because we also needed to know the boxing language. If I said, 'jab' or 'upper cut' to Priyanka, I should also know what it's about."

The training and arrangements were detailed, complex and torturous at all times.

"We got Rob Miller (US boxer) and Christie, an Olympic trainer in boxing, to form the games and bouts. We also brought in Hemlata who had boxed with Mary Kom. We put together a good, solid team. We built a boxing ring in Sanjay's office. We got in real boxers. PC was the only one in the cast who was not from the North East. The rest of the cast was from Manipur for Priyanka to familiarise herself with the language and to make her look real. Darshan Kumar who played Onler is not from the North East but he had those eyes which made it easy for me. The others were all people who looked the part and who could make Priyanka more believable.

"Full vigorous training went on for three months," he filed the details. "Dedicated gymming, body building, eating *bhar bhar ke* (heartily). Priyanka was doing other films also, so it was difficult for her to build muscle and hide it while shooting for the others. We went to Goa and did a workshop and narrations. She took the trainer with her. Finally, we began to see the build, the forearms, the muscles emerging. She would post videos and tell me, see my wings. And this was a person who'd never before gone to a gym," he threw in as a reminder. "Professional trainer Prashant really built her up. There were two parts to her training. Gymming and building muscle formed one aspect, training in boxing was the other."

In the midst of all this, tragedy struck. *Mary Kom* was on the verge of starting when Dr Ashok Chopra fell seriously ill. A week before they began shooting, he passed away.

Sandeep was one of Priyanka's many friends who saw her go through trauma in her personal life while retaining her dedication to her work.

"When her father was ailing and in hospital, she was coming to the boxing ring every day to practise for *Mary Kom*," he said in admiration. "I used to go to Kokilaben Hospital every day. She would be crying because we all knew that it was a matter of days. At that time, she was toning her body, practising her boxing, meeting Mary Kom and preparing for the role in every which way. The shoot was to start in three days. We kept telling her, 'If you want us to push the shoot, tell us.' She said, 'Put up the set.' Bhansali was really concerned because while we could understand and be sympathetic to the situation, at the same time, it would cost a lot of money to erect the set if the shooting was going to be cancelled."

It was when her father passed away that Priyanka showed what commitment meant to her.

Sandeep recalled, "After the cremation where Deepika, Bhansali, Shah Rukh, everybody was there, when we went to meet the family who was standing in a line, she was weeping all through. It was about 4:30 in the afternoon. When I went up to meet her, she hugged me and said, 'See you at 7:30 in the boxing ring.' I'd been actually worried because we had called trainers from abroad for her boxing. But she just said that one line to me and moved on to the next guest while I kept looking at her face, completely astonished at her focus. Actors in my experience give excuses not to shoot. Everybody works towards being a star, not towards becoming an actor. And here was this person who had achieved so much, such a big star. From that day to today, PC is Durga for me," he finished dramatically.

"We had to stall the film just a bit," remembered Omung, her director. "But in about a week's time, she was ready to get back to work. She wanted to. *Mary Kom* was the film she started after her dad passed away."

But in the tragic loss of her father, in the final fifteen days when she had sat by his bedside, she'd lost the muscle she'd built with such tenacity. "She simply said, *karenge*, we'll do it, and she built it all over again," added Omung.

"I started with filming the fights. For the first twenty days, all I did was shoot all the fights. I shot even the climax." So that all the scenes requiring her muscles and the presence of all the boxers who'd been assembled, were canned and done with.

"The shooting itself was crazy," he recounted as he listed vital information on the making of *Mary Kom*. "It

was my first time as director to say, 'Action, roll camera.'
It was Priyanka's first action film and biopic. Sanjay came
to wish me luck on the first day and then maybe came once
in between. My wife was the production designer. We built
a huge set and it was so smartly done, you couldn't tell
that Delhi, China and Kerala were all shot in the same
place. The fight in China was a big, larger-than-life match.
We shot it right here in the studio. The whole world was
filmed on one set – at Filmistan Studio. We kept changing
the background, the walls kept going back and back and
back with a green screen." (Green screen is a background in
front of which moving subjects are filmed and then merged
for the final image.)

Apart from also ensuring that a double was available
for Priyanka's practice shots, her back shots and so on,
there was the additional tension of having real boxers
in the film. They added authenticity to the shots but they
also packed a real wallop and it was Priyanka who had to
take their punches.

"That was really tough on her," Omung grinned at
what he'd put her through. "While she was still acting her
part, the boxers didn't know how to act. She'd be saying,
'Hello, Omung, *maar rahen hain*, they're really hitting
me.' They were boxers, they'd get angry if Priyanka hit
them and would hit back. How could they lose? For me, it
worked well because it looked so real. We had boxers from
everywhere, Australia, the US, China, India."

Those punches spelt trouble and it happened one day
when Priyanka had a little boil on her forehead.

"I was at the monitor and I couldn't see her being hit,"
Omung detailed the incident. "Here I was saying, 'Hit her,
I can't see the punch, it looks like you're ducking.' There
she was saying, '*Yeh* really *maar rahen hain*, they're really

hitting me.' When I kept saying, 'I can't see the punch,' the boxer landed *fatak*, one solid punch on her forehead and the boil just burst open; it oozed, and we had to stop shooting. Her mother was around, so she put some *patti* (bandage) on her forehead and took care of it. But Priyanka kept shooting. It was hurting her but she kept shooting."

Were all those blows worth it? For Priyanka they provided the satisfaction of a job well done.

"I pushed her so hard but she was also one who wouldn't give up for anything. *Maar khaayi* (she took blows) right through the picture. We knew that once we'd finished with the set, we couldn't shoot with all those boxers again. So when we were shooting the fights, we had to keep taking extra back-up shots just in case we needed them later."

With people brought together from all over, nightmare situations were bound to be a part of the experience.

"One boxer who was in the final match suddenly had to go back because her father who was a soldier was going to Afghanistan. We desperately needed her for the final fight, so we had to call her to come in (from the US) on just the last day and shoot extra footage with her before sending her back. Gosh, there was so much tension."

Through it all, Priyanka's application and sense of resolve stood firm.

"I was scared because I was getting extra work out of her," Omung remarked. "But if I'm a major taskmaster who goes into a lot of detail, she's also the same. She's very finicky too. Her clothes, her look, the hair. What she wore had to look very real. Together we'd do the trials right here in this office. We finally decided to take somebody's used clothes which she wore for the initial scenes. Then as Mary Kom progressed and sponsors came into her life, the clothes became better. We showed it that way. We planned her styling, her growth, everything together."

Two sticky problems when telling the story of a real flesh-and-blood person turned out to be Mary Kom's hair and her eyes.

"The film had a lot of changes in her hair," Omung laughed as he remembered. "At first her hair was haphazard like in her childhood. She was moody, so after she began training, one day Mary Kom just went and shaved her head. When her hair grew back, small bits sprouted at first. We had a full progression chart for just her hair – in which year what her hair looked like. While shooting, we had to keep referring to the chart and go back and forth. *Poori picture mein baal ka bahut panga tha* (Right through the film, her hair posed a huge challenge). In some scenes, where we required real short hair, we gave Priyanka a scarf to hide her hair which was longer than required. Fortunately for us, Mary Kom wears scarves in real life.

"Priyanka had never done anything like this before. There was nothing glamorous or beautiful in her look, no lipstick, nothing. Mary Kom likes nail polish and sunglasses, so we let Priyanka paint her nails and use shades. We followed all that from the real Mary Kom.

"Priyanka met Mary Kom who was always just a phone call away. If we got stuck in some detail, we'd call her. We'd ask her things like, 'How do you give *gaali*s (expletives) in Manipuri?'"

What also posed a problem was that Priyanka didn't have the typical North-Eastern eyes.

"Four months earlier, we'd tried prosthetics, got experts from abroad to get the right effect. But ultimately, this was about boxing and one blow would find the prosthetics flying off."

That was when Omung's talent as an extremely gifted artist (he paints too) came to the rescue. He revealed that two years before the film took off, when they were still working on the script, he had sketched the whole storyboard. (Incidentally, world renowned filmmaker, the late Satyajit Ray was also known to personally sketch the storyboard of his films.)

"In my storyboard, I had sketched her face with freckles," Omung revealed. "Mary Kom doesn't have freckles. But I had sketched her with freckles and a fringe. I gave that look to Priyanka and it worked. With just under-eye make-up and no prosthetics at all, we managed her eyes. Priyanka loved the freckles so much, she'd go home with it. They became the highlight of her look. When the first poster came out, the same people who had said, 'Priyanka doesn't look anything like Mary Kom,' started saying, 'She looks just like her.'"

What made the assignment tougher for Priyanka was that the film was not shot at one stretch.

"After the first twenty days, we didn't have Priyanka's dates. While we waited for the next schedule, I edited all the fights we'd shot. It took me ages to do that. I had the editing machine installed right here in my office," said Omung.

"She got busy with other films. She was shooting for *Gunday* then and her director there used to curse me, saying, 'What have you guys done to my heroine? She's got muscles and now I have to hide her beauty, hide those muscles under long sleeves.' Even that sexy dance in *Ram-Leela* happened in between the shooting of *Mary Kom*. It was six to eight months before she could shoot with us again."

And so it happened again – by the time she reported for the next shoot, the assiduously built muscles had disappeared and the whole process had to start again.

"She had to build muscle twice because I had to show the muscles during her training. In fact, we had to show even more than what we had shot during the fights because when she's supposed to be in training, those muscles really had to ripple. Prashant, the trainer was back on the job. We had a full anthem sequence where she's building her body; that's where we had to show her muscles. But this time we knew how to pump it in."

Most of the next schedule was filmed in Manali and Dharamshala which was made to look like Manipur. After that, they returned to Mumbai to shoot Mary Kom's house and other such locations on sets erected in the studio.

But it was Manali-Dharamshala where Priyanka's endurance was put to the test.

"Over there, the training was very hectic. We had taken Prashant and others with us. She had only two months this time around and not the three months that were needed. By then, we'd all become experts at how to build the body," he chuckled.

"Priyanka would ask me to let her off early, so she could train at night. But we were shooting late, so that couldn't be done. She said, 'Then give me time in the morning.' But we needed morning shots, therefore, that wasn't possible either. So she'd be pumping iron on the sets itself.

"It was freezing cold in Manali and pouring too, and for a sequence, I was making her run in a banian. She was completely cooperative. Her vanity van was parked a kilometre away. She'd say, 'Forget it, I'll get someone to hold a towel and I'll change behind it.' She had to run down a long road in different clothes. I was shooting with the ATB (camera) in a vehicle. She had to run and pass me by; I'm making her go faster to catch up with us and pass us. Then she'd change and come back and do it again. I have pushed her and she likes it. She's a male version of herself. Her 'I want to do it' helps us. There was a fight in a *mandir* at Dharamshala. It was the sequence where she fights a goon for money. At that time, she didn't have muscles, so I made her wear a long-sleeved shirt. We did our fair share of cheating," he admitted sheepishly.

"I can't even think of who else I could've worked with. The kind of dedication, the *maar khaana* (getting beaten up)... I had her hang from under a bridge, do rigorous sit-ups on the rocks. We wanted to show unbelievable strength and she did it."

The story of Mary Kom, the mother of two, meant that Priyanka would have to shoot with kids.

"We had twins on the set. We had to keep track of their growth too. If one got tired or cranky, we'd shoot with the other."

And then the heroine showed her kiddish side.

"There was Farex on set for the kids," Omung smiled. "Priyanka developed a taste for it, found it yummy and she'd keep eating bowls of Farex. It was snowing in Manali; we couldn't show snow in Manipur. We had to shoot indoors. In between shots, our lady would keep eating Farex. She would roam around with the *dabba* (tin). She'd say, 'I'll get more *dabba*s for the kids but I want this.'

"The demand of the role was so gruelling that, of course, I also heard her say, 'I don't want to get up in the morning, I don't want to do this.' That also happened," he laughed. "It was toughest for her because even if we were all slogging, it was she who had to go exercise. But we got fantastic body shots, the sweat too. We shot our first poster in Dharamshala. We got everybody to come there and shoot it because that's when she had those rippling muscles and it couldn't be photoshopped."

There was the exhilaration of building something together and also the trepidation of making a female-oriented biopic, a first.

"Luckily, *Queen* also happened that year. The same year, some other female-oriented cinema also happened (like *Gulab Gang, Revolver Rani, Highway, Khubsoorat*). But *Mary Kom* set a standard for biopics and for female-oriented cinema. By then, *Bhaag Milkha Bhaag* had also been released and had done well." In fact, one of the visitors on the set of *Mary Kom* was Farhan Akhtar (who played Milkha Singh); he dropped in to see the shooting of a boxing scene.

Besides winning the National Award for Best Popular Film Providing Wholesome Entertainment, *Mary Kom* fetched handsome returns on the investment and got Priyanka a bunch of awards for her performance. Most of all, it gave her one of the biggest highs of her career.

"Priyanka works twenty-four hours," remarked Sandeep Singh. "If she's just landed at the airport when you call her for something urgent that's to be discussed, she'll say, 'Come to the airport and we'll talk in the car on the way.' She doesn't waste time, she's always on the go."

"I don't drink coffee but it's like I've got caffeine in my blood" – Priyanka

She described herself to me: "I'm very restless. I work twenty hours a day but I'm still restless. I think very fast. I'm impatient, I need things done right now. I need people to keep pace with me. I need things to be done as fast as I think. I'm like I'm on coffee. I don't drink coffee but it's like I've got caffeine in my blood. I need instant results, super fast."

She doesn't waste time on sleep either.

"Sleep is something I will not do for many years to come because I just don't get the time for it. When I say I work for eighteen hours a day, I really do. I'm not saying it as an exaggeration. I'm a living example of the adage, 'I have miles to go before I sleep'. I'm an energiser, I should endorse Boost," she laughed. "Of course, I get tired but sleep is something I miss because I love to sleep, love to have an afternoon nap. But I feel I'm young right now, this is the time to work the way I do. *Poori zindagi hai na sone ke liye* (Haven't I got my whole life to sleep)? So it's never like I'm dying to go home and sleep. This is the time to be on the set, to meet people, to do things. Even when I'm sleeping, my mind doesn't sleep. I wake up suddenly at 2 am, write something in my to-do list and go back to sleep."

One of Priyanka's little-known secrets is that she loves a catnap. "The most important part of my life is a catnap. I work so much that I have the ability to sleep even for ten minutes. I'm really blessed that way. Like if I'm sitting here, I can doze off and have my ten-minute power nap."

But she had a little nettle as well about her silent dozes.

"I've never got caught (catnapping), I'm very good at not getting caught," she said. "I hate being caught when I'm sleeping. I really hate it, it's one of my pet peeves. I hate to be seen when I'm sleeping."

The main question: why does Priyanka push herself so much?

Neil Nitin Mukesh made an interesting observation.

"Never would I use the word 'luck' for Priyanka Chopra. She's a self-made, hard working woman who has made Brand Priyanka Chopra all by herself. I will never say, 'She's so lucky, she's in Hollywood.' She reminds me of that poem by Shiv Khera:

He worked by day
And toiled by night.
He gave up play
And some delight...

And forged ahead,
Success to earn...

And when he won,
Men called it luck.

"She just exemplifies that beautifully."

Priyanka herself has talked about wanting to leave behind a legacy. And about being on an eternal quest, "To discover, to find me. I've never known me. Even in the company I keep, there's a strange solitariness that I have. In a way, I'm very aloof and a loner but I'm a very friendly person. There's a certain quality of looking at everything from another point of view like almost as if I'm not there. So I may be surrounded by a million people but I'd still feel like I was all alone. I've become a little more aware of it. When I was fifteen-sixteen, I was just an obnoxious teenager.

"It's not a quest to find myself in a spiritual sort of way. I'd like to know what I'm capable of. I'm learning about myself... There's so much more to do, so much to learn. Every day, when I walk on to the set, I'm petrified. Will I be able to live up to expectations? I want to be the best. If somebody asked me to be a wallpaper, I'd want to be the best wallpaper ever."

Into that quest, she mixed the practicality that pushes aside pride and other corrosive emotions to play Bajirao's wife Kashibai when Bhansali went back to her once again with an offer that was not the title role in *Bajirao Mastani*.

"She was never Mastani in our head, in Sanjay's head," said Sandeep. "When we went to her for the role of Kashibai, she again said, 'Why not the title role?' Kashi was my favourite role always. But it took us time to convince her to do that role. We were nervous until the day of shooting *ki karegi ki nahin* (will she do it or not), nervous that she might turn it down. But she played Kashi out of respect for the director. And we all know what happened once she played Kashi. I don't know how as an actor, she's not insecure," he wondered aloud.

Bhansali, the director who made the spectacular historical by combining fine aesthetics with commercial acumen, had his own way of looking at Priyanka. Circuitous though it may seem, the route he took led to Priyanka.

"She's a great girl in terms of not letting the process of filming a song, filming a scene or a shot, get cumbersome. The process is light and enjoyable within which you discover nuances as you laugh, you converse, you eat, you chill. All those processes are actually about discovering those nuances. Finding a way of how to play the character, how to say a particular line, all this is a process. This process is very exciting for Priyanka."

However, when Kashibai reported for work, "I found her howling," a startled Bhansali remembered. "She was saying, 'I don't know if I'll be able to work, if I'll be able to do this.' And I said, 'What's all this nonsense?' I'd never seen an actor do this. Was she hamming, lying, trying to get attention? I couldn't understand any of it. I said, 'Bunk it, I'm not a sucker for all this nonsense, just do the shot. Once you've got the character, once you've got Kashi, once you realise how Kashibai would walk, she cannot walk like Priyanka, she cannot have the swagger of a star on the red carpet, it'll start flowing.' All that understanding came in the first two days and then she just flowed.

"Insecurities, yes, there are, as an actor. I won't paint a completely rosy picture and say, 'Priyanka has no flaws.' Every human being has them, every artiste should have them. Because only when you have flaws do you want to overcome them. And only when you overcome them, do you start excelling. When you succumb, you stagnate. When you don't listen to what other people are saying, to what's right and wrong, you'll never find yourself.

"That search for excellence is a process," he continued. "Just because you've done very well in an earlier film, if you've done really good work in say, *Barfi!*, it doesn't mean you're going to excel in your next one too. That search for excellence is constant in each project."

He conceded, "It took a lot of time to convince her to play Kashi in *Bajirao Mastani*. 'It's not in the title, I don't get to do songs, I don't have….' I said, it's high time Indian actors went beyond measuring a role in terms of how many songs, how many romantic scenes... Actresses in the '90s would do this. In the 2000s, they would do it. Why were we getting into this? Move on. Look at the West. Judi Dench did an eight-minute role in *Shakespeare In Love* and walked away with an Oscar. It's about your conviction, your confidence. It's not about whether your character's name is in the title or not.

"Priyanka's a sharp girl. She has cinematic intelligence. She understands the importance of every character, what the character is to the script and, therefore, how the character will turn out to be. So she finally came around to doing Kashibai and she did it beautifully."

It led to inevitable comparisons. But Bhansali stayed loyal to both his women – to Mastani Deepika Padukone who played the other woman in Bajirao's life and to Kashibai, his wife.

"I personally feel Deepika's performance was completely different," he said, speaking up for both actresses without leaning towards either. "Mastani was fragile, she was walking a very thin line because she was the other woman, very sensuous, very refined, and Deepika made it so goddamn beautiful. Kashi was lovable, reachable, accessible, somebody we know, graceful in her own way, a woman who doesn't know how to handle a situation but ultimately finds a way. There is no comparison, there is no, 'one is better than the other'. Some related to one character, some to another. When we watch *Sholay*, some would say, Jaya was excellent because she played a quiet role while some others would like Hema Malini because she played the over-the-top Basanti so beautifully. Both were so relevant, so valid. So we should stop making actors compete amongst themselves. Is Shahid better or Ranveer? (They were the two heroes of *Padmaavat*, Bhansali's next after *Bajirao Mastani*.) That's not important. The film is important. Each character plays a part. Otherwise it will stop a lot of actors from doing a lot of important films together because of 'I didn't get this, I didn't get that.' It's not about you and me, it's not about the actor and the director; it's the film that's important. Let that story be told, let that story be told to the world. It's only when Ranveer, Deepika and Priyanka do a *Bajirao Mastani* that it reaches the world in so many ways because they're such important and loved stars. So it's important that actors contribute."

He pointed out, "Priyanka is one such actor who realises the importance of contributing to a film, contributing to Indian cinema. It's not about Me. Her attitude is, 'You want me to do a song in *Ram-Leela*, come, I'll give it my best and it'll be the most talked about song too. Let's see where it goes.' Contributing to your industry where you're not important is a very rare quality. Nowadays, to get two female actors to come together is very difficult."

In his earlier films, "Madhuri (Dixit) wouldn't even bother to come to the monitor and check when they were doing a shot together. (Madhuri and Aishwarya Rai were cast together in his *Devdas*.) So much confidence. For her, it was all about, 'I know I'm playing Chandramukhi, I know my character, I know what I'm doing.' So much ease. If Suchitra Sen and Vyjayanthimala didn't come together, there wouldn't have been a *Devdas*. If Madhuri and Aishwarya didn't come together, I wouldn't have had a *Devdas*. So I feel Priyanka is one such actor who realises the importance of leaving landmarks or milestones in Indian cinema. You don't know if they'll turn out to be milestones but she participates in them. She'll go abroad and do a film, she'll cut an album, do *Quantico*. Adventurous.

"The adventure is very important. How do you tap your energies unless you go climb the unknown?" he queried. "It's only when you go climb the Himalayas that you discover all your strength and energies; you learn how to live, with the gashes, the storm, the falls, everything. That's a very important quality in Priyanka."

One of the highlights of *Bajirao Mastani* was 'Pinga' where Bhansali had both of Bajirao's women dance together. It was difficult to tell who was better – Priyanka and Deepika were that evenly matched.

"I enjoy putting two women together for a dance," he acknowledged. He had earlier done the same by pitting two consummate dancers, Madhuri Dixit and Aishwarya Rai against each other in 'Dola Re Dola'.

"People were saying, where's *Devdas* going – Paro and Chandramukhi coming together, blasphemous, bastardisation of literature. Today they talk of 'Dola Re Dola' as the most memorable part of the film," he snorted.

He grinned that there was no way he would let go of such an outstanding opportunity when he got Priyanka and Deepika to outstep each other in a dance sequence.

As always, it ruffled many feathers.

"A lot of people got upset. How can Kashibai dance? But when you have a Priyanka and a Deepika, you know the grace with which they will dance within the limits of the character."

The actresses also danced like their lives depended on it without tripping each other.

"It wasn't about who's dancing better than the other. Is my waist showing more than hers? Is my body more sensuous than hers? Deepika was least interested in that, so was Priyanka," the director said before he laughed, "I tried to make them fight, argue, not be friends. I wanted them to sit with back-to-back chairs, fighting over whose best shot was better. I would tell them, 'You're supposed to be competitors, not friends.' Because they'd be chatting about shopping and I'd say, 'What the f--- are you up to? You're supposed to be rivals. I need stories to give to the media.' And they'd both say, 'No, no, no, we don't want these stories, we're happy doing our song.' They did 'Pinga' with such ease."

Criss-crossing between both his historicals, *Bajirao Mastani* and his next film *Padmaavat*, he spelt out his cinema before tying it all up to Priyanka.

"A lot of people had objections to 'Pinga'. But I felt when you express through music, which in India we do a lot more than anywhere else in the world, when you express an emotion, two characters are expressing themselves and coming together through a song, what's wrong? What's wrong in Bajirao singing a song? Or if Padmavati dances to 'Ghoomar' (in *Padmaavat*)? Why can't a king or queen or warrior celebrate life, or enjoy with music or celebrate with his fellow warriors or in Padmavati's case, with women in her *zenana* (women's quarters)? How does it matter? People love watching dance and music. In my cinema, it's an important part of my storytelling. My expression comes through a lot of music and dance."

One of the many voices of dissent was that of legendary playback singer Asha Bhosle.

"Asha Bhosle called me and said, 'You know what, the thought of Bajirao singing and dancing was not acceptable to me, I was very angry. How could this happen?'" Sanjay disclosed. "Then she went and saw the film and she called me twice; she saw the film four times. '*Kitne acche se kiya* (You presented it so well). He's won a *jung* (war) and *ek mardana* (manly) warrior dance *hua* (happened).'"

Bhansali explained, "Bajirao could laugh, he could eat, he could ride, he could make love to his wife, he was a healthy normal man. So why shouldn't he have celebrated life? Why should Kashibai not dance? Mastani was not a courtesan at that moment; she was his wife in many ways, he'd brought her home. It was two wives dancing. There were so many objections to it. But the grace with which they danced, the grace with which it was shot, the grace with which it was choreographed, the whole world got to know that there's a dance form in Maharashtra called Pinga. 'Ghoomar' (which he picturised in *Padmaavat*) got revived. It got revived after so many years; people had forgotten Ghoomar. Now schoolchildren, everybody everywhere is dancing to Ghoomar. They (those objecting to it) were saying, '*Naak katwa diya*, you've shamed us.' But I have revived the dance; it's reached every part of the world. Let folk art survive, even if it's been a little Bollywoodised, you're reviving it and keeping folk art alive. It's very important. Because that's our tradition, our roots, our *mitti ki khushboo* (fragrance of our soil). If we lose our cultural connect, we'll be foreigners in our own land. We won't know our music, we won't know our own literature. Cinematically, *Bajirao* or *Padmaavat* will be different from a history chapter in our schoolbooks. Cinema is a different medium, like a painting or a ballad. Considering the art form of making a film, where was the need to react so much?

"When I was making these films, initially some actors also questioned why I was making a historical, who'll watch a historical. But people like Priyanka didn't. They said, 'You want to make it? We're with you.' They connected the youth to our history. Today's generation is a great audience, it's a great cinema-viewing audience. There's a great culture of going and watching a movie in our country; it's sacrosanct, it's a religion of its own. This genre had to come back. *Devdas* was not a historical, it was literature. A novel. But *Bajirao* and *Padmaavat* were.

"When these stars come around and play great parts in a historical, it's important. Priyanka playing Kashi in *Bajirao* was extremely important."

It was during the filming of *Bajirao Mastani* that Priyanka simultaneously leapt across the Atlantic to transform into Alex Parrish, the trouser-wearing federal agent of *Quantico*. She'd film the ABC serial in New York and elsewhere in the US until Friday night, sleep on the long-haul flight to Mumbai and report for work over the weekend in the traditional nine-yard saree of Kashibai before going back to filming *Quantico* from Monday morning.

By the time *Bajirao Mastani* was released in her home country, she'd vaulted to the West.

"You've never arrived enough not to explore new opportunities" – Priyanka

Exhorting her audience to become "the best version of you," she said, "At every step, I set a higher standard... There's only one of you. You're never too old or too experienced not to learn something new."

For her, the competition was never over. And Pradeep Guha's old observation about her positivity and fearlessness would take over. Tarun Mansukhani described how her mind worked when she took the big leap from the glossy Indianness of *Bajirao Mastani* to the gritty crime scene of *Quantico*.

"When *Quantico* was still being thought about, she'd read the script, we had conversations about it. At no point did she feel, am I going to end it all? That was never the question," Tarun disclosed. "Whether it was about ending it here or doing television that may not succeed, wasn't the debate. It was a question of, 'What will I achieve by doing this?' The answer would be, 'You'll become the first Indian girl to cross over and make a mark for yourself.' Which became a goal for her, more than the money or the fame. She doesn't look at the negatives. She doesn't come to you and say, 'Oh shit, this may happen to me, I'll get screwed.' She doesn't think of those things. Which can sometimes bother me because she doesn't think of the consequences. It's more of, why not rather than why? Utterly inspiring but I get scared for her. What if it goes wrong for her?"

Like most of her other leaps, *Quantico* too was something she went into after deliberating over it with friends and family.

"She will take opinions from all her friends. Possibly never listen to any of them," Tarun smiled. "But ask, she will. Like she did discuss *Quantico* with me. She had lengthy conversations about it with me. I'd ask her, 'Are you the central character? What if they suddenly screw you over and change the character to some American girl?' She had answers, she was on that side, I was asking the questions. As a friend, it was my job to play Devil's Advocate. She wasn't pessimistic. Her answer would be, 'It's contractual, they can't do that, so move on, next.'"

Move on, is exactly what she did, charting her course by breaking into the West first as singer, going to the glitziest of functions and being interviewed on the most-watched talk shows. For her, it was simply the next step northward but the physical distance also gave breathing time to an imminent heartbreak back home. Additionally, she made the most of Hollywood's new hunt for diversity and pitched herself as the perfect candidate for the job. As Ranjita Ganesan and Manavi Kapur observed in *Business Standard*:

"In retrospect, PC's 2013 pop track set in Miami Beach and featuring rapper Pitbull could easily have been the pitch that led to her recent big break. The Bollywood actress-turned-singer who crooned about being 'exotic' and 'hotter than the tropics' has emerged two years later as the newest find in US television's growing bid for diversity."

Priyanka herself claimed that it was more about spotting an opportunity than a strategised move. She said to friend and editor Jitesh Pillai of *Filmfare* that her current manager Anjula Acharya who ran a record label called Desi Hits in America, heard her in Abhishek Bachchan's rap number 'Right Here Right Now' from *Bluffmaster* (2005) in which she had co-starred. That was the time Abhishek had famously nicknamed her Piggy Chops and it was he who had rapped the popular number. Priyanka had largely lip-synced to lines sung by playback singer Sunidhi Chauhan. But Vishal-Shekhar, the music directors of *Bluffmaster*, had heard Priyanka sing a line and had recorded a number with her, a number that lies unreleased to this day, a number that Anjula happened to hear which made her repeatedly call Priyanka, asking her to come to London and record a couple of songs with Universal Music. The songs went from Universal to Interscope Records where co-founder Jimmy Iovine loved what he heard. Catching the ear of a big name like Jimmy in the music business put Priyanka on the road to becoming a legitimate recording artiste. Starry-eyed and dizzy, she found herself in the world of Pitbull and will.i.am and spent months going back and forth between India and America. "I went through this whole magical phase of flying to Los Angeles every four months even as I was doing films like *Gunday, Mary Kom,*" she told *Filmfare*.

It was Jimmy who pointed her in the direction of Hollywood as an actor. And a chance meeting with Keli Lee of ABC at a party turned her into Alex Parrish.

It didn't come to her on a platter. She followed one of her own self-set rules, "You've never arrived enough not to explore new opportunities" which was easier said than done. But she did it; few in her position would have. As Sanjay Bhansali said, "Priyanka gives her all to an opportunity, so they keep coming to her." She shed her pride, didn't carry along the baggage of the celebrity status she was used to, went through the process of introducing herself, "I'm Priyanka Chopra, I'm an Indian actor", auditioned the part and won the crown again. Like the ingénue from

Bareilly who'd stood at the Millennium Dome in 2000 and then done the star trek in Hindi cinema, the Desi Girl from India presented her credentials to the West, living out the rules she had set in stone *en route*.

Like many, Priyanka speaks two kinds of English. With her own countrymen, it's the sophisticated Indian English that she always spoke fluently. But Alex Parrish and Victoria Leeds of *Baywatch* spoke like Americans – it entailed training with a dialect coach. She became an American in those roles, not an Indian playing a part in an American series or movie. That was her biggest achievement, that was what she'd signed up for, making American kids want to be like Alex Parrish, the kickass agent who greeted New Yorkers from huge hoardings announcing the arrival of *Quantico*.

She did everything a celebrity in Hollywood would do. She walked the red carpet at the Oscars, she was on massive hoardings, she was on magazine covers all year long and she had her pinch-me moment when *Time* magazine put her on the cover as one of the 100 most influential people in the world.

She knew the importance of the media, always did. Unlike actresses who grimaced and looked on interviews as a chore they'd rather not be doing, she sparkled and once told me, "I love giving interviews, I just love it. I get to know myself when I give interviews. I never get to think about myself, I don't have the time. I'm not one of those actors who think only about their life and talk (only) about themselves. I don't. I'm a real girl with lots of things in my life. So when I give interviews, I get to know myself better. When you ask me things which provoke my mind, I think about it and say, oh, do I actually like that? I didn't think about that. So I like to give interviews. What I don't like are people who haven't done their homework. I hate those,

'How are you feeling?' kind of questions. 'How do you feel coming to the industry?' I hate those generic questions."

Americans liked her, she was more articulate than Aishwarya Rai, more earthy. Certainly well-read too, having compensated for not going further than Std 12 by turning into a knowledge fiend. As she said to me, "Google is my answer to every question. I have information about everything because of Google. I google for anything. Like I google to know why there is an 'H' in Jesus H Christ. I like trivia. It actually comes from Holy, different sects believe different things. If Google was a man, I'd marry him!"

Her thirst for knowledge also led her to the vast world of books. "I like reading, I'm a voracious reader. I read a lot, fiction and non-fiction. I prefer non-fiction, I read a lot of biographies. I can spend a lot of time in a bookstore. I buy all sorts of books. I have a lot of favourites. One of my all-time favourites is *Letters From A Father To His Daughter* by Jawaharlal Nehru. It's lovely and I found it very interesting. I don't follow authors as much as I follow books. I love reading, so I read a lot of screenplays for my friends, I do a lot of proofreading for them because I enjoy it. Reading is my world away from everything."

The knowledge thus gathered added so much to her personality that Sanjay Leela Bhansali found it worthy of compliment. It was a personality that was well-rounded and suitable for life beyond movies.

"There are some wonderful actors, great on screen, wonderful stars, great body of work but very inarticulate because their language is only cinema. They come alive only when they come before a camera. There's an imaginary wall between you and them. But Priyanka has a wonderful personality. She's a public speaker, she has a mind and she wants to say so many things. She's tuned into the events of the world, she knows how to speak about them, has the intellect to speak about them. When she walks in, she changes the atmosphere of the room with her sheer presence, her sheer sense of being alive. She's so alive, always excited. Even if she has no set agenda in her mind when she comes in, there's a purpose to her walk. She gets something out of it, she gives something to you and she leaves. When she goes out of a room, something dims because she's such a livewire, such sparkling eyes. I won't say that she's the best face in the industry but she's one of the most beautiful women I've ever seen. Because she's very alive, she has a love for life, she has appreciation for nice things around her, she wants to experience it all. She knows how to take her tough moments. She's a very tough girl, she's seen life, from success to failure, to personal incidents in her life which have changed her mindset, so many things. She has such tremendous zest for life, her smile has so much sunshine in it," he said, like he was describing one of the most beautiful women he created on celluloid.

Well-informed, Priyanka boarded America's diversity express just in time when the country was discovering Columbian Sofia Vergara (in the television series *Modern Family*) and Kenyan-Mexican Lupita Nyong'o, the latter a star after *12 Years A Slave* (2013), now top-lining the biggest like *Black Panther*. In fact, Priyanka featured in the *Forbes* list of highest-paid TV actresses along with Sofia who was the No 1 with a whopper $ 43 million income that included endorsements. Priyanka herself was No 8 with an annual earning of $11 million.

She homed in on the 'Asian in the West' profile and became its champion. As she said in several interviews, "South Asians in international entertainment are still a novelty. At the Emmys, Aziz Ansari won for writing *Master*

Of None. Riz Ahmed won for best actor in a drama; it was the first time an Asian had ever won an Emmy for best actor in a drama. At the after-party, there were just four of us in a room of 400. Aziz said, 'Eight years ago, there was just one.' So we're taking steps.

"We're ⅕th of the world population; we damn well have a representation in international entertainment," she underscored.

She put her money where her mouth is by insisting that she didn't want to be a part of, "The big fat Punjabi wedding" in an American television series or a Hollywood film but be known as "a kickass actress."

She'd put her arm candy days behind her a long time ago even in Hindi cinema, seeking to be relevant in what she did as an actress.

Priyanka also became relevant as a person by turning to philanthropy. She said, time and again, that she knew she was privileged to have been born to progressive parents, growing up in an environment where freedom prevailed in all spheres. She, therefore, woke up to the reality of the rest of India when her housekeeper's daughter who loved reading books had stopped going to school because her parents couldn't afford to educate all their children and sent only the boys to study. The general tendency, especially among the underprivileged, was to look at the education of the girl child as a waste since she'd get married anyway and go away soon. It made practical sense for the parents to invest their meagre earnings in the male and not the female child.

That kind of discrimination had never happened to Priyanka. It touched the sensitive side of the actress who instinctively took on the education of her housekeeper's daughter and led to the establishment of the Priyanka Chopra Foundation for Health and Education. Ten per cent of her earnings began to be earmarked for the foundation that today takes care of the medical care and education of over eighty children, of which more than half are girls. She has taken on the responsibility of seeing the children all the way through college.

Additionally, she has been a Goodwill Ambassador with UNICEF.

"Appreciate every day of this beautiful journey," she told her audience at a lecture. And she instilled in those who were listening that everybody had to give back to society. "It's not very difficult," she said, "to be kind, to be compassionate, to be human. There's always someone who's less fortunate than you. It's one world, we need to heal it. Give back."

Perhaps her story, *The Dark Horse* too will make a difference to the lives of millions of readers. Priyanka's triumphs over tribulations are an inspiration, the route to finding success and fulfilment. And to contributing to a better world.

It's believed that whatever you give, comes back to you. It did for Priyanka, although one is sure she gave because it warmed her heart and not because she wanted the universe to reward her even more. But it did, it does.

Priyanka soon settled into a luxury apartment in Manhattan with her own private theatre (although she had no time to watch any movies there), a well-stocked gym, a wine cellar and a pool table too.

She loved the good life, she'd earned it. And Priyanka's doors were open to all her friends from back home to visit her. Manish Malhotra did. Pradeep Guha did. So did Anupama Chopra, among many others.

She welcomed Guha with a bottle of wine, opened and ready.

"When I went to New York, there were 100-ft posters of her on Madison Avenue. I don't think any Indian reached that position so far," remarked Guha. "Meeting her was like it was in the good old days. It did not matter that today she was there and I was here.

"Unlike many others, she always mentions where she has come from. She has no hesitation in talking of her roots publicly or privately while others would like to give the impression that they've *tapkaoed* (descended) from the heavens. To that extent, Priyanka is pretty grounded.

"That said, if I went to her and said, 'PeeCee (or PC), I want to do a movie with you', she won't be any less money-minded about it. She'd say, 'Okay, if I have to do business with you, then let's talk business.' In that sense, she's not a Salman who'd tell a friend, 'Bro, *kab aana, bol* (tell me when you want me).'"

Pradeep did approach her when he started Culture Management, a talent management company that represented Kajol and a few others. Costume designer Ana Singh's husband Jaiveer ran the business along with Guha. But Priyanka didn't want to be a part of his company's clientele. 'You are too close to me. You are family, I can't do business with you,' she told Guha upfront. "And I respected her for it," said Guha, "which was far better than hemming and hawing. She is one of a kind."

Over time, Guha did find that she's, "Perhaps become a little cynical and less trusting of people. But I don't blame her, it happens with everybody.

"But as a friend, she has stayed warm, friendly and accessible. Obviously, I cannot expect her to turn up if I say, 'Come over to my house.' That way, there is a bit of an estrangement because of the time factor. But there are people here who'll toss you over because *abhi yeh kaam ka nahin hai* (he's no longer of use to me). Priyanka is not like that."

Anupama related to her success as a woman would.

"Hindi cinema always had these restrictions around women. We've all seen it where there were no women on the film set, we've seen the whole evolution. There was a marked, 'You're done after thirty' feeling even about women like Priyanka. What she did by going abroad was to completely change the goalpost. The goalpost was no longer to be only the A-List Bollywood star. The goalpost became global stardom. I've told her, 'You have changed the game. Forget about winning it, you've changed the damn game.'

"It's very irrational but I can't tell you the surge of pride I had at an airport somewhere, maybe it was Frankfurt when I was going to the Berlin Film Festival, where I walked by the magazine stand, and saw Priyanka on the cover of some publication or endorsing something. I was like, 'Damn, it's one of us.' What she has achieved has been incredible, and I've seen her work ethic. I spent a day with her in New York and saw the relentless sort of work she was doing.

"She's on a set (of *Quantico*), she's shooting, in between shooting, she is talking to me and doing my interview, and after all of that, she changes and goes to a party where they are honouring her for being on the cover of some magazine. She's been out since 8:30 in the morning, but she's got to look great, and be glamorous and be personable to everyone. I was standing there ready to drop, and this was just one day in her life.

"Meeting her in her apartment in New York was more intimate than it is here because you feel like you are two *desi*s connecting somewhere. For me, that was really lovely, and to see her in her home and her space. It was a gorgeous apartment. She said, 'Have tea', and feigned surprise that the tea magically appeared and laughed. Of course, she had her staff to do it all for her. But I was very proud of her.

"She's absolutely the star out there. We drove to the studio outside of Manhattan, I think it was in Queens, and when she walked in, it was very much like the top-liner had arrived. It's very egalitarian. She had her own room but make-up was done in one space where all the actors were getting ready. In that space, she had her own mirror. She had to adjust to all of that, to a new work culture. For me, it was also incredible for her to go from being an A-List person to somebody who needs to go out there and say, 'This is who I am.' That's very hard. Which is why most of our actors until now have not been able to cross over like she has.

"There you start off as a nobody. This is global, the headquarters of world cinema, and there are 50, 100, 200 actors who are as good-looking and as talented as you are. It's really hats off to her to stand out there and to land the deal. She has just said to every woman who works here, 'It doesn't end at whatever absurd date that someone has made up.' She's just so much on the go all the time.

"I interviewed her in September at the Toronto Film Festival, and there was no pause in her life. She walked in, she was there to promote her Assamese film, she did a Master Class, she did the screening. Next morning, she did a spate of interviews and afterwards, she was leaving to do her UN work.

"I'd think the fact that you are willing to work that hard when you are that famous and that successful, is really what sets you apart. Because it was just, tick, tick, tick, tick. There was nothing like, now I will sit back and take in what I have done. It's just not there in her."

Anupama appraised Priyanka's career in the West and laid it out without wallpapering any of it. "Is she the Jennifer Lawrence of Hollywood? She's not. *Baywatch*, the one film that's been released, didn't do well; it wasn't a very good film in any case. In fact, it was pretty bad. So of course there are miles to go. But she has gotten farther than anyone else in this country has, and she's a massive star. She's big on television and there's no caste system out there. Reese Witherspoon is on television, Nicole Kidman is on television. So that caste system which exists in our heads, is not there. And she's huge."

En passant, *Quantico* was not the first time Priyanka went on TV. In 2010, she was the first and so far the only female host of the daredevil television show *Khatron Ke Khiladi: Fear Factor*. Akshay Kumar had hosted the first, second and the fourth seasons of the series and she had stepped into his audaciously adventurous shoes to lead a gang of adrenaline-dripping male contestants in the third edition. At the presser to introduce her, Priyanka had come in riding a motorbike to set the mood for a show that tested the contestants' adventurousness, bravery and fitness levels. It was once again, Priyanka testing herself as she ventured into what was so far a male game.

But of course, *Quantico* in another part of the world was a different ball game altogether.

Anupama had heard a little bit about her being an Army kid and mused that perhaps the nomadic gene came from there.

"She has talked to me about how, because her parents were in the Army, she had to work in the summers, pitch in with all the charitable work they were doing, and how that sort of helped her to open up her head. And also, as an

Army kid, you have a sense of reality, a certain rootedness and awareness of how the world really is.

"So maybe all those things have helped shape her into the person that she is. And also, the constant moving, it's a sort of nomadic gene in you. You don't put your roots down, you go wherever the work is. I think that also makes you very resilient because you are constantly adjusting.

"She's very strong; I don't think anyone can keep up with this sort of dual career, unless you are very driven. It's her career 24×7 and she's told me, 'There are twenty-five people who manage me, and help me, and enable me to have this sort of life where I am shuttling between continents; I am doing so much.' But that strength and the drive has to come from her."

However, it wasn't always successful. *Baywatch*, Priyanka's first Hollywood film, not just tanked but also had quite a few people (she'd be surprised, but some of her filmmaker friends too) asking with a snigger, if 'breaks' like that were worth re-settling in another continent and making friends anew at this stage of her life and career.

Anupama did talk to her about *Baywatch*.

"I interviewed her for *Hello* magazine in December, and I said, 'Perhaps that wasn't the best choice'. But she explained, 'Look, people in India don't really have an understanding of how it works here, and how hard it is to even land a film like *Baywatch* in the first place.' Essentially she was saying that it's not as simple as it looks."

Priyanka herself had laughed it off with a witty, 'Can you imagine anyone intimidating The Rock (Dwayne Johnson, her co-star in *Baywatch*)? Me and my high heels can do it well.'

As she'd always claimed, "I'm like the Phoenix, I rise from the ashes," she hadn't vanished like Freida Pinto did after that astounding debut in *Slumdog Millionaire*.

"Correct. It's not like she's been side-lined," agreed Anupama, as Priyanka wrapped up the third season of *Quantico* and in 2017 she completed the filming of two more Hollywood projects, *Isn't It Romantic* and *A Kid Like Jake*.

That fantastic connect she maintained with those at home was spelt out by Anupama who also heads the MAMI (Mumbai Academy of the Moving Image) festival of films in Mumbai. When Anupama reached out to her for the festival, Priyanka put her on to her agent. "She was amazingly helpful," said Anupama. "She introduced me to Brad Slater, the agent, who was very nice and said, 'Let me check who is looking to come, who is available.' And we finally got Cary Fukunaga to come, which was brilliant for us. It was absolutely because of her. Most others wouldn't give a shit about a festival on the other side of the world. It was her way of saying, 'I believe in this festival, I want it to succeed, so let me enable you in whatever small way I can.' Those things really speak of her generosity."

Priyanka managed an all-consuming career in two different parts of the world, made time for her friends old and new, and by turning producer in Mumbai, steered her life into a position where she gradually became the boss who called the shots.

"You're really writing your own narrative, that's very interesting," Anupama said in her praise. "She's completely moved out of the position where you are sitting and waiting for offers, you are now propelling your own life, which is fab."

Staying in touch, those flowers, those gifts, those phone calls, were vintage Priyanka, sometimes with a bit of a prod from her mother.

Long after he'd finished *Barsaat*, his last film with Priyanka, Suneel Darshan was at Trishna, the seafood restaurant in Mumbai, when she walked in. After Madhu told her that she'd met Suneel there, Priyanka went up to his table to make polite conversation.

That was of course years ago. But after she shifted to the US, her friends marvelled at the way she stayed in touch.

"A note will come from her, something will come on your birthday or on Diwali. I like that. I mean, she's in New York but flowers and a personal note will be there. I don't know if I could do that," said Manish.

Aseem Merchant who had no contact with her, had a different sort of experience with her rather recently.

With a company that does celebrity endorsements, he said that he got a call, "For a Brand Ambassador for the state of Assam and they were very keen on Deepika. I knew someone there, so we spoke to them and we zeroed in on Priyanka and got the contract for her. I wasn't in touch with her; it was with her mother and her managers and her team. We worked out the deal together, how much money, all of that. She was probably unaware that I was involved with it. But the deal went through; she did the endorsement and I was travelling when my office called me to say that our money (a hefty commission) hadn't come through. Apparently, they were saying that they got her the assignment directly. So I sent her a text message saying, 'I always thought you were ethical.' Within five minutes, her office was calling me up and saying, 'Let's sort this out.' It was a very sizeable chunk of money that was due to us.

"The fact that she responded so promptly was enough to tell me she was still the same. And that is going to take her very far. Because ethics is very important in life. She didn't need to ask her office to call and sort it out."

The whisper was that she inked the deal to be Brand Ambassador of Assam for Rs 6 crore.

If the ethics were in place, so was her etiquette. She was the first Hindi film actress to usher in the culture of addressing every person around as 'Sir' or 'Ma'am'; perhaps it was a part of her being an Army kid. Saying 'Thank you' and 'Sorry', and standing up when someone else did, also came easily to her. The face she projected in public never slipped. But the famous equanimity, the perfect behaviour every time she put a stilettoed-step out, on set, in public, had a release button, a hidden side that she talked about to me.

"Sometimes, I'm obnoxious with my close ones. I'm always so correct with everyone, and I like it that way because I like being on my guard. So when I'm with my family, my friends, my team, I can be pretty obnoxious. I will yell, I will throw a tantrum; my mom will come and hold me and I'll go and sit on her lap, I behave like a six-year-old. I've locked myself in my room when I've had to go somewhere. When my team was at the door asking me to come out, I was like, 'I'm not coming out, I'm going to sit here and I'm going to cry. I don't want to go there, I don't want to talk to you.' And I love doing that because I know I can get away with it with them. I won't get away with it anywhere else."

It was extreme, as always.

"I am extreme in my behaviour, in everything that I do," she accepted. "I'm a complete extremist. I'll either suddenly be hot or suddenly very cold. Anybody who has to keep up with me will go crazy. My mood swings are extreme. Also, being an artiste, I think most artistes are a little warped. I use it sometimes as an excuse to gain sympathy."

But she didn't look for a shoulder to weep on when her relationship with the one man who held her under his spell for six years began to fray.

Way back in 2011, she had tweeted, "Here's wishing the true king of hearts @iamsrk a super happy birthday... May u always have happiness, peace and love..."

But she soon turned wary of even talking about him and said that in so many words in an interview to Pinkvilla.

However, it took six years for the relationship to be finally called off. It's only recently that Priyanka was willing to officially refer to the end of a six-year relationship (without naming the man). Where did it leave the girl who'd always dreamt of being the typical Indian bride with a robust Punjabi celebration, the girl who wanted a cricket team of children?

"The one fear she has is that there shouldn't come a day when she'll be alone. I don't think she herself realises how major a star she is. She's got everything going for her, she's talented, she's a great actress, she sings, she's got great carriage, beautiful voice, speaks beautifully, what has she not got? *Par usko ek darr hai ki main akeli na reh jaoon* (But she's always got this one fear of ending up lonely)," observed Sandeep Singh.

A close friend also said that although parallels were often drawn between her and Rekha, in her personal life, she had no intentions of ending up like the senior actress.

Pradeep Guha understood, "Priyanka needs love. That I am absolutely certain about. She's eternally searching for love, constantly in search of it. She needs love, love, love. It's a very thin line, love/sex is a very thin line. I know deep down that it's love she craves for."

She's only thirty-five. No reason why love, marriage and the cricket team can't happen especially when she asks the universe for it. And be wise in her choices.

But as she described herself to me, "I'm very emotional. It's a good thing and a bad thing for me. I am hyper-sensitive.

I get stupidly emotional over the smallest of things. The Cancerian in me takes over. Anything can set it off. I'm a self-made person, so there's a lot of pride. I don't like asking for things just in case I don't get them. I like living my life on my own terms in a way. So I guess I'm very sensitive in a lot of things. It works because I'm very attached to people, I'm warm, I care. And it works in the kind of work I do. I'm emotional, not practical and detached and I prefer it that way. I like being delusional, I'm completely dervish to my work; my life is almost constantly surrounded by dreams. Practicality is not a part of it."

Practicality stepped in when it came to her work as Priyanka added a very impressive chapter to her life by turning producer in India, choosing to back small, regional films that gave respectability to her fledgling production outfit.

"Film, that's all I know (how to do)" – Priyanka

Her turning filmmaker had a purpose. She could keep a firm foot in the terrain she knew, loved and wanted to stay connected with while she worked her way around an unmined territory in another part of the world.

"Film, that's all I know (how to do). I've never known how to do anything else," she'd told me. "I started working in films at nineteen. I learnt everything on my own, nobody taught me anything, nobody supported me. My failures and my successes are my own. That's why films play such an important part in my life."

She was not the clichéd crossover star; she did a balancing act between two continents, producing films in India while making waves as an actress in America.

Rajesh Mapuskar who wrote and directed *Ventilator*, her biggest success so far as producer, got the whole

Priyanka experience when he made the film for her company Purple Pebble Pictures (PPP), a company magnificently managed by her mother, Madhu.

"There's something about these Chopras, *kuch hai Chopras mein*," laughed the genial filmmaker who had made his first film, *Ferrari Ki Sawaari* (2012) in Hindi for Vidhu Vinod Chopra. *Ventilator* for Priyanka was his second, this time in his mother tongue, Marathi. "Vidhu Vinod was also like this, *ghode pe rehte hain*, they're all the time riding a horse. I never saw Priyanka tired, never ever heard her say, 'Let it be, let's do this later.'

"I'd never met Priyanka or her mother Madhuji before *Ventilator*. Her mother has a very warm, unique way of handling things. She takes a back seat, she lets Priyanka lead, she'd let me lead, she won't be in your face, she won't raise her voice. But she had her own way of telling you if something was not working."

This was a company that mother and daughter set up, after the death of her father, Dr Ashok Chopra. While the world saw Priyanka sport her sentiment on her arm with the tattoo, 'Daddy's lil girl…', a tattoo in her father's writing that she got inked reportedly in Malibu before the launch of her single 'In My City', only the few who'd interacted closely with Madhu knew of a touching daily tribute she paid her husband each time she sat in her car.

"She will sit behind the driver and never on the other side of the back seat where Dr Chopra used to sit," Mapuskar observed. "She will always leave that space for Dr Chopra, she never sits there."

How Priyanka, a person he'd never met, turned out to be his producer, is another tale of how when something's meant to be, it happens. Rajesh had written *Ventilator* and was looking for producers but even big names like Zee were backing off, wondering how the film could be made. While everybody reacted positively to the script that had great entertainment written in despite its sombre premise of a patient on the ventilator, it revolved around a hospital, and potential producers were worried about erecting a set that would cost them about one crore rupees. Marathi films were made on a total budget of Rs 3.5 crore, no more.

But in one of those fortuitous coincidences that life sometimes surprises you with, his CA knew Ishan, the CEO of PPP, and he told Mapuskar that Priyanka was looking for subjects to produce. Mapuskar's initial reaction was to shrug it off. "I told my CA, 'Why would she produce a Marathi film and why would she produce mine? She has all the power and money to do a Hindi film. Why would she make a regional film?' I just didn't get it. But he insisted that I don't give up, so I went along to meet them saying, 'Okay, let's try this out too.'"

The filmmaker met and left a one-pager with CEO Ishan. The next thing he knew was that he was face-to-face with Madhu who told him that she liked it but wanted Priyanka (who was then busy with *Quantico*) to also hear it. But even before the star flew into Mumbai, negotiations to put together a contract started in right earnest. "It went on for a long time. At one point, they dropped the project because the financials were not going in their favour. Actually, I was more adamant than them, I wanted certain things in a certain way," Rajesh admitted. The differences were over IPR and profit-sharing.

What Madhu Chopra did then was a good indication of where Priyanka got her skills of putting pride aside to pursue something that held promise.

"Madhuji called me to the office and asked me, 'What do you want?' By then I had warmed up to her, she was easy to talk to and I could open my heart to her. She asked me what number I had in mind and when I mentioned a certain figure, she simply said, 'Done.' There was no discussion, nothing. She just said, 'Set up this project; we love it, we want to do it.' And then came Priyanka."

She was flying in after a long spell and had much lined up on her arrival itself. Mapuskar asked her mother if he should give her a couple of days to relax before giving her a narration of the film. But Madhu told him, 'No, no, she won't relax; she wants all the meetings lined up on day one.' Rajesh was asked to come at 10 am but all he did for the next few hours was to keep looking at his watch.

"When my turn finally came in the afternoon, I went into her office and Priyanka stood up saying, 'I'm so sorry I made you wait. I have heard so much about your story that I didn't want anything to disturb me while I heard you. I wanted to finish everything else and spend time with you.' She didn't have to say that because I was comparatively a nobody and Priyanka Chopra was such a big star. But she didn't have that air about her. When I started the narration, she reacted openly like a child, laughing, getting emotional and enjoying it as the scenes unfolded. At the end of it, she said enthusiastically, 'I want to do this.' We were even ready with the 'Baba' song and she loved it."

'Baba' (father, in Marathi), a number composed by two young boys Rohan-Rohan, touched all the right chords in Priyanka. Actually, the whole premise moved the Chopras as they'd just lost Dr Ashok Chopra and had gone through some of the experiences that Mapuskar had detailed in his story. To encapsulate the story in one line, it had a whole bunch of relatives descending on the hospital where a patient was on the ventilator, each person coming in with his or her own personal agenda. But told with much humour. Ashutosh Gowariker, the filmmaker whose Aamir Khan-starrer *Lagaan* had gone as India's entry to the Oscars and whose *Jodhaa Akbar* set a precedent for aesthetically told historicals on a lavish scale, had directed Priyanka in a film called *What's Your Raashee?*. Mapuskar cast Ashutosh, who also acts ably, in the central role as himself, the glamour name around whom all the relatives buzzed at the hospital. So there was a lot in Mapuskar's story that made it personal for Priyanka.

The next time she came to India, she saw the unedited rushes of the film and was so pleased with the way it was shaping out that she hugged her director. A much-encouraged Mapuskar recalled, "She said, 'This is amazing. Though it's not edited, I can feel the vibe. I can feel a certain purity in it.' This way, at every stage there was a lot of encouragement, never interference. Priyanka had all the power to come up with creative suggestions but she didn't. It also worked that our wavelengths matched."

Rajesh agreed that Madhu and Priyanka had made an expeditious connect with the story. "Yes, there was, *fatak*, an immediate connection. Priyanka's father had been on the ventilator and she told me, 'Rajesh, forty of my relatives whom I'd never seen had come from all over. Everybody turned up and I was tired just talking to them; it's exhausting at the end of the day.'

"She was so close to her father, she was going through her own trauma, plus relatives were pouring in. And each time you have a conversation, you tell the same story. It can really exhaust you. With Priyanka being such a big star, there was another motive behind relatives meeting her. I tried showing that through Ashutosh, to illustrate the glamour that's attached to the industry."

The film progressed with Mumbai-based Madhu, the more active partner, while Priyanka stayed in touch with the director all through its making. In the digital world, it was possible for Rajesh to send her tracks of shots that were canned and other stuff to check out, knowing that the workaholic on the other end of the world wouldn't delay her response even by a day. Priyanka was so hands-on that once he hit the 'Send' button, he was sure her answer would be in the mail by the time he woke up next morning.

Priyanka and he also clicked on the importance of family. "At the end of the day, our families are family. There will be good, bad, irritating, all kinds of people, and they will have their way. They may not necessarily be evil or bad-intentioned but something makes them do what they do. So acceptance of family members as they are, was something we both felt strongly about. Family is important. People are important. Family should be one's priority. That was a common ground between us."

What was different was Priyanka's sharp focus, "Which I tried to learn from her. Otherwise I have ADD (Attention Deficit Disorder)," he laughed. "I also admired her energy. She's always in a '*Bolo, bolo* (Quickly tell me), next, next' mode, never cuts herself any slack."

Rajesh too pointed to her fearlessness. "She's not scared of failure, *bilkul darti nahin* (she never gets scared). Because it is a bold decision for somebody like her who has so much power, to start producing regional films which you know will not fetch you money or fame. But she did it to get her production house off the ground with smaller and different projects and to test the waters and see how it's turning out. You know she could easily get any star, get financial backing and launch a project, a project that could fetch her 200 crore rupees. She could have done that but she chose to go with a film, not a project, and she chose to produce regional cinema." Among the many who've shot a film for PPP are two National Award directors, Aruna Raje who has made *Firebrand*, another Marathi film for Priyanka's company, and Assamese filmmaker Jahnu Barua whose film *Broken Window*, she took over. There are other films in Bhojpuri, Bengali, Punjabi and other languages ready to roll out of PPP. None of it has been a cakewalk.

"I as a producer sitting right here in India, find it difficult to manoeuvre my project and there she is, so far away, coordinating all her productions through her mother. There are more chances of failure than success when backing such different cinema. But this mother and daughter have the patience and the persistence to keep at it and not lose it. They're seeing ups and downs but learning and smartly managing the whole ship," remarked Mapuskar.

Ventilator put additional responsibilities on Priyanka because Rajesh also got her to act in the film and sing in it, out of sheer greed. Neither requirement existed in the original script.

"When my first script went to her, there was no scene featuring Priyanka," he blithely accepted. "Once she came on board as a producer, I thought of how to get her into the film. I wanted to do something, I got greedy." He gave a small chuckle as he went on, "I wrote a scene for her. With Ashutosh cast as a director in the film, I put in a scene where after he leaves some editing work unfinished to go to the hospital, Priyanka Chopra is seen waiting for him. That way my protagonist also gets elevated because someone as important as Priyanka Chopra is waiting for him but he's still in the hospital. Ashutosh had his own persona and with Priyanka in it, it got magnified. I very shyly sent her the scene and she said, 'Of course I'll do it.' I was thrilled.

"Her only query was, 'When are you planning to do it?' I said, 'Whenever you are here, you give me one day and I'll do this with you.' When she did come to Mumbai the next time, I'd conceived a certain way of presenting her which she changed – for the better. Initially it was, she wears track pants or a track suit and she comes in from the gym sometime in the morning. But she understood the character and said, 'You want to show me as a diva, right? I'll show you something I want to wear.' And she wore that amazing outfit which is in the film and I went, 'Wow, this almost looks like a flame to me.' Once she came to the shoot, she listened carefully to the instructions. She has this very endearing quality of listening and being attentive, not doing her own thing. But she takes the instructions and then projects her role in such a way, it goes to another level. I can't wait to direct her in a full-fledged role. I keep telling Madhuji that I have a story which I'll pitch to her when I am ready with it."

When it came to the heartwarming number 'Baba' in Marathi, it was one of the two Rohans, composer Rohan Gokhale who came up with the idea of Priyanka singing it herself. They felt it would be a great marketing tool.

"So once again, I mailed her the idea and once again her reply was, 'Yes'. But how was she intending to find time to record it? Madhuji was anxious. She said, 'She's gone and made a commitment to sing it but how will you record it with her? She'll have to find time to learn it, to learn Marathi, to do this and that.' But my god, she did it. She asked me to find a teacher who could coach her in Marathi diction in New York. We found a classical singer, a Maharashtrian staying in New York who coached her. We sent Priyanka the whole song in Devanagari script."

It was classic Priyanka in action. In the same Manhattan area where she had to learn and hold on to speaking English like an American, she now learnt to pronounce the Marathi lyrics correctly. When it was time to shoot the video of her singing 'Baba', Mapuskar told her that Maheep Dhillon would be directing it. Priyanka said, 'Send her to me.' Rajesh couldn't believe his ears.

"I said, 'No, it's not Andheri-Jogeshwari. We can do it over Skype', and she said, 'Are you mad? Send her here because I want to be with her and personally understand the video we're shooting.' Maheep made a concept and was flown down to New York specially for that video. Then in one of the studios of New York, that girl (Priyanka) shot for eight hours without tiring while we watched and interacted with them on Skype from Mumbai. After a point, all of us stopped saying anything because we could see that she had just taken off.

"So she shot 'Baba' in a studio in New York with the tutor and with the video director around her. With four cameras facing her, they went on shooting her and she was in a world of her own, unaware of where the cameras were. That focus was unbelievable. I wish I had fifty per cent of her concentration powers. *Kamaal hai* (It's fascinating). She is who she is because of that focus. It's not easy that you sleep so little when you have to also look your best as an actor. She's an actor, a producer, a singer, you don't do anything that's substandard and you have to look good at the end of the day. Madhuji was telling me what a huge responsibility it was to do a show of that magnitude in New York (reference, *Quantico*), how strict they were with their timings, how they shot sixteen hours a day. Actors don't leave the set, everybody has to sit right there. Nobody goes to the make-up room or vanity van. So it's all quite strenuous, very strenuous.

"In the midst of all that, she shut herself off from everything else and sang 'Baba' with her heart, in a language she did not even know. She was very close to getting the pronunciations right. I was okay with that and told her, 'Even if it's not one hundred per cent perfect, it's fine because then people will know it's Priyanka Chopra and not think we've got someone who sounded like her.'"

Priyanka tweeted, '#Baba..My first Marathi song. Forgive me if there are any mistakes...this one is all heart https://www.youtube.com/watch?v=ByikEd9Oa3A ...'

When the trailer of *Ventilator* was out, it said, 'In loving memory of Dr (Lt Col) Ashok Chopra'.

It was personal for Madhu and Priyanka but it was also so professionally made that it fetched them heaps of awards and great returns at the box-office. Interestingly, *Ventilator* was released on November 4, 2016, four days before Prime Minister Narendra Modi announced the overnight demonetisation of 500 and 1000-rupee currency notes in India. Its short-term repercussions were that long queues and many hours of wait had to be endured by the public to lay their hands on a small, limited amount of cash. It had a rippling and crippling effect at the box-office where even bigger films like Farhan Akhtar's *Rock On 2* crashed.

In this grim scenario, a small, regional film like *Ventilator* held steady which was the biggest indicator of its commercial success. It's now being made in other Indian languages including Gujarati in which Jackie Shroff will be playing Ashutosh's role.

Most of all, it set a record by bagging three National Awards (including Best Director for Mapuskar), probably a first for any Marathi film.

"Every week, there used to be some good news," the jubilant director reported with glee. "Then it was all about awards shows where we collected around forty-one trophies. Priyanka would call from the US every time we won an award. But after a while, the awards became so routine that she tired of calling and stopped. That was probably the only time she tired," he cheekily added.

When they won the National Award, she called up each of the winners to congratulate them. But long before that, she had sent flowers and a personal note to each and every member of the cast on the release of the film.

"Every actor would happily tell me, '*Arre*, Priyanka Chopra *se phool aa gaye* (Wow, we got flowers from Priyanka Chopra).' After the National Award, she spoke to me, to the others who won and to the press from there.

"I troubled her so much. I'd ask her, 'Priyanka please tweet this for *Ventilator*', and she'd do it. TV channels would ask for her bytes. We'd write and send it to her in Marathi. She'd make videos in between her shooting there and send them across for various channels. When there were screenings of the film, she made a list from there, called up people from the US and invited them personally. She was involved at every turn, very hands-on."

On her guest list was Abbas-Mustan, the duo who had directed her in *Aitraaz*.

"To this day, whenever she has a film screening or a party, she always remembers us, invites us," said Abbas-Mustan. "Whenever she's here, she'll always call. She has maintained relations very well. We were very happy that she has gone international. When she was here in December, she had a party (for her directors) where she personally called and invited us. She accords us the same affection and respect that she always did.

"When they made the Marathi film *Ventilator*, Priyanka was in New York but she made sure we were invited for the screening they had in Mumbai. She told us, 'You must see it.' When there was the trailer launch of her Punjabi film also, we were invited. People here generally stay in touch only as long as a film is on the floor. She goes beyond it; it's a rare quality." It sounded like something one had heard far too many times before but every time somebody mentioned it, it was emphatically underlined and drove home the point that 'staying in touch' was something she put special effort into.

The astonished Hindi film industry that saw her move her goalpost frequently was left wondering what her next move would be.

Farah Khan said, "If she wants something, she goes for it. And works her ass off. I think she likes being a workaholic. When I was doing the ad with her (after she became a star), she'd come down for one day, she was going to LA, doing something else. She thrives on this manic energy."

And she's a total diva, her entourage a part of her persona.

"I've never seen any other heroine with such an entourage. It's like a mini crew, she's always had the biggest entourage. Even here, she'd have twelve people around her," remarked Farah.

"She has always had the first-mover advantage over everybody else. She was the first to get on Twitter; she's aware, so she tries out things before others."

Farah's guess at the future was, "She's capable of running her own studio one day."

Madhur Bhandarkar believed, "Many of our actors have gone to Hollywood but always come back. They couldn't stay there and achieve what PC has done there. I see her intensifying her work there, reaching the top and intensifying her Hollywood presence."

Subhash Ghai predicted, "I see her as a director. You mark my words. In a few years, you'll find her directing a film. She's finally going to be a filmmaker. That's my prediction. She's a smart girl, knows how to enter a field. She's multi-talented, she knows dance, music, singing, acting, storytelling. She's got it all. Other heroines don't have it, they can only act and look good. She's gone beyond that."

Rakesh Roshan observed, "She's been going step by step to evolve into a better Priyanka Chopra and she'll continue to do that. The world already knows that she's an Indian actor doing well in the West too. She has everything in her to keep going further and further in her present acting career and that's what I think she'll do in the next few years."

Anurag Basu foresaw, "Two things. I could be completely wrong but one foot will be firmly planted in the West, she'll not be taking off that foot from there and coming back here. So she'll be there designing her own shows, on her own terms, where she's spearheading the project. Movie, show, anything.

"What I'm very sure about is that she'll also come here to create a different space for content. I know she's looking for it. She doesn't want to be a Yashraj or a Dharma Productions. She wants to be a Priyanka Chopra, have her own voice for content creation as a production house. That's where her future will be. All this, besides acting (here and there) which she'll continue doing.

"She's curious about where technology is going, she talks to people about it, she's taking in the expertise, she's aware of where entertainment is heading and she's getting ready for it. Right now, it might seem like she's going slow but she's actually ahead of time."

Bhansali was blunt. "I've told her, I'm waiting for you to come back to do cinema in the language that you were born into and have grown up watching. It's not important to be the flavour of the month and discover where you're the queen. It's necessary for you to be here where you've been crowned; that's very important. I think filmmakers here miss her a lot. I know I do. It's important to see one Priyanka film at least once every two years if not every year. There are some actors who're special to us, to the audience.

"With her talent she could go, well, not to Mars, but she could be everywhere. She's found that connect, found that liberation, broken the shackles of *only Bollywood*. It's not just Bandra and Mehboob Studio but Beverley Hills and whatever for Priyanka today. She could do anything, be in some underground experimental cinema being shot in Paris or whatever," he laughed. "We don't know where Priyanka will go. With Priyanka, you never know. I never thought she'd go to Hollywood. It just happened. So it's a very feel-good shock to know, oh, did she really manage that?"

The way Priyanka has positioned herself, there's a good chance that she could one day go into public life as well. She is already the voice of Asia, the brown voice in the West. She's also been the voice of women. When she was on a list of powerful people, she exclaimed, "Why is there only one of me? Why am I the only one who can stand shoulder-to-shoulder with the Top 10 men of the industry?"

"Life's journey," she told her audience, "is not to arrive at your brave side safely in a well-preserved body but to skid inside, completely worn out and say, 'Holy shit, that was a ride.'"

It has been one hell of a ride, a life that continues to be well lived, marked with milestones that could galvanise the ambitious into sprinting to the goal, never mind the bruises.

"Heartbreak is a bitch," she told Jitesh Pillai of *Filmfare*. Whatever the larger plan, after three years in the West, Priyanka's next move is the ambitious Hindi film, *Bharat* (reportedly inspired by the Korean film *Ode To My Father*). To be shot in 2018 in Spain, Abu Dhabi, Delhi and other places, it will be the big Eid release of 2019. It is the home production of her new friend, Salman Khan – her answer to the other Khan who couldn't work with her anymore. Making flying visits to Mumbai was easy. This time she'll be checking into the vicinity of Heartbreak Hotel for a longer period. But facing the tough and triumphing has always been the leitmotif, the courage-chant of Priyanka Chopra.

For most who try to follow her template without the accompanying conviction and courage, it would be onerous. Priyanka herself doesn't follow rules, she makes them, and she enjoys the process enormously, thriving on the energising vitality of her self-made rules.

She is a tough act to follow.

For when Priyanka inked that tattoo, 'Daddy's lil girl', on her arm, she forgot to add one word – 'Daddy's *brave* li'l girl'.

Filmography, Films Produced, Television & Music Videos

Thamizhan (2002) (Tamil)
Producer: G. Venkateswaran
Director: A. Majid
Screenplay: S.A. Chandrashekhar
Music: D. Imman
Cinematography: N.K. Ekambaram
Main cast: Priyanka Chopra, Joseph Vijay, Nassar, Revathy, Ashish Vidyarthi

The Hero: Love Story Of A Spy (2003)
Producer(s): Dhirajlal Shah, Hasmukh Shah, Pravin Shah
Director: Anil Sharma
Screenplay: Shaktimaan Talwar
Music: Uttam Singh
Cinematography: Kabir Lal
Main cast: Priyanka Chopra, Sunny Deol, Preity Zinta

Andaaz (2003)
Producer: Suneel Darshan
Director: Raj Kanwar
Screenplay: Robin Bhatt, Shyam Goel, Jainendra Jain

Music: Nadeem-Shravan
Cinematography: Ishwar R. Bidri
Main cast: Priyanka Chopra, Akshay Kumar, Lara Dutta

Plan (2004)
Producer(s): Sanjay Gupta, Dharam Oberoi
Director: Hriday Shetty
Screenplay: Yash-Vinay
Story: Sanjay Gupta
Music: Anand Raj Anand, Vishal-Shekhar
Main cast: Priyanka Chopra, Sanjay Dutt, Dino Morea,
              Sanjay Suri, Sameera Reddy, Riya Sen

Kismat (2004)
Producer(s): Dhirajlal Shah, Hasmukh Shah, Pravin Shah
Director: Guddu Dhanoa
Screenplay: Robin Bhatt, Sutanu Gupta
Music: Anand Raj Anand
Cinematography: Shripad Natu
Main cast: Priyanka Chopra, Bobby Deol, Kabir Bedi

Asambhav (2004)
Producer: Gulshan Rai
Director: Rajiv Rai
Screenplay: Rajiv Rai
Music: Viju Shah
Cinematography: Sukumar Jatania
Main cast: Priyanka Chopra, Arjun Rampal

Mujhse Shaadi Karogi (2004)
Producer: Sajid Nadiadwala
Director: David Dhawan
Screenplay: Anees Bazmee, Rumi Jaffery
Music: Sajid-Wajid, Anu Malik
Background score: Salim-Sulaiman
Cinematography: Sanjay F. Gupta
Main cast: Priyanka Chopra, Salman Khan, Akshay Kumar

Aitraaz (2004)
Producer: Subhash Ghai
Director: Abbas-Mustan
Screenplay: Shiraz Ahmed, Shyam Goel
Music: Himesh Reshammiya
Cinematography: Ravi Yadav
Main cast: Priyanka Chopra, Akshay Kumar, Kareena Kapoor

Blackmail (2005)
Producer(s): Narendra Bajaj, Shyam Bajaj
Director: Anil Devgan
Screenplay: Robin Bhatt, Javed Siddiqui
Music: Himesh Reshammiya
Cinematography: Nirmal Jani
Main cast: Priyanka Chopra, Ajay Devgn, Sunil Shetty, Dia Mirza

Karam (2005)
Producer: Pammi Baweja
Director: Sanjay F. Gupta
Screenplay: Suparn Verma
Music: Vishal-Shekhar, Pankaj Awasthi
Main cast: Priyanka Chopra, John Abraham, Shiney Ahuja

Waqt: The Race Against Time (2005)
Producer(s): Vipul Amrutlal Shah, Kumar Mangat
Director: Vipul Amrutlal Shah
Screenplay: Aatish Kapadia
Music: Anu Malik
Cinematography: Ashok Mehta, Santosh Thundiyil
Main cast: Priyanka Chopra, Akshay Kumar, Amitabh Bachchan,
        Shefali Shah, Boman Irani

Yakeen (2005)
Producer: Sujit Kumar Singh
Director: Girish Dhamija
Screenplay: Vikram Bhatt
Music: Himesh Reshammiya

Cinematography: Anshuman Mahaley
Main cast: Priyanka Chopra, Arjun Rampal

Barsaat (2005)
Producer: Suneel Darshan
Director: Suneel Darshan
Screenplay: Robin Bhatt, Shyam Goel; **Writer(s):** Rumi Jaffery, K.K. Singh (dialogue)
Story: Suneel Darshan
Music: Nadeem-Shravan
Cinematography: W.B. Rao
Main cast: Priyanka Chopra, Bobby Deol, Bipasha Basu

Bluffmaster! (2005)
Producer: Ramesh Sippy
Director: Rohan Sippy
Screenplay: Shridhar Raghavan, Rajat Arora (dialogue)
Music: Vishal-Shekhar, Trickbaby, Sameeruddin
Cinematography: Himman Dhamija
Main cast: Priyanka Chopra, Abhishek Bachchan, Ritesh Deshmukh

Taxi No. 9 2 11 (2006)
Producer(s): Ramesh Sippy, Rohan Sippy
Director: Milan Luthria
Screenplay: Rajat Arora
Music: Vishal-Shekhar
Cinematography: Vijay Karthik
Main cast: Nana Patekar, John Abraham, Sameera Reddy, Sonali Kulkarni, Shivaji Sata, Priyanka Chopra (cameo)

36 China Town (2006)
Producer: Subhash Ghai
Director: Abbas-Mustan
Screenplay: Shyam Goel
Music: Himesh Reshammiya
Cinematography: Ravi Yadav

Main cast: Shahid Kapoor, Akshaye Khanna, Kareena Kapoor, Vivek Shauq, Isha Koppikar, Upen Patel, Paresh Rawal, Payal Rohatgi, Johnny Lever, Tanaaz Currim, Priyanka Chopra (cameo)

Alag (2006)
Producer: Subi Samuel
Director: Ashu Trikha, Jim Mulligan
Screenplay: Ashu Trikha, Sanjay Masoom, Tagore Almeda
Music: Aadesh Shrivastava
Main cast: Akshay Kapoor, Dia Mirza, Priyanka Chopra (cameo)

Krrish (2006)
Producer: Rakesh Roshan
Director: Rakesh Roshan
Screenplay: Sachin Bhowmick, Rakesh Roshan, Akash Khurana, Honey Irani, Robin Bhatt
Dialogue: Sanjay Masoomi
Story: Rakesh Roshan
Music: Rajesh Roshan
Background score: Salim-Sulaiman
Cinematography: Santosh Thundiyil
Main cast: Priyanka Chopra, Rekha, Hrithik Roshan, Naseeruddin Shah

Aap Ki Khatir (2006)
Producer(s): Ganesh Jain, Ratan Jain
Director: Dharmesh Darshan
Screenplay: Sunil Munshi
Music: Himesh Reshammiya
Cinematography: W.B. Rao
Main cast: Priyanka Chopra, Akshaye Khanna, Ameesha Patel, Dino Morea, Suniel Shetty

Don (2006)
Producer(s): Ritesh Sidhwani, Farhan Akhtar
Director: Farhan Akhtar

Screenplay: Javed Akhtar, Farhan Akhtar (based on *Don* by
	Salim-Javed)
Music: Shankar-Ehsaan-Loy
Cinematography: K.U. Mohanan
Main cast: Priyanka Chopra, Shah Rukh Khan, Arjun Rampal,
	Boman Irani, Isha Koppikar, Om Puri

Salaam-E-Ishq: A Tribute To Love (2007)
Producer(s): Mukesh Talreja, Sunil Manchanda
Director: Nikhil Advani
Screenplay: Nikhil Advani, Saurabh Shukla, Suresh Nair
Music: Shankar-Ehsaan-Loy
Cinematography: Piyush Shah
Main cast: Priyanka Chopra, Salman Khan, Anil Kapoor,
	Govinda, John Abraham, Sohail Khan,
	Akshaye Khanna, Vidya Balan, Juhi Chawla,
	Shannon Esra, Ayesha Takia, Ishaa Koppikar

Big Brother (2007)
Producer: Ninth Jan Jeet Entertainment
Director: Guddu Dhanoa
Screenplay: Bhagwan Chitra Mandir
Music: Sandesh Shandilya, Anand Raj Anand
Main cast: Priyanka Chopra, Sunny Deol, Danny Denzongpa,
	Farida Jalal, Suhasini Mulay

Om Shanti Om (2007)
Producer: Red Chillies Entertainment
Director: Farah Khan
Screenplay: Farah Khan, Mushtaq Shiekh
Dialogue: Mayur Puri
Music: Laxmikant Pyarelal, Vishal-Shekhar
Background Score: Sandeep Chowta
Cinematography: V. Manikandan
Main cast: Shah Rukh Khan, Deepika Padukone, Arjun Rampal,
	Shreyas Talpade, Kirron Kher, Priyanka Chopra (cameo)

My Name Is Anthony Gonsalves (2008)
Director: Eeshwar Nivas
Screenplay: Lajan Joseph, Mayur Puri
Dialogue: Mayur Puri
Music: Pritam, Himesh Reshammiya
Cinematography: Prakash Kutty
Main cast: Nikhil Dwivedi, Amrita Rao, Mithun Chakraborty, Priyanka Chopra (cameo)

Love Story 2050 (2008)
Producer: Pammi Baweja
Director: Harry Baweja
Screenplay: Harry Baweja
Dialogue: Mayur Puri
Music: Anu Malik
Cinematography: Kiran Deohans
Main cast: Priyanka Chopra, Harman Baweja, Boman Irani, Archana Puran Singh

God Tussi Great Ho (2008)
Producer(s): Afzal Khan, Sohail Khan
Director: Rumi Jaffrey
Screenplay: Rumi Jaffery, Yunus Sajawal
Music: Sajid-Wajid
Cinematography: Ashok Mehta
Main cast: Priyanka Chopra, Salman Khan, Sohail Khan, Amitabh Bachchan

Chamku (2008)
Producer: Vijayta Films Pvt. Ltd
Director: Kabeer Kaushik
Screenplay: Kabeer Kaushik
Music: Monty Sharma
Cinematography: Gopal Shah
Main cast: Priyanka Chopra, Bobby Deol, Irrfan Khan, Riteish Deshmukh, Danny Denzongpa

Drona (2008)
Producer(s): Shrishti Arya, Sunil Lulla, Amitabh Bachchan
Director: Goldie Behl
Screenplay: Goldie Behl, Jaydeep Sarkar
Music: Dhruv Ghanekar
Cinematography: Sameer Arya
Main cast: Priyanka Chopra, Abhishek Bachchan,
           Kay Kay Menon, Jaya Bachchan

Fashion (2008)
Producer(s): Madhur Bhandarkar, Deven Khote,
             Ronnie Screwvala, Zarine Mehta
Director: Madhur Bhandarkar
Screenplay: Ajay Monga, Madhur Bhandarkar, Anuraadha Tewari
Music: Salim-Sulaiman
Cinematography: Mahesh Limaye
Main cast: Priyanka Chopra (also narrator), Kangana Ranaut,
           Mugdha Godse, Arjan Bajwa, Samir Soni, Arbaaz Khan

Dostana (2008)
Producer(s): Hiroo Yash Johar, Karan Johar
Director: Tarun Mansukhani
Screenplay: Tarun Mansukhani
Music: Vishal-Shekhar
Background score: Salim-Sulaiman
Cinematography: Ayananka Bose
Main cast: Priyanka Chopra, Abhishek Bachchan, John Abraham

Billu (2009)
Producer: Shah Rukh Khan
Director: Priyadarshan
Screenplay: Manisha Korde, Mushtaq Shiekh
Story: Sreenivasan
Music: Pritam
Cinematography: V. Manikandan
Main cast: Irrfan Khan, Lara Dutta, Shah Rukh Khan, Om Puri,
           Rajpal Yadav, Asrani, Priyanka Chopra (cameo)

Kaminey (2009)

Producer: Ronnie Screwvala
Director: Vishal Bhardwaj
Screenplay: Vishal Bhardwaj, Sabrina Dhawan,
    Abhishek Chaubey, Supratik Sen
Music: Vishal Bhardwaj
Cinematography: Tassaduq Hussain
Main cast: Priyanka Chopra, Shahid Kapoor, Amole Gupte

What's Your Raashee? (2009)

Producer(s): Ronnie Screwvala, Sunita A. Gowariker
Director: Ashutosh Gowariker
Screenplay: Naushil Mehta, Ashutosh Gowariker (based on
    Kimball Ravenswood by Madhu Rye)
Music: Sohail Sen
Cinematography: Piyush Shah
Main cast: Priyanka Chopra, Harman Baweja

Pyaar Impossible! (2010)

Producer: Uday Chopra
Director: Jugal Hansraj
Screenplay: Uday Chopra
Music: Salim Sulaiman
Cinematography: Santosh Thundiyil
Main cast: Priyanka Chopra, Uday Chopra, Dino Morea

Jaane Kahan Se Aayi Hai (2010)

Producer(s): Mukesh Talreja, Nikhil Advani
Director: Milap Zaveri
Music: Sajid-Wajid
Cinematography: Attar Singh Saini
Main cast: Ritesh Deshmukh, Jacqueline Fernandez,
    Sonal Sehgal, Ruslaan Mumtaz, Priyanka Chopra
    (cameo)

Anjaana Anjaani (2010)

Producer: Sajid Nadiadwala

Director: Siddharth Anand
Screenplay: Advaita Kala, Siddharth Anand
Music: Vishal-Shekhar
Background score: Salim-Sulaiman
Cinematography: Ravi K. Chandran
Main cast: Priyanka Chopra, Ranbir Kapoor

7 *Khoon Maaf* (2011)

Producer(s): Ronnie Screwvala, Vishal Bhardwaj
Director: Vishal Bhardwaj
Screenplay: Matthew Robbins, Vishal Bhardwaj (based on
Susanna's Seven Husbands by Ruskin Bond)
Music: Vishal Bhardwaj
Cinematography: Ranjan Palit
Main cast: Priyanka Chopra, Neil Nitin Mukesh, John Abraham,
Irrfan Khan, Aleksandr Dyachenko, Annu Kapoor,
Naseeruddin Shah, Vivaan Shah, Usha Uthup

Ra.One (2011)

Producer: Gauri Khan
Director: Anubhav Sinha
Screenplay: Anubhav Sinha, Kanika Dhillon, Mushtaq Shiekh,
David Benullo
Music: Vishal-Shekhar
Cinematography: Nicola Pecorini, V. Manikandan
Main cast: Shah Rukh Khan, Arjun Rampal, Kareena Kapoor,
Armaan Verma, Priyanka Chopra (cameo)

Don 2 (2011)

Producer(s): Farhan Akhtar, Ritesh Sidhwani, Shah Rukh Khan
Director: Farhan Akhtar
Screenplay: Farhan Akhtar, Ameet Mehta, Amrish Shah
Music: Shankar-Ehsaan-Loy
Cinematography: Jason West
Main cast: Priyanka Chopra, Shah Rukh Khan, Lara Dutta,
Kunal Kapoor, Boman Irani, Om Puri

Agneepath (2012)
Producer(s): Karan Johar, Hiroo Yash Johar
Director: Karan Malhotra
Screenplay: Ila Dutta Bedi, Karan Malhotra (based on *Agneepath*
by Mukul S. Anand)
Music: Ajay-Atul
Cinematography: Kiran Deohans, Ravi K. Chandran
Main cast: Priyanka Chopra, Rishi Kapoor, Sanjay Dutt, Hrithik
Roshan, Om Puri, Zarina Wahab

Teri Meri Kahaani (2012)
Producer(s): Kunal Kohli, Vicky Bahri, Sunil Lulla
Director: Kunal Kohli
Screenplay: Robin Bhatt, Kunal Kohli
Music: Sajid-Wajid
Background Score: Sandeep Shirodkar
Cinematography: Sunil Patel
Main cast: Priyanka Chopra, Shahid Kapoor

Barfi! (2013)
Producer(s): Ronnie Screwvala, Siddharth Roy Kapur
Director: Anurag Basu
Screenplay: Anurag Basu, Tani Basu
Music: Pritam
Cinematography: Ravi Varman
Main cast: Priyanka Chopra, Ranbir Kapoor, Ileana D'Cruz,
Ashish Vidyarthi, Jisshu Sengupta, Roopa Ganguly

Deewana Main Deewana (2013)
Director: K.C. Bokadia
Music: Bappi Lahiri
Main cast: Priyanka Chopra, Govinda

Girl Rising (2013) (Documentary)
Producer(s): Kayce Freed, Tom Yellin, Holly Gordon
Director: Richard E. Robbins

Narrator: Priyanka Chopra
Featuring: Anne Hathaway, Cate Blanchett, Selena Gomez, Liam Neeson, Priyanka Chopra, Chloé Grace Moretz, Freida Pinto, Salma Hayek, Meryl Streep, Alicia Keys and Kerry Washington

Shootout At Wadala (2013)

Producer(s): Sanjay Gupta, Anuradha Gupta, Ekta Kapoor, Shobha Kapoor
Director: Sanjay Gupta
Screenplay: Sanjay Gupta, Sanjay Bhatia, Abhijit Deshpande
Story: Sanjay Gupta, Hussain Zaidi (based on *Dongri to Dubai* by Hussain Zaidi)
Music: Anu Malik, Mustafa Zahid, Anand Raj Anand, Meet Bros Anjaan
Background score: Amar Mohile
Cinematography: Sameer Arya, Sanjay F. Gupta
Main cast: John Abraham, Anil Kapoor, Kangana Ranaut, Sonu Sood, Manoj Bajpayee, Ronit Roy, Mahesh Manjrekar, Tusshar Kapoor, Priyanka Chopra (cameo)

Bombay Talkies (2013)

Producer: Ashi Dua
Director(s): Karan Johar, Dibakar Banerjee, Zoya Akhtar, Anurag Kashyap
Screenplay: Karan Johar, Dibakar Banerjee, Zoya Akhtar, Anurag Kashyap, Reema Kagti
Music: Amit Trivedi
Cinematography: Anil Mehta, Carlos Catalan, Nikos Andritsakis, Rajeev Ravi, Ayananka Bose, Pankaj Kumar
Main cast: Rani Mukerji, Randeep Hooda, Saqib Saleem, Vineet Kumar Singh, Nawazuddin Siddiqui, Sadashiv Amrapurkar, Naman Jain, Swati Das, Katrina Kaif, Amitabh Bachchan, Priyanka Chopra (cameo)

Planes (2013) (**Animation**)

Producer: Tracy Balthazor-Flynn

Director: Klay Hall
Screenplay: Jeffrey M. Howard
Story: John Lasseter, Klay Hall, Jeffrey M. Howard
Music: Mark Mancina
Featuring (voiceover): Priyanka Chopra, Dane Cook, Stacy Keach, Teri Hatcher, Brad Garrett, Julia Louis-Dreyfus, Roger Craig Smith, John Cleese, Carlos Alazraqui, Val Kilmer, Anthony Edwards

Zanjeer (2013)

Producer(s): Reliance Entertainment Puneet Prakash Mehra, Sumeet Prakash Mehra Flying Turtle Films
Director: Apoorva Lakhia
Screenplay: Suresh Nair, Apoorva Lakhia
Dialogue: Chintan Gandhi
Story: Salim-Javed, Apoorva Lakhia (additional story); based on *Zanjeer* by Salim-Javed
Music: Meet Bros Anjjan, Anand Raj Anand, Chirantan Bhatt
Background Score: Amar Mohile
Cinematography: Gururaj R. Jois
Main cast: Priyanka Chopra, Ram Charan Teja, Sanjay Dutt, Prakash Raj

Krrish 3 (2013)

Producer: Rakesh Roshan
Director: Rakesh Roshan
Screenplay: Rakesh Roshan, Honey Irani, Robin Bhatt
Music: Rajesh Roshan
Background Score: Salim-Sulaiman
Cinematography: Tirru
Main cast: Priyanka Chopra, Hrithik Roshan, Vivek Oberoi, Kangana Ranaut

Goliyon Ki Raasleela Ram-Leela (2013)

Producer(s): Sanjay Leela Bhansali, Chetan Deolekar, Kishore Lulla, Sandeep Singh

Director: Sanjay Leela Bhansali
Screenplay: Sanjay Leela Bhansali, Siddharth-Garima (based on *Romeo and Juliet* by William Shakespeare)
Lyrics & Dialogue: Siddharth-Garima
Music: Sanjay Leela Bhansali, Hemu Gadhvi
Background Score: Monty Sharma
Cinematography: Ravi Varman
Main cast: Ranveer Singh, Deepika Padukone, Priyanka Chopra (cameo)

Gunday (2014)
Producer: Aditya Chopra
Director: Ali Abbas Zafar
Screenplay: Ali Abbas Zafar
Music: Sohail Sen
Background score: Julius Packiam
Cinematography: Aseem Mishra
Main cast: Priyanka Chopra, Ranveer Singh, Arjun Kapoor, Irrfan Khan

Mary Kom (2014)
Producer(s): Sanjay Leela Bhansali, Ajit Andhare
Director: Omung Kumar
Screenplay: Saiwyn Quadras
Music: Shashi Suman, Shivam
Background Score: Rohit Kulkarni
Cinematography: Keiko Nakahara
Main cast: Priyanka Chopra, Darshan Kumaar, Sunil Thapa

Dil Dhadakne Do (2015)
Producer(s): Ritesh Sidhwani, Farhan Akhtar
Director: Zoya Akhtar
Screenplay: Reema Kagti, Zoya Akhtar
Music: Shankar-Ehsaan-Loy
Cinematography: Carlos Catalan
Main cast: Priyanka Chopra (Also playback singer for song, 'Dil Dhadakne Do'), Anil Kapoor, Shefali Shah, Ranveer Singh, Anushka Sharma, Farhan Akhtar

Bajirao Mastani (2015)

Producer(s): Sanjay Leela Bhansali, Kishore Lulla
Director: Sanjay Leela Bhansali
Screenplay: Prakash R. Kapadia (based on *Raau* by
Nagnath S. Inamdar)
Music: Sanjay Leela Bhansali
Background score: Sanchit Balhara
Cinematography: Sudeep Chatterjee
Main cast: Priyanka Chopra, Ranveer Singh, Deepika Padukone,
Tanvi Azmi

Jai Gangaajal (2016)

Producer(s): Prakash Jha, Milind Dabke
Director: Prakash Jha
Screenplay: Prakash Jha
Music: Salim-Sulaiman
Cinematography: Sachin Krishn
Main cast: Priyanka Chopra, Prakash Jha, Manav Kaul

Baywatch (2017)

Producer(s): Ivan Reitman, Michael Berk, Douglas Schwartz,
Gregory J. Bonann, Beau Flynn
Director: Seth Gordon
Screenplay: Damian Shannon, Mark Swift
Story: Jay Scherick, David Ronn, Thomas Lennon, Robert Ben
Garant (based on *Baywatch* by Michael Berk,
Douglas Schwartz, Gregory J. Bonann)
Music: Christopher Lennertz
Cinematography: Eric Steelberg
Main cast: Priyanka Chopra, Dwayne Johnson, Zac Efron,
Alexandra Daddario, David Hasselhoff

A Kid Like Jake (2018) (forthcoming)

Producer(s): Paul Bernon, Jim Parsons, Eric Norsoph, Todd
Spiewak, Rachel (Xiaowen) Song
Director: Silas Howard

Screenplay: Daniel Pearle; (based on *A Kid Like Jake* by
Daniel Pearle)
Music: Roger Neill
Cinematography: Steven Calitri
Main cast: Priyanka Chopra, Claire Danes, Jim Parsons,
Octavia Spencer

Isn't It Romantic (2019) (**forthcoming**)
Producer(s): Todd Garner, Grant Scharbo, Gina Matthews
Director: Todd Strauss-Schulson
Screenplay: Erin Cardillo, Dana Fox, Katie Silberman, Paula Pell
Cinematography: Simon Duggan
Main cast: Priyanka Chopra, Rebel Wilson, Adam DeVine, Liam
Hemsworth, Betty Gilpin

Producer

Bam Bam Bol Raha Hai Kashi (2016) (**Bhojpuri**)
Producer(s): Priyanka Chopra, Dr. Madhu Chopra
Director: Santosh Mishra
Music: Rajesh Rajnish, Madhukar Anand
Main cast: Dinesh Lal Yadav, Amrapali Dubey,
Samarth Chaturvedi, Sanjay Pandey, R. Shandilya

Ventilator (2016) (**Marathi**)
Producer(s): Priyanka Chopra, Dr. Madhu Chopra
Director: Rajesh Mapuskar
Screenplay: Rajesh Mapuskar
Music: Rohan-Rohan
Cinematography: Savita Singh
Main cast: Ashutosh Gowariker, Jitendra Joshi, Sulabha Arya,
Sukanya Kulkarni Mone

Sarvann (2017) (**Punjabi**)
Producer(s): Priyanka Chopra, Dr. Madhu Chopra,
Deepshikha Deshmukh
Director: Karan Guliani
Screenplay: Amberdeep Singh

Music: Jatinder Shah
Cinematography: Vineet Malhotra
Main cast: Amrinder Gill, Simi Chahal, Ranjit Bawa,
               Sardar Sohi, Dilnoor Kaur

Kay Re Rascalaa (2017) (**Marathi**)

Producer: Priyanka Chopra
Director: Giridharan Swamy
Music: Sonu Nigam, Rohan Rohan, Shaan
Main cast: Gaurav Ghatnekar, Nihar, Nagesh Bhosale, Nikhil
               Ratnaparakhi, Akshar Kothari, Bhagyashree Mote

Pahuna: The Little Visitors (2017) (**Sikkimese**)

Producer: Priyanka Chopra
Director: Pakhi Abbas Tyrewala
Screenplay: Biswas Timshina (dialogue), Paakhi A. Tyrewala
Music: Sagar Desai
Main cast: Ishika Gurung, Anmol Limbu, Sujoy Rai, Rupa Tamang

Television

2010	*Fear Factor: Khatron Ke Khiladi*	Host
2015-2018	*Quantico*	Lead role
2016	*It's My City*	Producer; also guest role

Music videos

2000	'Sajan Mere Satrangiya' with Daler Mehndi; Album: Ek Dana
2010	'Phir Mile Sur Mera Tumhara'
2011	'Mind Blowing' for Ganesh Hegde, Album: Let's Party
2012	'In My City' (featuring will.i.am)
2013	'Exotic' (featuring Pitbull)
2014	'I Can't Make You Love Me'
2016	'Don't You Need Somebody' (featuring Enrique Iglesias, R. City, Shaggy and Serayah)

Compiled by Ipshita Mitra

Awards & Honours

Civilian Awards
2016   Padma Shri

National Film Awards
2008   Best Actress for *Fashion*

Filmfare Awards
2004   Best Female Debut for *Andaaz*
2005   Best Performance in a Negative Role for *Aitraaz*
2009   Best Actress for *Fashion*
2012   Best Actress Critics Award for *7 Khoon Maaf*
2016   Best Supporting Actress for *Bajirao Mastani*

Producers Guild Film Awards
2009   Best Actress in a Leading Role for *Fashion*
2010   Best Actress in a Leading Role for *Kaminey*
2012   Entertainer of the Year for *7 Khoon Maaf* and *Don 2*
2013   Star of the Year for *Agneepath* and *Barfi!*
2015   Best Actress in a Leading Role for *Mary Kom*
        Hindustan Times Celebrity for a Cause
2016   Guild Global Honour

Global Indian Film Awards

2005   Best Villain Female for *Aitraaz*

2007   Most Searched Female Actor on the Internet

Screen Awards

2005   Best Actor in a Negative Role for *Aitraaz*

2009   Best Actress for *Fashion*

2012   Best Actor in a Negative Role – Female for *7 Khoon Maaf*

2012   Jodi No. 1 (along with Shah Rukh Khan) for *Don 2*

2013   Jodi No. 1 (along with Ranbir Kapoor) for *Barfi!*

2015   Best Actress for *Mary Kom*

2016   Best Supporting Actress for *Bajirao Mastani*

Bengal Film Journalists' Association Awards

2005   Best Actress for *Aitraaz*

IIFA Awards

2007   Best On-Screen Beauty for *Krrish*

2009   Best Actress for *Fashion*

2011   Green Globe Award for Contribution to a Greener Earth

2014   Woman of Substance

2016   Woman of the Year

2016   Best Supporting Actress for *Bajirao Mastani*

Stardust Awards

2004   Best Supporting Actress for *The Hero: Love Story of a Spy*

2005   Superstar of Tomorrow – Female for *Mujhse Shaadi Karogi*

2009   Star of the Year – Female for *Fashion* and *Dostana*

2013 Best Actress – Drama for *Barfi!*
   Star of the Year – Female
2014 Best Actress – Drama for *Mary Kom*
2016 Global Icon Award

Star Box Office Awards
2014 Ms. Money Bags for *Gunday* and *Mary Kom*

Zee Cine Awards
2013 Best Actor – Female for *Barfi!*
2014 International Female Icon

BIG Star Entertainment Awards
2010 New Talent of the Decade – Female
2012 Most Entertaining Film Actor – Female for *Barfi!*
2014 Most Entertaining Actor in a Social/Drama Film – Female for *Mary Kom*
   Most Entertaining Film Actor – Female

Lions Gold Awards
2009 Favourite Actor in a Leading Role – Female for *Fashion*
2011 Favourite Popular Film Actor – Female for *Anjaana Anjaani*
2012 Favourite Actor in a Leading Role – Female for *Don 2*
2013 Favourite Actor in a Leading Role – Female for *Barfi!*
2015 Favourite Actor in a Leading Role – Female for *Mary Kom*
2017 Favourite Marathi Film for *Ventilator*

Asian Film Awards
2009 'Nielsen Box Office Award' for Outstanding Contribution to Asian Cinema

Times of India Film Awards

2013   Best Actor – Female for *Barfi!*

2016   Best Supporting Actress for *Bajirao Mastani*

People's Choice Awards (India)

2012   Favourite International Music Debut for 'In My City'

Filmfare Marathi Awards

2017   Best Film for *Ventilator*

Maharashtra State Film Awards

2017   Best Film for *Ventilator*

Nickelodeon Kids' Choice Awards India

2013   Best Movie Actress for *Barfi!*

Mirchi Music Awards Marathi

2017   Listeners' Choice Song of the Year for 'Baba'

Mother Teresa Awards

2017   Mother Teresa Memorial Award for Social Justice

International Awards

People's Choice Awards

2016   Favourite Actress in a New TV Series for *Quantico*

2017   Favourite Dramatic TV Actress for *Quantico*

Shanghai International Film Festival

2009   'Golden Goblet' (Jin Jue) Award for Contribution
        to Cinema

MTV Europe Music Awards

2015   Best Indian Act

Other Recognitions

2007   Kelvinator's Gr8 Women Awards for Contribution
        to Indian Cinema
2008   Zee Astitva Award for Contribution to Indian Cinema
2009   NDTV Profit Car and Bike Award for Brand
        Ambassador of the Year
        FICCI Frames Excellence Honours for Most
        Powerful Entertainer of the Decade
2010   NDTV Indian of the Year Awards-Female
        Entertainer of the Year
2011   Dadasaheb Phalke Academy Award for Most
        Memorable Performance for 7 *Khoon Maaf*
        The South Asians in Media, Marketing and
        Entertainment Association 'Trailblazer Award'
2012   Big Star Young Entertainer Award for Style Icon
2013   MTV Video Music Award India for Super Achiever
        of the Year
        India Leadership Conclave Awards for Actress of
        the Decade
        South African Indian Film and Television Awards,
        Best Actress for *Barfi!*
2014   IAA Leadership Awards for Brand Ambassador of
        the Year — Female
        Gaana Awards, Most Popular English Song for
        'Exotic'
        Priyadarshini Academy Global Awards, Smita Patil
        Memorial Award for Best Actor for *Mary Kom*
2015   Arab-Indo Bollywood Awards, Best Actress in a
        Leading Role for *Mary Kom*
2016   Dadasaheb Phalke Academy Awards, Best Actress
        for *Bajirao Mastani*
        Instyle Awards, Breakthrough Style Star

2017   National Award for Best Direction for *Ventilator*
National Film Award for Best Editing for *Ventilator*
National Film Award for Best Audiography for *Ventilator*
Sanskriti Kaladarpan Awards, Best Film for *Ventilator*
Dadasaheb Phalke Academy Awards, Best Film for *Ventilator*
Zee Talkies Comedy Awards, Best Film for *Ventilator*
Variety Power of Women Awards, Philanthropy

Media Honours

2006   World's Sexiest Asian Woman by *Eastern Eye*
Style Diva of Year by *eBay*

2009   Most Desirable Woman by *Indiatimes*

2011   India's Best Dressed by *People India*
Hottest Woman of the Year by *Maxim India*

2012   India's Glam Diva by *Big CBS Love*
Most Influential Indian in the Social Media Circuit by *Pinstorm*
Punjabi Icon by Punjab Government
World's Sexiest Asian Woman by *Eastern Eye*

2013   Ambassador of Beauty and Substance by *Femina Miss India*
Hottest Woman of the Year by *Maxim India*

2014   World's Sexiest Asian Woman by *Eastern Eye*

2015   World's Sexiest Asian Woman by *Eastern Eye*
World's Sexiest Woman by *FHM India*
Sexiest Woman on Television by *BuddyTV*
25 Most Intriguing People of the Year by *People*

2016   Sexiest Eyes by *Victoria's Secret*
100 Most Influential People in the World by *Time*

Most Desirable Woman by *Indiatimes*
Hottest Woman of the Year by *Maxim India*
2017 World's 100 Most Powerful Women by *Forbes*
World's Sexiest Asian Woman by *Eastern Eye*

Pageants

2000 Femina Miss India World
Miss World
Miss World Continental Queen of Beauty — Asia & Oceania

Compiled by Ipshita Mitra

Acknowledgements

Would such a book – perhaps the first of its kind in India that doesn't pull its punches in its deep study of an achiever – have been possible without the backstage information and generous support of some of the most eminent names in show business?

For their contribution in terms of time and the delightful supply of behind-the-scenes details that have gone into the making of Priyanka Chopra and her landmark films along with photographs, I am immensely grateful to (in alphabetical order):

Abbas-Mustan, Anil Sharma, Anurag Basu, Aseem Merchant, Farah Khan, Hrithik Roshan, Jaywant Thakre, Madhur Bhandarkar, Manish Malhotra, Neil Nitin Mukesh, Omung Kumar, Pradeep Guha, Rajesh Mapuskar, Rakesh Roshan, Sandeep Singh, Sanjay Leela Bhansali, Subhash Ghai, Suneel Darshan, Tarun Mansukhani, and Vijay Galani;

General Nandwani, Yash Roy and Ratna Manucha for their tiny but welcome bits from the Army end;

Girish Agarwal of *Dainik Bhaskar* and Nari Hira of Magna Publishing for the generous use of their respective libraries;

My friends and media colleagues Anupama Chopra, Bharti Dubey, Jyothi Venkatesh, KS Sanjay, Meena Iyer, Parull Gossain and the large-hearted Yogen Shah whose photographs enliven *The Dark Horse*;

Publisher Ajay Mago and my dear fellow-owl and Chief Editor Dipa Chaudhuri who worked like me till the milk bottles arrived, and their talented team of Arijit Ganguly and Ipshita Mitra at Om Books International for sharing my belief in such a different book;

Priyanka Chopra herself for becoming the symbol of success worthy of emulation by the ambitious and the industrious;

And most of all to the warm Madhu Chopra and late Dr Ashok Chopra who I have known socially, for parenting an inspiration.

Dhanyavad!